Ancient Puzzles

Ancient Puzzles

CLASSIC BRAINTEASERS AND OTHER TIMELESS MATHEMATICAL GAMES OF THE LAST 10 CENTURIES

Dominic Olivastro

BANTAM BOOKS

NEW YORK   TORONTO   LONDON   SYDNEY   AUCKLAND

ANCIENT PUZZLES

A Bantam Book/December 1993

See page 280 for acknowledgments.

Book design by Glen M. Edelstein.

Library of Congress Cataloging-in-Publication Data

Olivastro, Dominic.
    Ancient puzzles : classic brainteasers and other timeless
mathematical games of the last ten centuries / Dominic Olivastro.
        p.   cm.
    ISBN 0-553-37297-1
    1. Mathematical recreations.   I. Title.
QA95.045   1994
793.7′4—dc20   93-1985
                                                       CIP

Published simultaneously in the United States and Canada

Bantam Books are published by Bantam Books, a division of Bantam
Doubleday Dell Publishing Group, Inc. Its trademark, consisting of the
words "Bantam Books" and the portrayal of a rooster, is Registered in
U.S. Patent and Trademark Office and in other countries. Marca
Registrada. Bantam Books, 1540 Broadway, New York, New York 10036.

PRINTED IN THE UNITED STATES OF AMERICA

0 9 8 7 6 5 4 3 2 1

KING NEFERKIRĒ HAS BEGUN COUNTING

ON HIS FINGERS

—*THE BOOK OF THE DEAD*

To my Mother, Mary,
and my Father, Manfredo . . .

. . . and to King Neferkirē

Ancient Puzzles

Introduction

IT WOULD HAVE BEEN SIMPLE TO WRITE A BOOK CALLED *THE Classic Puzzles of All Time*, and a second book called *The Histories of Classic Puzzles. This* book is neither. *This* book is an attempt to merge the two into a single work. The obvious danger is that I will disappoint readers who would have been interested in either of the two books separately, but I hope I have struck such a note that everyone will find a familiar friend in an unfamiliar setting.

My obsession with ancient puzzles started early on. Like many in my generation, I grew up on Martin Gardner's monthly essay on mathematical games in *Scientific American*, and when a specific puzzle attracted my attention I spent an improper amount of time tracking down its origins in libraries. Often it turned up in the manuscripts of a pharaoh's scribe or the letters of a medieval monk; in these cases the puzzle, once merely interesting, became more like a relic. So much of this ancient writing has an enduring charm, largely because the older writers were able to find mysteries in simple things.

Consider the story of Eve's stay in paradise—here we have what the author believes to be the origin of life and sin, yet there is no thunder or lightning. Instead, it begins with a bone and it ends with a tree. All deep and abiding literature is couched in simple terms like this. I hope some of that charm can be garnered from this book. Certainly there are puzzles enough to hold anyone's attention, especially novices; but even experts, or those who do not especially care to solve puzzles, will find food for thought in the anecdotal sections.

In digging up the ruins of ancient puzzles, we are something like archaeologists of logic. In this undertaking, we may have two experiences that are as rewarding as, say, uncovering a lost city. First, we may find a modern puzzle occurring only slightly changed at an improbably early date. Second, we may find a dead puzzle, now hardly a puzzle at all, attracting an inordinate amount of attention in a past civilization. The Egyptians, for example, had a difficult time dividing five loaves of bread among three workers. Is the latter type of puzzle uninteresting? With our modern puzzle-solving methods, yes. But to anyone interested in the development of these methods, no. In our modern notation, simply stating the problem is solving it: 5 divided by 3 is, well, $^5/_3$. But the Egyptians did not possess our notation. In cases like this, it is important to keep in mind exactly how the ancient people themselves went about solving their own problems, even if this forces us to abandon our tried-and-true methods. Solving a problem in this ancient way, without the essential tools, is actually a very difficult task—like thinking without words. But it is well worth doing because it will tell you a great deal about both thinking and words.

My first attempt at writing this book was an article I wrote for *The Sciences*, that marvelous, lively, and—this is unusual these days—highly accurate journal of popular science.[1] Even while writing the article, I was struck by an inevitable question: Why do puzzles arise at all? Some answer this with the analogy of a roller coaster. We invent problems that do not exist in the real world—adding nothing to our lives when we solve them—for the sheer pleasure of it, like seeking out rides that rise and fall at breakneck speeds, taking us nowhere. I think a better analogy is that of the earliest primitive carpenter. He has just invented the first hammer. What does he do with it? Unfortunately, the poor fellow lives in a village of grass huts, so there is nothing around him that needs building. To pass his time, he bangs together crazy lopsided wooden structures just for the sake of using his hammer. No

---

[1] "A sampler of Ancient Conundrums," *The Sciences*, January/February 1990. Interested readers may wish to obtain subscriptions at $18.00 per year. Write to *The Sciences*, 2 East 63rd Street, New York, NY 10021. Or call 1-800-THE-NYAS.

one asks to have them built; no one uses them after they are built. The structures are junk, but if you don't understand them you might think the carpenter, who is really a genius, is just a lunatic who makes a lot of noise.

Puzzles are logical junk. They arise when our reasoning ability outpaces any problem in the real world that needs to be reasoned about. They are meaningless, profitless, unusable, silly, insignificant, inconsequential—but without them highly intelligent people would just be lunatics who make a lot of noise.

The hammer in our analogy is the number system—the ten digits 0, 1, 2, 3, 4, 5, 6, 7, 8, 9—and the notation, in which the value of a digit depends on its position in the number. In the number 110, for example, the middle "1" represents 10, while the left-most "1" represents 100. When I was young, we were taught to call this the "Hindu-Arabic number system," which not too inaccurately explained its historical origins. Sometime later, it was decided that the numbers should be given a functional name, and so they were denuded of their culture. Most readers probably have been raised to call it simply the "positional number system." In the course of human development, nothing is of greater consequence—not the wheel, not fire, not nuclear energy—than this number system. We, today, are a little jaded, so we think our numbers are nothing more than a counting aid, no different from any other number system. But the way in which our numbers tick off from 0 to 9, push the next digit up, then start all over, is actually an extraordinary device that is capable of mirroring the purely logical workings of the world. It is not farfetched to say that the history of puzzles is the history of ancient people groping toward the positional number system. Whenever appropriate, I have included in each chapter the numbers and arithmetic that were used to solve that chapter's puzzles. This will add flesh to the bare bones of the puzzles, and perhaps, too, it will return some of the history that was lost.

This book is meant to be fun, but the introduction to any book, even one that aspires only to entertain, is meant for pontificating. So, before the fun begins, let me worry the reader about some thoughts that have dogged me during the last few months.

There are two modern trends that may lead some to misinterpet this book. The first is a movement that has coined the terrible words "multiculturalism" and "ethnocentrism." It is a movement that resents the center that Europe, or the West, has occupied for so many years. By way of correction, it has tried to emphasize the importance of other parts of the world—thus, we have "multicultural science," even "ethnocentric mathematics." Like most horrors, this started innocently enough, but lately it has degenerated into a kind of snotty ancestor worship. In the following chapters there will be many examples in which Europe is compared unfavorably to other parts of the world. This is unavoidable. One cannot go far in the history of anything "Western," especially science and mathematics, without finding that much of it actually originated in places like China. But I hope I have never adopted the scolding attitude of some writers. Reading history should be entertaining. In any case, the history of mathematics can never be more important than mathematics itself, and for better or worse (I choose the former) today and for the foreseeable future mathematics is largely a Western affair.

The second trend is a movement toward irrationality, by which I mean the disturbing rise in interest in such superstitions as astrology, numerology, psychic phenomena, and so on. Just as you may find examples of multiculturalism in this book, you may also find examples of superstitions. In ancient times puzzles were intimately connected with spiritual matters. This may seem strange at first, but actually it is quite reasonable. Puzzles explain something that is invisible, an orderliness that cannot actually be touched—the "obscure secrets" of the world, as the scribe Ahmes once put it, believing he caught a glimpse of the Deity's mind. One is reminded of what Gottfried Wilhelm Leibnitz once said: "The Supreme Being is one who has created and solved all possible games." There may be some truth in this. Perhaps God first created all possible magic squares, then decided that every action should have an equal and opposite reaction. Perhaps God first solved all configuration games, then decided that space should have exactly three dimensions. Perhaps God first solved all possible odd-coin problems, then decided that every physical system would tend toward maximum entropy. As we solve these puzzles, are we not really discovering the workings of the world? It is likely that ancient people thought this way.

The superstitions that arose in ancient times should not be dismissed out of hand; they are an important part of the puzzles themselves. Consider the cult of Isis that flourished in Egypt around the time of

Christ. Plutarch describes it as a blend of gibberish and surprisingly good mathematics:

> The Egyptians relate that the death of Osiris occurred on the seventeenth [of the month], when the full moon is most obviously waning. Therefore the Pythagoreans call this day the "barricading" and they entirely abominate this number. For the number seventeen, intervening between the square number sixteen and the rectangular number eighteen, two numbers which alone of plane numbers have their perimeters equal to the areas enclosed by them, bars and separates them from one another, being divided into unequal parts in the ratio of nine to eight. The number of twenty-eight years is said by some to have been the extent of the life of Osiris, by others of his reign; for such is the number of the moon's illuminations and in so many days does it revolve through its own cycle. When they cut the wood in the so-called burials of Osiris, they prepare a crescent-shaped chest because the moon, whenever it approaches the sun, becomes crescent-shaped and suffers eclipse. The dismemberment of Osiris into fourteen parts is interpreted in relation to the days in which the planet wanes after the full moon until a new moon occurs.

That is nonsense, of course, but it is interesting nonsense. It was said by a people who have just discovered that numbers rule the world, and who just can't get over the fact. Notice that it claims, quite correctly, that the only two rectangles having an area equal to their perimeters are rectangles with areas of 16 and 18.[2]

It is typical of ancient superstitions that they lead to solid discoveries like this, and then quietly disappear. Not so modern superstitions. I can point to innumerable examples, but one that seems appropriate is what might be called the "psychoanalytic barricading." This is not the

---

[2] Let the two sides of the rectangle be x and y. Then $x \cdot y = 2x + 2y$. A little algebra changes this to $y = 2 + 4/(x-2)$. Now if y is to be an integer, as is called for in the problem, then $(x-2)$ must be a divisor of 4, otherwise the right side of the equation is 2 plus "some fraction." This means $(x-2)$ must be either 1, 2, or 4, and we have only three possibilities:

$x = 3, y = 6, xy = 18$
$x = 4, y = 4, xy = 16$
$x = 6, y = 3, xy = 18$

So it is true that the area of the rectangle can only be either 16 or 18.

number 17, but the numbers 23 and 28. Modern psychoanalysts, beginning with Sigmund Freud and Wilhelm Fliess, believe these numbers "bar and separate" men from women. The first is the length of the ideal male cycle and the second the length of the ideal female cycle. They see great significance in these two numbers, since all possible integers can be generated from them. For example, the number 13 equals $(3 \times 23) + (-2 \times 28)$. In a similar way, men and women who break the barricade and come together can produce offspring.

This, too, is nonsense, but now it is dull and childish nonsense.[3] Unlike ancient number mysticism, it does not lead to new insights and it will never disappear. It is said by a people who have grown disenchanted with the world. Ancient supersitions were always forward-looking. Modern irrationalities look backward. The apricot pit that cures cancer, the herb that prolongs life, the mystic surgeon in some third world country—always the tendency is to a distant time and distant place. Although this book contains a few (very interesting) superstitions, I hope it will be taken the right way. It is meant to flesh out ancient puzzles; it is not meant to support modern foolishness.

My attempt in each chapter is to begin with ancient puzzles and move as quickly as possible to more modern problems that suggest themselves. One could write several volumes this way, but by necessity I have had to pick my way through several fascinating examples. I've tried to sample much of the world across several centuries. Starting with Africa and China is unavoidable. Including yet another chapter on magic squares may seem like overkill to some but not to others, and perhaps the history will be interesting to everyone. After that I pass to Europe and the Middle East. It may seem surprising that I have included only Abu Kamil's *The Book of Precious Things in the Art of Reckoning*, but I do not find it mentioned often elsewhere, and it gives me the opportunity to bring in puzzles of indeterminate equations. There are many glaring omissions, and the one of which I am most ashamed is the complete absence of Native Americans. Since the chapters are arranged in a roughly chronological order, the book as a whole follows a similar ancient-to-modern design.

It begins with a bone, and it ends with a tree.

---

[3] It is not so much wrong as it is meaningless. *Any* two numbers that are relatively prime—that share no divisors in common—have this property. For example, you can generate all integers by adding multiples of 6 and 13.

The First Etches

IT MUST HAVE REQUIRED MANY AGES TO REALIZE THAT A BRACE OF PHEASANTS AND A COUPLE OF DAYS WERE BOTH INSTANCES OF THE NUMBER TWO.

—BERTRAND RUSSELL

HOW ANCIENT IS THE MOST ANCIENT PUZZLE?
It is a fairly simple matter to find an ancient manuscript recounting the popular puzzles of its time, but such manuscripts will take us back to the second millennium B.C. at the earliest. Surely, the greatest puzzles of all must be those that were never recorded, the ones that were invented at the dawn of civilization. When humankind first left its animal origins behind, and first walked on only its hind legs, and first acquired a reasoning mind that enjoyed being puzzled—what were the puzzles? We may never know exactly, but there is one artifact that provides some tantalizing hints.

A SIMPLE BONE

About 11,000 years ago—and possibly much longer—a tiny fishing village flourished around Lake Edward in Zaire, situated in central Africa. The people of the village are now called the Ishango. The evidence that can be excavated around the lake suggests that the Ishango practiced cannibalism, as did others at the time, and built certain crude tools, mostly used for fishing, hunting, and gathering. They are our intellectual forefathers, the people who took the first faltering steps toward rational thinking. Much of the excavation around

Lake Edward was done by the archaeologist Jean de Heinzelin in the early 1970s. Little pieces of bone and teeth can be put together to obtain a fairly detailed account of the people. If the age—11,000 years—does not create a sense of awe, then keep in mind that de Heinzelin believes the Ishango represented the emergence in Africa of its indigenous population:

> . . . some of the molars we found were as large as those of *Australopithecus*, the pre-human "man-ape." Moreover, the skull bones were thick . . . approximately the thickness of Neanderthal skulls . . . On the other hand, Ishango man did not have the overhanging brow of Neanderthal and other earlier forms . . . his chin was shaped like the chin of modern man . . . the long bones of his body were quite slender . . . this adds up to a unique picture. No other fossil man shows such a combination.

A more complete picture is created by looking at their tools. They were "crude and completely unlike any unearthed at other African sites," and they included some tools that were apparently used to "pound seed and grain for food." One tool, dating to about 9000 B.C., is of particular interest. It was a "bone tool handle with a small fragment of quartz still fixed . . . at its head . . . it may have been used for engraving or tattooing, or even for writing of some kind."

Even more interesting, however, are its markings: groups of notches arranged in three distinct columns. The pattern of these notches leads me to suspect that they represent more than pure decorations.

Figure 1 is an illustration of the Ishango bone and its curious notches. The tip at the end is the quartz point that we assume was used for engraving purposes.

There are many other bones like this. For example, the shin bone of a wolf found in Czechoslovakia has similar markings and it is very likely much older than the Ishango bone. Such notched bones are the earliest examples of tally sticks, the most direct kind of counting system. The use of a tally stick was by no means restricted to primitive people. In France, an etched stick actually became the subject of one of the first examples of modern law. It is found in the Code Napoléon, issued in 1804:

Figure 1. The Ishango bone (Reprinted from de Heinzelin, 1962)

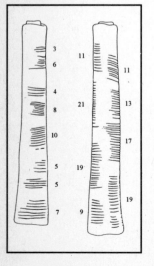

The tally stick which match their stocks have the force of contracts between persons who are accustomed to declare in this manner the deliveries they have made or received.

It is, in fact, a little startling to find how recently they were still in use throughout much of the world. As recently as the 1800s, for example, they were commonplace in England's banking system. If an individual made a loan to a bank, the amount of the loan was etched onto a stick, and the stick was split laterally to create two copies. The one held by the bank was called a "foil," and the one held by the individual making the loan was called a "stock"; hence, the individual was a "stockholder." When the loan was called, the stock was "checked" against forgery by seeing if it matched the foil in the size and spacing of its etches. The word "check" was later used for written certificates as well. The custom continued in England long after more accurate methods were available. The British Parliament finally abolished the practice in 1826; when all of the tally sticks were gathered together and burned in the furnaces that heat the House of Lords, the fire became unmanageable and destroyed both Houses of Parliament.

WHAT DO THE NOTCHES MEAN?

In Figure 1, you can see the pattern of notches. Often these are grouped together by a large space occurring between groups. Along one column there are 11, 21, 19, and 9 notches. Along another there are eight groups of 3, 6, 4, 8, 10, 5, 5, and 7 notches. Along the third column there are 11, 13, 17, and 19 notches. "I find it difficult to believe," de Heinzelin continues, "that these sequences are nothing more than a random selection of numbers." Indeed not. We may have in Figure 1 the earliest number system possible, and as befits a people who flourished 11,000 years ago, it is a very simple system: It is the unary number system, in which one notch means 1, two notches means 2, and so on.

It is worthwhile to keep in mind exactly what the Ishango accomplished in this number system, even though it may seem to us ridiculously simple and straightforward. A good exercise in this regard is to jump outside our skins and try to count while divorcing ourselves from the numbers that we have. This is difficult, but fortunately there are many people even today who have a counting system that is not very different from the Ishango system. For example, in central Brazil the Bakairi have words for only "one" and "two." To count higher they must combine these words. Thus, one is *tokále*, two is *ahága*, and three is *ahága tokále*. Four, of course, is *ahága ahága*. Five and six follow logically, but for seven there is no word at all. We might expect *ahága ahága ahága tokále* (meaning 2 + 2 + 2 + 1), but such a phrase requires the listener (and the speaker) to count the number of times the word *ahága* is uttered, which is not the same as the number of objects being counted. To get by, the Bakairi instead point to certain fingers and say *méra*, meaning "this many." In this way, *méra* becomes seven when pointing to the index finger of the left hand. *Méra* becomes eleven when pointing to the big toe of the right foot. After twenty, the Bakairi simply tussle their hair while saying *méra, méra*, as though to say "more than the hairs on my head" or simply "a great multitude."

The truth is, the discovery of a number system, even one as simple as the unary number system, is an extraordinary achievement, one that we are far too likely to take for granted. And quite possibly, it all began on the Ishango bone. If we knew what urged them to etch the bone as they did, we would know an important aspect of the human mind in its early stage of development—namely, what it was that first set it to count. It would be similar to knowing what a newborn sees when it first opens its eyes, before it has words for the colors and shapes around it. But newborns can't speak and the Ishango left no records, so we must be satisfied with simple conjectures.

Consider first one column with four sets of notches, 11, 21, 19, and 9. This seems to be 10 plus 1, 20 plus 1, 20 minus 1, and 10 minus 1. Is this an emphasis on the number 10, or merely a coincidence?

Consider next the second column, with eight groups: 3, 6, 4, 8, 10, 5, 5, and 7. The three and the six are very close together. Then, after a very large gap, there is a group of four and a group of eight, also close together. Then, after another large gap, there is a group of ten followed by two groups of five. There is no simple explanation for the final group of seven at the end of the bone, but the other markings strongly suggest the idea of doubling a number. You can almost see the Ishango (working from left to right) etching in a set of 5, then another set of 5, then a set of 10, as it suddenly occurs to him that twice five is miraculously the same as ten. Then rapidly (from the right) he etches in 3, and doubles it to 6. Then 4, and 8. Or is this another coincidence?

The third side of the bone is a little more confusing. The notches this time are 11, 13, 17, and 19. These are all the prime numbers—numbers that can be divided only by themselves and one—between ten and twenty. Again, is this a coincidence?

De Heinzelin believes the bone represents "an arithmetical game of some sort, devised by a people who had a number system based on 10 as well as a knowledge of duplication and of prime numbers." If so, this is certainly the most ancient puzzle.

The evidence for this is admittedly slim—only 16 numbers etched into a bone. And there is absolutely no reason to see in it a "number system based on 10" as de Heinzelin thinks, although it may be the beginnings of such a system. In general, mathematicians are far more likely than archaeologists to dismiss the bone, but it is still fascinating to find how often the ideas we see on it—or the ideas we *think* we see there—would later appear throughout the regions around the Ishango village. In this sense, the puzzle on the bone is the puzzle of the number system itself, a very fitting puzzle for 9000 B.C. Each of the three sides of the bone is like a little flashpoint in the birth of the number system.

First, consider the way the bone dwells on the number 10. We find something similar to it in *The Coming Forth by Day*, or as it is usually called, *The Book of the Dead*, an Egyptian work from about the sixteenth century B.C. The book is a collection of spells, incantations, prayers, and vignettes that was placed in the tombs of the newly deceased, to be used when the soul "came forth by day," that is, arose in the afterlife. Like the modern Bible, some of the prayers contained blank lines to be filled in with the deceased's name. One vignette is called "The Spell for Obtaining a Ferry-boat." In it, a king tries to convince the ferryman to let him cross one of the canals to the netherworld. The ferryman objects: "The august god [on the other side of the canal] will say, 'Did you bring me a man who cannot number his fingers?' " But the king is a magician who knows a rhyme that numbers his ten fingers. The ferryman is thus satisfied and takes the king across. In Buddhism, too, we find this close association between 10 and spirituality. In one myth concerning the early life of Buddha, the powers of 10 are used repeatedly, up to 10^{153}. Perhaps it is the beginnings of this notion of a magical number ten that we find on the first side of the Ishango bone.

Next, consider the way the carvers of the bone were mystified by doubling a number. This is another common feature of ancient mathematics, found in many regions of Africa and elsewhere. An extended use of doubling, certainly of very ancient origins, is found in modern Ethiopia. The story is told of a colonel who wished to purchase seven bulls, each costing 22 Maria Theresa dollars. The owner of the stock called the local priest, who performed the necessary multiplication by digging a series of holes (called houses) arranged in two parallel columns. At the top of one column, he placed 7 pebbles (the number of bulls to be purchased) and at the top of the second column he placed 22 pebbles (the cost of each bull). The colonel reports:

> It was explained to me that the first column is used for multiplying by two: that is, twice the number of pebbles in the first house are placed in the second, then twice the number in the third, and so on. The second column is for dividing by 2: half the number of pebbles in the first house are placed in the second, and so on down until there is one pebble in the last house. Fractions are discounted.
>
> The division column is then examined for odd or even number of pebbles in the cups. All even houses are considered to be evil ones, all odd houses good. Whenever an evil house is discovered, the pebbles are thrown out (from both columns) and not counted. All pebbles left in the remaining cups of the multiplication column are then counted, and the total of them is the answer.

The colonel's problem looks like this:

First Column (for Multiplication)	Second Column (for Division)
~~7~~	~~22~~
14	11
28	5
~~56~~	~~2~~
112	1
154	

In other words, $7 \cdot 22 = 154$. If you look carefully at the numbers that are not crossed out in the first column, you will see that we are actually multiplying by powers of two. The multiplication above amounts to saying $7 \cdot 22 = 14 + 28 + 112 = 7 \cdot (2^1 + 2^2 + 2^4)$. This may seem strange, but it is actually a very logical way of proceeding for

people who do not have a full number system. The method is still in
common use in certain parts of the Soviet Union.

A computer, too, does not have a full number system, at least not one
that counts to 10. It prefers, like the Ethiopians, to express numbers in
powers of two (called a binary representation), and for much the same
reason: It is easiest for a computer to duplicate a number. Modern
textbooks in computer science often begin with a simple trick for
changing numbers into a computer's binary representation. A little
eerily, these books are repeating the principle discovered by the Ethiopians. First take the original number and successively divide by two,
throwing out fractions when they arise. (In our story, the colonel said
the priest also threw away the fractions.) If the number is even (an evil
house) write a 0 next to it, effectively throwing it away, and if it is odd (a
good house) write a 1 next to it, effectively keeping it. The numbers
read from bottom up are the computer's representation of the original
number. For example, to find how a computer stores the number 22, do
the following:

$$
\begin{array}{ccc}
22 & \rightarrow & 0 \\
11 & \rightarrow & 1 \\
5 & \rightarrow & 1 \qquad 10110 = 22 \text{ in binary} \\
2 & \rightarrow & 0 \\
1 & \rightarrow & 1
\end{array}
$$

Does the Ethiopian's trick seem a little mystifying? If so, then the
computer's trick of changing a number to its binary form may throw
some light on it. By calling numbers "good" and "evil" houses, the
Ethiopian, in modern terminology, is "reducing a number modulo 2."
That sounds like a mouthful, but it only means we are finding the
remainder of a number after dividing by 2. Evil houses are even
numbers that leave a remainder of 0, and good houses are odd numbers
that leave a remainder of 1. Instead of throwing out and keeping various
houses, the Ethiopian is merely multiplying by this remainder.

There is nothing magical about the modulus 2. We can go one up on
the Ethiopian by using a different modulus, as in Figure 2, where we
find the product of 7 • 58 using modulus 3. Again we use two columns,
headed by 7 and 58; but because we are using modulus 3, the first
column is tripled instead of doubled, and the second column is divided
by 3 instead of 2. To help the procedure along, I have included a third

Figure 2. How a modern
Ethiopian might multiply
7 by 58 in modulus 3

First Column	Second Column	Remainders	Remainder Times First Column		
7	58	1	1 x	7 =	7
21	19	1	1 x	21 =	21
63	6	0	0 x	63 =	0
189	2	2	2 x	189 =	378
					406

Figure 2. How a modern Ethiopian might multiply 7 by 58 in modulus 3

column, which lists the remainder when the corresponding number in the second column is divided by three.

Just multiply the first column by the third column and sum up the products. In effect this throws away the evil houses, which are numbers that leave a remainder of 0, and keeps the two types of good houses, which are numbers that leave a remainder of either 1 or 2. This rule works for any modulus whatsoever, including the Ethiopians' choice of modulus 2. (The reader may like to try other examples using higher moduli.) By the way, can you find the number 58 in its ternary form in Figure 2? In general, using modulus n will produce a method that changes a number to its n-ary representation.

Finally, consider the listing of prime numbers on the bone. That these numbers are meant to be prime, and not merely random, has always been hard to swallow, since primes are a fairly advanced concept. But fundamental concepts quite often are the ones that first arise to the novice, something like beginner's luck.

We do not know why the bone stops at 19. Quite possibly, at a time when numbers were at best a fuzzy concept, it was meant to be a complete listing of *all* primes. Even today, many people who first encounter the idea of primes believe that they must come to an end at some point, as though to say that if a number is big enough it must be composed of other smaller numbers. But the opposite is true as Euclid first proved. Assume you have a complete list of known primes, p_1, p_2, $p_3 \ldots p_n$, in which p_n is the largest. Now add one to the product of all the primes: $1 + p_1 \cdot p_2 \cdot p_3 \cdot \ldots \cdot p_n$. This number cannot be evenly divided by any known prime, since it will always leave a remainder of 1. Therefore, it is either a prime number greater than p_n, or a composite number that has a prime divisor that is greater than p_n. In either case, there must always be a prime number greater than the last known prime. In essence, the primes never end.

It is tempting to think of Ishango Man, sitting at the lake, pondering those four prime numbers on his bone. What was he thinking? "11 . . . 13 . . . 17 . . . 19 . . . Is there some sort of order here?" Remember, according to our reconstruction, he has just discovered that twice three is always 6, just as twice five is always 10. Numbers seemed to represent the hidden orderliness of the world around him. Perhaps he thought, "Upon looking at these numbers, one has the feeling of being in the presence of one of the inexplicable secrets of creation." There is a primitive mysticism in this, but it was not said by Ishango; it was actually said by a modern mathematician, Don Zagier, when he looked upon another Ishango bone, a modern computerized version that lists not just four but 50 million primes. A page of it may be found in Figure 3. Why did he create this list? Perhaps for the same reason Ishango carved his bone, to glimpse the "inexplicable secrets of creation." These primes are the indivisible units, or the atoms, of the number system that Ishango had just discovered. We expect them to show some sort of order.

What is that order? We cannot say precisely, but we can gain teasing hints of it if we look at the distribution of primes. There are many surprising regularities. For example, if you pick a number n that is greater than 8, then there must be at least one prime between n and $1.5n$. Or, more interestingly, say you want to find the nth prime. You can only find it by counting off the first n numbers in Figure 3, but if you find the two values $0.91 \cdot \ln(n)$ and $1.7 \cdot \ln(n)$, then the nth prime will be somewhere between the two. You're a little limited, but you will be able to test both theories in Figure 3.

An even more startling attempt to find order in the distribution of primes may be found in Figure 4, where we list the number of primes less than or equal to successive powers of ten, for example, 10, 100, 1000. There seems to be something orderly here, and we can get at it if

	0	1	2	3	4	5	6	7	8	9	10	11	12	13	14	15	16	17	18	19	20	21	22	23	24
1	2	547	1229	1993	2749	3581	4421	5281	6143	7001	7927	8837	9739	10663	11677	12569	13513	14533	15413	16411	17393	18329	19427	20359	21391
2	3	557	1231	1997	2753	3583	4423	5297	6151	7013	7933	8839	9743	10667	11681	12577	13523	14537	15427	16417	17401	18341	19429	20369	21397
3	5	563	1237	1999	2767	3593	4441	5303	6163	7019	7937	8849	9749	10687	11689	12583	13537	14543	15439	16421	17417	18353	19433	20389	21401
4	7	569	1249	2003	2777	3607	4447	5309	6173	7027	7949	8861	9767	10691	11699	12589	13553	14549	15443	16427	17419	18367	19441	20393	21407
5	11	571	1259	2011	2789	3613	4451	5323	6197	7039	7951	8863	9769	10709	11701	12601	13567	14551	15451	16433	17431	18371	19447	20399	21419
6	13	577	1277	2017	2791	3617	4457	5333	6199	7043	7963	8867	9781	10711	11717	12611	13577	14557	15461	16447	17443	18379	19457	20407	21433
7	17	587	1279	2027	2797	3623	4463	5347	6203	7057	7993	8887	9787	10723	11719	12613	13591	14561	15467	16451	17449	18397	19463	20411	21467
8	19	593	1283	2029	2801	3631	4481	5351	6211	7069	8009	8893	9791	10729	11731	12619	13597	14563	15473	16453	17467	18401	19469	20431	21481
9	23	599	1289	2039	2803	3637	4483	5381	6217	7079	8011	8923	9803	10733	11743	12637	13613	14591	15493	16477	17471	18413	19471	20441	21487
10	29	601	1291	2053	2819	3643	4493	5387	6221	7103	8017	8929	9811	10739	11777	12641	13619	14593	15497	16481	17477	18427	19477	20443	21491
11	31	607	1297	2063	2833	3659	4507	5393	6229	7109	8039	8933	9817	10753	11779	12647	13627	14621	15511	16487	17483	18433	19483	20477	21493
12	37	613	1301	2069	2837	3671	4513	5399	6247	7121	8053	8941	9829	10771	11783	12653	13633	14627	15527	16493	17489	18439	19489	20479	21499
13	41	617	1303	2081	2843	3673	4517	5407	6257	7127	8059	8951	9833	10781	11789	12659	13649	14629	15541	16519	17491	18443	19501	20483	21503
14	43	619	1307	2083	2851	3677	4519	5413	6263	7129	8069	8963	9839	10789	11801	12671	13669	14633	15551	16529	17497	18451	19507	20507	21517
15	47	631	1319	2087	2857	3691	4523	5417	6269	7151	8081	8969	9851	10799	11807	12689	13679	14639	15559	16547	17509	18457	19531	20509	21521
16	53	641	1321	2089	2861	3697	4547	5419	6271	7159	8087	8971	9857	10831	11813	12697	13681	14653	15569	16553	17519	18461	19541	20521	21523
17	59	643	1327	2099	2879	3701	4549	5431	6277	7177	8089	8999	9859	10837	11821	12703	13687	14657	15581	16561	17539	18481	19543	20533	21529
18	61	647	1361	2111	2887	3709	4561	5437	6287	7187	8093	9001	9871	10847	11827	12713	13691	14669	15583	16567	17551	18493	19553	20543	21557
19	67	653	1367	2113	2897	3719	4567	5441	6299	7193	8101	9007	9883	10853	11831	12721	13693	14683	15601	16573	17569	18503	19559	20549	21559
20	71	659	1373	2129	2903	3727	4583	5443	6301	7207	8111	9011	9887	10859	11833	12739	13697	14699	15607	16603	17573	18517	19571	20551	21563
21	73	661	1381	2131	2909	3733	4591	5449	6311	7211	8117	9013	9901	10861	11839	12743	13709	14713	15619	16607	17579	18521	19577	20563	21569
22	79	673	1399	2137	2917	3739	4597	5471	6317	7213	8123	9029	9907	10867	11863	12757	13711	14717	15629	16619	17581	18523	19583	20593	21577
23	83	677	1409	2141	2927	3761	4603	5477	6323	7219	8147	9041	9923	10883	11867	12763	13721	14723	15641	16631	17597	18539	19597	20599	21587
24	89	683	1423	2143	2939	3767	4621	5479	6329	7229	8161	9043	9929	10889	11887	12781	13723	14731	15643	16633	17599	18541	19603	20611	21589
25	97	691	1427	2153	2953	3769	4637	5483	6337	7237	8167	9049	9931	10891	11897	12791	13729	14737	15647	16649	17609	18553	19609	20627	21599
26	101	701	1429	2161	2957	3779	4639	5501	6343	7243	8171	9059	9941	10903	11903	12799	13751	14741	15649	16651	17623	18583	19661	20639	21601
27	103	709	1433	2179	2963	3793	4643	5503	6353	7247	8179	9067	9949	10909	11909	12809	13757	14747	15661	16657	17627	18587	19681	20641	21611
28	107	719	1439	2203	2969	3797	4649	5507	6359	7253	8191	9091	9967	10937	11923	12821	13759	14753	15667	16661	17657	18593	19687	20663	21613
29	109	727	1447	2207	2971	3803	4651	5519	6361	7283	8209	9103	9973	10939	11927	12823	13763	14759	15671	16673	17659	18617	19697	20681	21617
30	113	733	1451	2213	2999	3821	4657	5521	6367	7297	8219	9109	10007	10949	11933	12829	13781	14767	15679	16691	17669	18637	19699	20693	21647
31	127	739	1453	2221	3001	3823	4663	5527	6373	7307	8221	9127	10009	10957	11939	12841	13789	14771	15683	16693	17681	18661	19709	20707	21649
32	131	743	1459	2237	3011	3833	4673	5531	6379	7309	8231	9133	10037	10973	11941	12853	13799	14779	15727	16699	17683	18671	19717	20717	21661
33	137	751	1471	2239	3019	3847	4679	5557	6389	7321	8233	9137	10039	10979	11953	12889	13807	14783	15731	16703	17707	18679	19727	20719	21673
34	139	757	1481	2243	3023	3851	4691	5563	6397	7331	8237	9151	10061	10987	11959	12893	13829	14797	15733	16729	17713	18691	19739	20731	21683
35	149	761	1483	2251	3037	3853	4703	5569	6421	7333	8243	9157	10067	10993	11969	12899	13831	14813	15737	16741	17729	18701	19751	20743	21701
36	151	769	1487	2267	3041	3863	4721	5573	6427	7349	8263	9161	10069	11003	11971	12907	13841	14821	15739	16747	17737	18713	19753	20747	21713
37	157	773	1489	2269	3049	3877	4723	5581	6449	7351	8269	9173	10079	11027	11981	12911	13859	14827	15749	16759	17747	18719	19759	20749	21727
38	163	787	1493	2273	3061	3881	4729	5591	6451	7369	8273	9181	10091	11047	11987	12917	13873	14831	15761	16763	17749	18731	19763	20753	21737
39	167	797	1499	2281	3067	3889	4733	5623	6469	7393	8287	9187	10093	11057	12007	12919	13877	14843	15767	16787	17761	18743	19777	20759	21739
40	173	809	1511	2287	3079	3907	4751	5639	6473	7411	8291	9199	10099	11059	12011	12923	13879	14851	15773	16811	17783	18749	19793	20771	21751
41	179	811	1523	2293	3083	3911	4759	5641	6481	7417	8293	9203	10103	11069	12037	12941	13883	14867	15787	16823	17789	18757	19801	20773	21757
42	181	821	1531	2297	3089	3917	4783	5647	6491	7433	8297	9209	10111	11071	12041	12953	13901	14869	15791	16829	17791	18773	19813	20789	21767
43	191	823	1543	2309	3109	3919	4787	5651	6521	7451	8311	9221	10133	11083	12043	12959	13903	14879	15797	16831	17807	18787	19819	20807	21773
44	193	827	1549	2311	3119	3923	4789	5653	6529	7457	8317	9227	10139	11087	12049	12967	13907	14887	15803	16843	17827	18793	19841	20809	21787
45	197	829	1553	2333	3121	3929	4793	5657	6547	7459	8329	9239	10141	11093	12071	12973	13913	14891	15809	16871	17837	18797	19843	20849	21799
46	199	839	1559	2339	3137	3931	4799	5659	6551	7477	8353	9241	10151	11113	12073	12979	13921	14897	15817	16879	17839	18803	19853	20857	21803
47	211	853	1567	2341	3163	3943	4801	5669	6553	7481	8363	9257	10159	11117	12097	12983	13931	14923	15823	16883	17851	18839	19861	20873	21817
48	223	857	1571	2347	3167	3947	4813	5683	6563	7487	8369	9277	10163	11119	12101	13001	13933	14929	15859	16889	17863	18859	19867	20879	21821
49	227	859	1579	2351	3169	3967	4817	5689	6569	7489	8377	9281	10169	11131	12107	13003	13963	14939	15877	16901	17881	18869	19889	20887	21839
50	229	863	1583	2357	3181	3989	4831	5693	6571	7499	8387	9283	10177	11149	12109	13007	13967	14947	15881	16903	17891	18899	19891	20897	21841
51	233	877	1597	2371	3187	4001	4861	5701	6577	7507	8389	9293	10181	11159	12113	13009	13997	14951	15887	16921	17903	18911	19913	20899	21851
52	239	881	1601	2377	3191	4003	4871	5711	6581	7517	8419	9311	10193	11161	12119	13033	13999	14957	15889	16927	17909	18913	19919	20903	21859
53	241	883	1607	2381	3203	4007	4877	5717	6599	7523	8423	9319	10211	11171	12143	13037	14009	14969	15901	16931	17911	18917	19927	20921	21863
54	251	887	1609	2383	3209	4013	4889	5737	6607	7529	8429	9323	10223	11173	12149	13043	14011	14983	15907	16937	17921	18919	19937	20929	21871
55	257	907	1613	2389	3217	4019	4903	5741	6619	7537	8431	9337	10243	11177	12157	13049	14029	15013	15913	16943	17923	18947	19949	20939	21881
56	263	911	1619	2393	3221	4021	4909	5743	6637	7541	8443	9341	10247	11197	12161	13063	14033	15017	15919	16963	17929	18959	19961	20947	21893
57	269	919	1621	2399	3229	4027	4919	5749	6653	7547	8447	9343	10253	11213	12163	13093	14051	15031	15923	16979	17939	18973	19963	20959	21911
58	271	929	1627	2411	3251	4049	4931	5779	6659	7549	8461	9349	10259	11239	12197	13099	14057	15053	15937	16981	17957	18979	19973	20963	21929
59	277	937	1637	2417	3253	4051	4933	5783	6661	7559	8467	9371	10267	11243	12203	13103	14071	15061	15959	16987	17959	19001	19979	20981	21937
60	281	941	1657	2423	3257	4057	4937	5791	6673	7561	8501	9377	10271	11251	12211	13109	14081	15073	15971	16993	17971	19009	19991	20983	21943
61	283	947	1663	2437	3259	4073	4943	5801	6679	7573	8513	9391	10273	11257	12227	13121	14083	15077	15973	17011	17977	19013	19993	21001	21961
62	293	953	1667	2441	3271	4079	4951	5807	6689	7577	8521	9397	10289	11261	12239	13127	14087	15083	15991	17021	17981	19031	19997	21011	21977
63	307	967	1669	2447	3299	4091	4957	5813	6691	7583	8527	9403	10301	11273	12241	13147	14107	15091	16001	17027	17987	19037	20011	21013	21991
64	311	971	1693	2459	3301	4093	4967	5821	6701	7589	8537	9413	10303	11279	12251	13151	14143	15101	16007	17029	17989	19051	20021	21017	21997
65	313	977	1697	2467	3307	4099	4969	5827	6703	7591	8539	9419	10313	11287	12253	13159	14149	15107	16033	17033	18013	19069	20023	21019	22003
66	317	983	1699	2473	3313	4111	4973	5839	6709	7603	8543	9421	10321	11299	12263	13163	14153	15121	16057	17041	18041	19073	20029	21023	22013
67	331	991	1709	2477	3319	4127	4987	5843	6719	7607	8563	9431	10331	11311	12269	13171	14159	15131	16061	17047	18043	19079	20047	21031	22027
68	337	997	1721	2503	3323	4129	4993	5849	6733	7621	8573	9433	10333	11317	12277	13177	14173	15137	16063	17053	18047	19081	20051	21059	22031
69	347	1009	1723	2521	3329	4133	4999	5851	6737	7639	8581	9437	10337	11321	12281	13183	14177	15139	16067	17077	18049	19087	20063	21061	22037
70	349	1013	1733	2531	3331	4139	5003	5857	6761	7643	8597	9439	10343	11329	12289	13187	14197	15149	16069	17093	18059	19121	20071	21067	22039
71	353	1019	1741	2539	3343	4153	5009	5861	6763	7649	8599	9461	10357	11351	12301	13217	14207	15161	16073	17099	18061	19139	20089	21089	22051
72	359	1021	1747	2543	3347	4157	5011	5867	6779	7669	8609	9463	10369	11353	12323	13219	14221	15173	16087	17107	18077	19141	20101	21101	22063
73	367	1031	1753	2549	3359	4159	5021	5869	6781	7673	8623	9467	10391	11369	12329	13229	14243	15187	16091	17117	18089	19157	20107	21107	22067
74	373	1033	1759	2551	3361	4177	5023	5879	6791	7681	8627	9473	10399	11383	12343	13241	14249	15193	16097	17123	18097	19163	20113	21121	22073
75	379	1039	1777	2557	3371	4201	5039	5881	6793	7687	8629	9479	10427	11393	12347	13249	14251	15199	16103	17137	18119	19181	20117	21139	22079
76	383	1049	1783	2579	3373	4211	5051	5897	6803	7691	8641	9491	10429	11399	12373	13259	14281	15217	16111	17159	18121	19183	20123	21143	22091
77	389	1051	1787	2591	3389	4217	5059	5903	6823	7699	8647	9497	10433	11411	12377	13267	14293	15227	16127	17167	18127	19207	20129	21149	22093
78	397	1061	1789	2593	3391	4219	5077	5923	6827	7703	8663	9511	10453	11423	12379	13291	14303	15233	16139	17183	18131	19211	20143	21157	22109
79	401	1063	1801	2609	3407	4229	5081	5927	6829	7717	8669	9521	10457	11437	12391	13297	14321	15241	16141	17189	18133	19213	20147	21163	22111
80	409	1069	1811	2617	3413	4231	5087	5939	6833	7723	8677	9533	10459	11443	12401	13309	14323	15259	16183	17191	18143	19219	20149	21169	22123
81	419	1087	1823	2621	3433	4241	5099	5953	6841	7727	8681	9539	10463	11447	12409	13313	14327	15263	16187	17203	18149	19231	20161	21179	22129
82	421	1091	1831	2633	3449	4243	5101	5981	6857	7741	8689	9547	10477	11467	12413	13327	14341	15269	16189	17207	18169	19237	20173	21187	22133
83	431	1093	1847	2647	3457	4253	5107	5987	6863	7753	8693	9551	10487	11471	12421	13331	14347	15271	16193	17209	18181	19249	20177	21191	22147
84	433	1097	1861	2657	3461	4259	5113	6007	6869	7757	8699	9587	10499	11483	12433	13337	14369	15277	16217	17231	18191	19259	20183	21193	22153
85	439	1103	1867	2659	3463	4261	5119	6011	6871	7759	8707	9601	10501	11489	12437	13339	14387	15287	16223	17239	18199	19267	20201	21211	22157
86	443	1109	1871	2663	3467	4271	5147	6029	6883	7789	8713	9613	10513	11491	12451	13367	14389	15289	16229	17257	18211	19273	20219	21221	22159
87	449	1117	1873	2671	3469	4273	5153	6037	6899	7793	8719	9619	10529	11497	12457	13381	14401	15299	16231	17291	18217	19289	20231	21227	22171
88	457	1123	1877	2677	3491	4283	5167	6043	6907	7817	8731	9623	10531	11503	12473	13397	14407	15307	16249	17293	18223	19301	20233	21247	22189
89	461	1129	1879	2683	3499	4289	5171	6047	6911	7823	8737	9629	10559	11519	12479	13399	14411	15313	16253	17299	18229	19309	20249	21269	22193
90	463	1151	1889	2687	3511	4297	5179	6053	6917	7829	8741	9631	10567	11527	12487	13411	14419	15319	16267	17317	18233	19319	20261	21277	22229
91	467	1153	1901	2689	3517	4327	5189	6067	6947	7841	8747	9643	10589	11549	12491	13417	14423	15329	16273	17321	18251	19333	20269	21283	22247
92	479	1163	1907	2693	3527	4337	5197	6073	6949	7853	8753	9649	10597	11551	12497	13421	14431	15331	16301	17327	18253	19373	20287	21313	22259
93	487	1171	1913	2699	3529	4339	5209	6079	6959	7867	8761	9661	10601	11579	12503	13441	14437	15349	16319	17333	18257	19379	20297	21317	22271
94	491	1181	1931	2707	3533	4349	5227	6089	6961	7873	8779	9677	10607	11587	12511	13451	14447	15359	16333	17341	18269	19381	20323	21319	22273
95	499	1187	1933	2711	3539	4357	5231	6091	6967	7877	8783	9679	10613	11593	12517	13457	14449	15361	16339	17351	18287	19387	20327	21323	22277
96	503	1193	1949	2713	3541	4363	5233	6101	6971	7879	8803	9689	10627	11597	12527	13463	14461	15373	16349	17359	18289	19391	20333	21341	22279
97	509	1201	1951	2719	3547	4373	5237	6113	6977	7883	8807	9697	10631	11617	12539	13469	14479	15377	16361	17377	18301	19403	20341	21347	22283
98	521	1213	1973	2729	3557	4391	5261	6121	6983	7901	8819	9719	10639	11621	12541	13477	14489	15383	16363	17383	18307	19417	20347	21377	22291
99	523	1217	1979	2731	3559	4397	5273	6131	6991	7907	8821	9721	10651	11633	12547	13487	14503	15391	16369	17387	18311	19421	20353	21379	22303
100	541	1223	1987	2741	3571	4409	5279	6133	6997	7919	8831	9733	10657	11657	12553	13499	14519	15401	16381	17389	18313	19423	20357	21383	22307

Figure 3. The first few primes (Reprinted from Davis and Hersch, 1981)

we take the power of ten and divide it by the number of primes. This is done in the third column below.

The third column seems to increase by about 2.3 at every stage. This general pattern will continue indefinitely. It is not a very good one, but it is sufficient to bolster our confidence in the orderliness that Ishango Man first contemplated over 9000 years ago.

(1) Powers of ten	(2) Number of primes less than or equal to the power of ten	(3) Column 1 divided by column 2	(4) Amount of increase in column 3
10	4	2.50	
100	25	4.00	1.50
1,000	168	5.95	1.95
10,000	1,229	8.14	2.18
100,000	9,592	10.43	2.29
1,000,000	78,498	12.74	2.31
10,000,000	664,579	15.05	2.31
100,000,000	5,761,455	17.36	2.31
1,000,000,000	50,847,634	19.67	2.31
10,000,000,000	455,052,512	21.98	2.31

Figure 4. The distribution of primes

The most sophisticated attempt to find a pattern in the distribution of primes may be found in the equation below. Do not be overly disturbed by the look of it.

$$R(n) = 1 + \sum_{k=1}^{\infty} \frac{1}{k\zeta(k+1)} \frac{(\log n)^k}{k!}$$

The function $\zeta(n)$ is the zeta function which equals

$$\zeta(z) = 1 + (1/2)^z + (1/3)^z + (1/4)^z + \ldots$$

We need not worry about any of this, however, because all we want to show is how close the function R(n) comes to predicting the number of primes less than or equal to n. We do this in Figure 5.

(1)	(2)	(3)	(4)
Powers of ten	Number of primes less than or equal to the power of ten	R(n)	Difference
100,000,000	5,761,455	5,761,552	97
200,000,000	11,078,937	11,079,090	153
300,000,000	16,252,325	16,252,355	30
400,000,000	21,336,326	21,336,185	-141
500,000,000	26,355,867	26,355,517	-350
600,000,000	31,324,703	31,324,622	-81
700,000,000	36,252,931	36,252,719	-212
800,000,000	41,146,179	41,146,248	69
900,000,000	46,009,215	46,009,949	734
1,000,000,000	50,847,534	50,847,455	-79

Figure 5. Predicting the distribution of primes

Notice that R(n) is never very far off the mark. It is enough to warm the hearts of the Ishango—orderliness in chaos, revealing one of the secrets of creation, the entrance into all obscure secrets.

THE SIEVE OF ERATOSTHENES . . .

Eratosthenes lived in Greece during the third century B.C. His compatriots nicknamed him "Beta," the second letter of the alphabet, since they believed he was only second best in most of his endeavors. The nickname, however, is not demeaning when one considers how varied his endeavors were. He was an astronomer, mathematician, historian, and geographer. And in at least one startling case his compatriots' judgments were flatly wrong, although they did not know it. This was Eratosthenes' estimate of the circumference of the earth. Based on only a few observations, he believed it to be somewhat more than twenty-five thousand miles, which is very nearly correct.

Like many others, Eratosthenes realized that there is no simple way of producing all the primes in sequence. Euclid's proof, which we have already seen, effectively produces an infinity of primes, but it leaves large gaps. The best approach is the rather naive one of taking a number, then seeing if it is evenly divisible by any number less than it other than 1. Is 2,956,913 prime? Is it divisible by 2,956,912? No. Is it divisible by 2,956,911? No . . . Continue this way and with enough patience you will get your answer. We can add a little sophistication to the process by checking not each number less than the number in question, but each number equal to or less than its square root. The reasoning here is that among the prime divisors of n at least one must be less than or equal to $\sqrt{n}$.

Eratosthenes saw that it is really a little more convenient to turn this process around. Instead of finding the divisors of a number, we will find the multiples of all other numbers. Once all of these have been eliminated, whatever remains must be prime. For example, write down all the numbers between 2 and 100. Which ones are prime? Begin at 2 and eliminate every second number, since these are multiples of 2: thus, cross out 2, 4, 6, 8, 10, and so on. Now move to 3. It is not crossed out, so it must be prime. Now eliminate every third number: 6, 9, 12, 15, and so on. Move to 4; it is crossed out, so it must be composite. Move to 5; it is prime, since no number less than 5 can claim it as a multiple, so we eliminate every fifth number. Continue in this way, and when you are done you have all the primes between 2 and 100. Since we are looking for primes less than 100, we can stop the process on 7, the largest prime less than $\sqrt{100}$. See Figure 6.

This process is now known as the Sieve of Eratosthenes. It is still naive, but quite simple to handle. Its major disadvantage is that you must limit your search beforehand.

Figure 6. The Sieve of Eratosthenes

	2	3	4	5	6	7	8	9	10
11	12	13	14	15	16	17	18	19	20
21	22	23	24	25	26	27	28	29	30
31	32	33	34	35	36	37	38	39	40
41	42	43	44	45	46	47	48	49	50
51	52	53	54	55	56	57	58	59	60
61	62	63	64	65	66	67	68	69	70
71	72	73	74	75	76	77	78	79	80
81	82	83	84	85	86	87	88	89	90
91	92	93	94	95	96	97	98	99	100

. . . AND THE SIEVE OF
JOHN HORTON CONWAY

John Horton Conway is a professor of mathematics at Princeton University, justly famous not only for his serious discoveries but also for his many puzzles and games. At least one compatriot has come close to nicknaming him "Alpha and Omega."[1]

He has created what might be called a new kind of sieve, and unlike that of Eratosthenes, it truly produces all the primes in sequence without any limits whatsoever. There is something enormously magical about it, and like all good magic it becomes even more wonderful when you dig beneath the surface to reveal its pristine simplicity. It is really nothing more than the set of fourteen fractions in Figure 7.

$$\frac{17}{91} \quad \frac{78}{85} \quad \frac{19}{51} \quad \frac{23}{38} \quad \frac{29}{33} \quad \frac{77}{29} \quad \frac{95}{23}$$

$$\frac{77}{19} \quad \frac{1}{17} \quad \frac{11}{13} \quad \frac{13}{11} \quad \frac{15}{14} \quad \frac{15}{2} \quad \frac{55}{1}$$

Figure 7. The Sieve of
John Horton Conway

You are to take a number and run through the fractions, from first to last, until you find one that will produce an integer. Once you get that integer, then run through the fractions again in order to get the next integer. Begin with 2. Will the first fraction give you a whole number? No, so move on to the second fraction. You will not be able to stop until you get to the next-to-last fraction, and then the product, at long last, is 15. With this new number we begin all over again. Fifteen becomes 825 when it is multiplied by the last fraction, and 825 becomes 725, and so on. We stop when we arrive at a number that is a power of 2. The power itself—that is the next prime!

Figure 8 shows the Conway fractions pumping out the first prime, 2. This, after 19 steps. You need 50 more steps to find the next prime, 3 (which appears as 2^3). And 211 more to find 5 (or 2^5). It's all a little like swatting a fly with heavy artillery, but remember these fourteen fractions alone have it in them to produce an infinity of primes, even those that no one yet knows about. Look at them carefully and you will begin to feel somewhat awestruck, perhaps like the Ishango must have felt when they first contemplated the etchings on their bone.

---

[1] I am thinking of Donald E. Knuth, a professor of computer science at Stanford University. His short novel, *Surreal Numbers*, is about an ancient text concerning one J.H.W.H. Conway, a mythical figure who created the rules "to bring forth all numbers large and small."

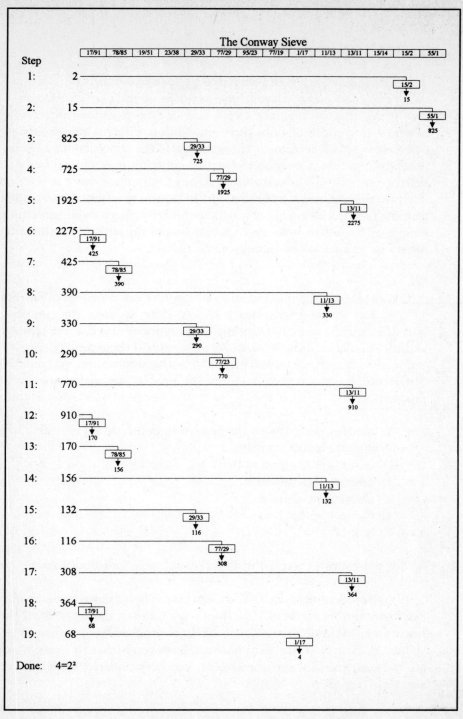

Figure 8. Finding the first prime with the Sieve of Conway

How in the world does it work? To answer that, let us look at something that may seem unrelated at first but which is really very similar to the Conway sieve. Imagine a simple computer with a small set of registers, or memory locations that can store an integer. The machine is capable of only three operations. First, it can increment (increase by 1) or decrement (decrease by 1) the contents of a register. Second, it can see if a register is zero. And third, it can jump to a new instruction. We might call this an Ishango computer, since it restricts itself to addition and subtraction within the unary number system. The purpose of introducing the Ishango computer is to give you something simple and solid to hold on to while grappling with ideas that may otherwise seem obscure and abstract.

Can we use an Ishango computer to subtract two numbers other than 1? Yes, and we need only two registers. First, we load the computer with the two numbers, putting the larger number into the first register, and the smaller into the second. We look to see if the second equals 0. If it does not, decrement both registers by 1; then repeat this last step. If it does, stop. The first register contains the answer. We can write a simple program:

0. Load register A with the large number. Load register B with the small number.
1. Is register B equal to 0? If yes, go to step 5.
2. Decrement register B.
3. Decrement register A.
4. Go to step 1.
5. Stop

The program is pictured in Figure 9 as a standard flowchart.

It may seem unnecessarily fussy, but this is because we are limited to the unary number system. The important point is that even with this limitation, higher-level tasks can be accomplished with sufficient patience. What might not seem obvious, however, is that this task—and all tasks on the Ishango computer—can be simulated with a set of Conway fractions.

The trick is the simple fact that every number can be decomposed into a unique set of primes; and conversely every set of primes, when multiplied together, will produce a unique number.

Here is how it works. Imagine you have an Ishango computer with only two registers, A and B, like the one we have just used. Certainly the state of the computer is completely determined when we give the contents of the registers. Now imagine you have a number of the form $2^A 3^B$. Then this number is completely de-

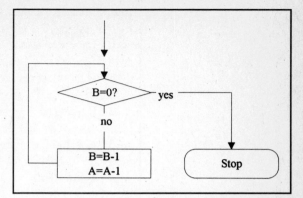

Figure 9. How an Ishango computer subtracts two numbers

termined when we give the values of A and B. Do you see what is happening? On the one hand, we have an Ishango who might say, "My computer has a 5 and 2 in its registers." On the other hand, we have John Horton Conway who replies, "288." They have said the same thing, since 288, and no other number, equals $2^5 3^2$. In this example, the "registers" are the primes 2 and 3. Any primes will do, but it is easiest to use the small ones.

The computer's ability to change the contents of a register by 1 is simulated by simple multiplication and division using the corresponding primes. An Ishango might say, "I have decremented the contents of register A." We reply, "$288/2 = 144$." Again we have said the same thing, since $144 = 2^4 3^2$. An Ishango might say, "I have incremented the contents of register B." We reply, "$144 \cdot 3 = 432$," since this gives us $2^4 3^3$.

Primes other than those used as registers enable us to turn an instruction on or off at any given moment, effectively simulating an Ishango computer's ability to jump about its program. An example will bring everything together. Consider the fraction

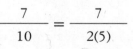

$$\frac{7}{10} = \frac{7}{2(5)}$$

Think of what this fraction means, not in terms of arithmetic but in the more concrete terms of a computer. Is the fraction usable? Only if the machine is currently in state 5 and register A is not equal to 0; otherwise the fraction will not produce a whole number. What happens

Figure 10. The meaning of the fractions

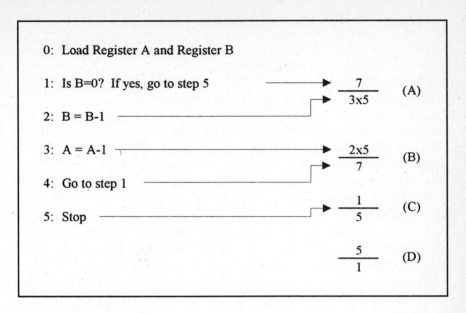

0: Load Register A and Register B

1: Is B=0? If yes, go to step 5 $\dfrac{7}{3 \times 5}$ (A)

2: B = B-1

3: A = A-1 $\dfrac{2 \times 5}{7}$ (B)

4: Go to step 1

5: Stop $\dfrac{1}{5}$ (C)

$\dfrac{5}{1}$ (D)

if we use it? It will decrement register A and shift the machine to state 7. In Figure 10, we change each line of our program to the fraction that simulates it. (Labels are assigned to the fractions for easier reference.)

In finding these fractions, we are not so much engaging in arithmetic as we are programming an Ishango computer. Let us use the computer to subtract 2 from 5. First load the numbers into the appropriate registers—that is, compute $2^5 3^2 = 288$. Now go through the fractions as before until you get a power of 2:

$$288 \to E \to 1440 \to A \to 672 \to B \to 240 \to$$
$$A \to 112 \to B \to 40 \to$$

$$C \to 8 \text{ (or } 2^3)$$

Notice that the power of 2—the contents of register A—is 3, just as it should be in the Ishango computer.

Can we use an Ishango computer to see if one number is divisible by another? Yes, and although it may not seem obvious, we have already done much of the work. A general flowchart is in Figure 11(a). In Figure 11(b) we list a corresponding set of fractions.

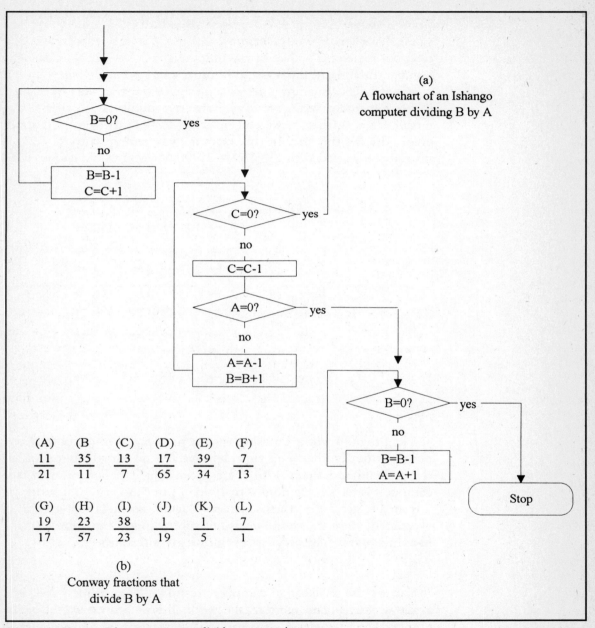

(a)
A flowchart of an Ishango
computer dividing B by A

(A)	(B	(C)	(D)	(E)	(F)
$\frac{11}{21}$	$\frac{35}{11}$	$\frac{13}{7}$	$\frac{17}{65}$	$\frac{39}{34}$	$\frac{7}{13}$

(G)	(H)	(I)	(J)	(K)	(L)
$\frac{19}{17}$	$\frac{23}{57}$	$\frac{38}{23}$	$\frac{1}{19}$	$\frac{1}{5}$	$\frac{7}{1}$

(b)
Conway fractions that
divide B by A

Figure 11. How an Ishango computer divides two numbers

Use the computer—use the fractions—to see if 3 is divisible by 2. This time we need three registers, since a third is used for temporary storage. We load the numbers into registers A and B respectively, and clear out register C—that is, we compute $2^3 3^2 5^0 = 72$. Now run this number through the fractions in the usual way, stopping when you get a power of 2. The program is designed in such a way that the power itself is the remainder when we divide the two numbers, so that if the remainder is 0 (that is, we end up with $2^0 = 1$) the second number evenly divides the first. In this example, you end up with $2 = 2^1$. If instead you started with $2^{13} 3^5 5^0 = 1,990,656$ you would end up with $8 = 2^3$.

$$72 \to L \to 504 \to A \to 264 \to B \to 840 \to$$
$$A \to 440 \to B \to 1440 \to$$

$$C \to 2600 \to D \to 680 \to E \to 780 \to$$
$$D \to 204 \to E \to 234 \to$$

$$F \to 126 \to A \to 66 \to B \to 210 \to$$
$$A \to 110 \to B \to 350 \to$$

$$C \to 650 \to D \to 170 \to E \to 195 \to$$
$$D \to 51 \to$$

$$G \to 57 \to H \to 23 \to I \to 38 \to$$

$$J \to 2 \ (\text{or } 2^1)$$

The program works by using the previous program to subtract one number from another. This time, however, we do not stop but subtract it out again and again until there is nothing left. For example, the computer is too simpleminded to divide 13 by 5, so instead it subtracts 5 from 13, getting 8, then subtracts 5 again, getting 3. (Even this is overstated, since the computer is not subtracting 5 but subtracting 1 five times over). The very last operation gives the answer.

Can we use an Ishango computer to find all the primes? Yes, and again we have done most of the work. Let us assume we have the number 15 in register A. Is it prime? We use the previous program to see if it is divisible by 14, then 13, then 12, and so on. If we reach the end, then it is prime. Here at last we have Conway's magic, and surprisingly, the general procedure is really no more complex than the very naive algorithm that predated even Eratosthenes. I will not give the flowchart in this case, but leave it to the reader instead. It is somewhat complicated, but accessible to anyone who sticks with it.

One more thing: What I have called an Ishango computer is more properly called a Minsky machine. And there is nothing ancient or primitive about it. It is, in fact, a fundamental tool of modern computer science.

OR IS IT REALLY A CALENDAR?

There is another way of interpreting the Ishango bone.

Remember that the Ishango were hunters and gatherers who lived by the lakeside. There were very definite times of the year when rains would make the lakeside village uninhabitable, and there were other times when it became more profitable to fish than to hunt. In both cases, and in many others we can imagine, it may have been necessary for the Ishango to distinguish the seasons of the year. Is it possible that the bone is actually a primitive kind of calendar? It was this possibility that attracted the attention of Alexander Marshack in *The Roots of Civilization*.

There is one obvious reason for thinking the bone is keeping a record of the heavens. Sum the numbers along the column that we thought was a listing of the prime numbers: $11 + 13 + 17 + 19 = 60$. Now sum the numbers along the column that we thought had played on the number ten: $11 + 21 + 19 + 9 = 60$. In both columns we have very nearly the number of days that make up two lunar months. (A true lunar month is only 29.5 days, but this is an astronomical precision we cannot credit to the Ishango.) Clocking the seasons by reference to the moon was common among people who left records of their work, such as the Babylonians, who developed a remarkably advanced system of astronomy. The curiosity that attracted their attention to the heavens may have developed first among the Ishango.

How can we test this hypothesis? If we believe that each notch on the bone represents a day, and the various groups of notches on the bone represent periods between different phases of the moon, we find ourselves up against a few roadblocks. First, we do not know in which order the notches were made. Did the Ishango record the days from right to left, or from left to right? Similarly, having reached the end of a line, was the tendency to "wrap around" and go in the other direction, as some ancient people did in their writing, or to begin over again and move in the same direction, as we do today? Even the idea of counting days is open to question. A lunar month is actually very uneven. The number of days between a visible moon could be one, two, or three, although on the average it is only two. Finally, even the notches are open to some interpretation. If you look closely at the illustration, you will see that it is a little arbitrary to lump some of them together. The first stretch of 19 notches is made up of two quite distinct groups, one with 5 little notches, and one of 14 larger ones.

Taking all this into account, there is far too much room for hedging, allowing us to prove almost any hypothesis. Nevertheless, Marshack has done a fairly credible job. We assume that Ishango Man held the bone in his left hand with the quartz end pointing to the right. The notches were made beginning at the quartz end and moving to the left. At the end of the first row, the bone was turned 180 degrees and the second series of notches were made in the same direction. In this way, the notches appear to keep track of various phases of the moon. The results are in Figure 12.

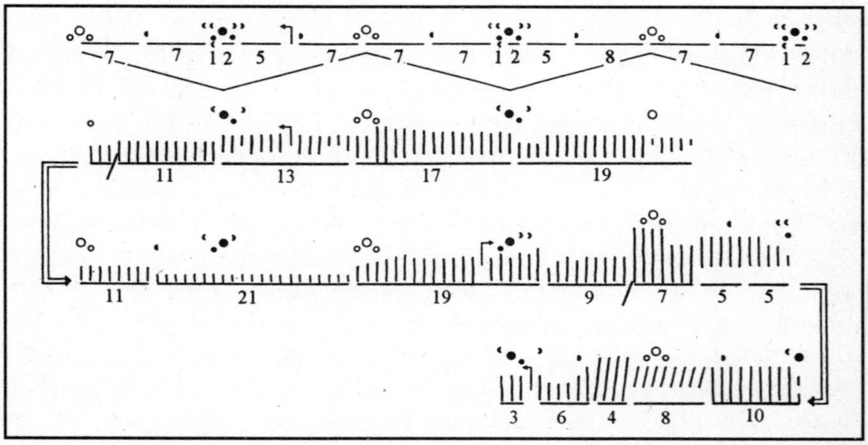

Figure 12. The Ishango bone as a calendar (Reprinted from Marshack, 1971)

Notice that different segments of notches appear to begin and end with different phases of the moon, although sometimes it is necessary to think of one segment of notches as two. This, however, is never done unless there is some reason for doing so on the bone itself, as when the notches appear to change shape or angle.

In all, Marshack's theory may seem a little strained, but there is nothing in it that is obviously wrong. ". . . I had an almost desperate desire to hold the bone in hand so that I could see and feel it," Marshack later wrote, having seen that his original hypothesis appeared to have some truth behind it. Indeed, there is something almost mystifying about the bone. Whatever its ultimate use may have been in the hands of its owner—and we may never know what that was—it cannot be denied that the notches are in fact some primitive form of counting. In that sense it is the beginning of all puzzles.

THE END OF ISHANGO

Not very long after the bone was first etched, a volcano erupted around Lake Edward and the ash blackened the sky. It settled on the tiny fishing village and in time the Ishango and their way of life was obliterated. Their time on earth may have been only a few centuries. We will never know what they did with that strange bone, but whether it was a game they played among themselves or a calendar to chart their seasons, it is undoubtedly one of the earliest uses of numbers that we know of. Nothing similar to it can be found in Europe during this time. "It is even possible," de Heinzelin wrote, "that the modern world owes one of its greatest debts to the people who lived at Ishango. Whether or not this is the case, it is remarkable that the oldest clue to the use of a number system by man dates back to the central Africa of the Mesolithic period."

It has been sad to watch the picture of Africa—including its fossil, the Ishango bone—become blurry and even comical over the years. One story in particular may seem appropriate at this point, since it involves the use of doubling a number. It was written in 1889 by a British anthropologist, Sir Francis Galton, who described an encounter with the Damara people of Namibia in his book *Narrative of an Explorer in Tropical South Africa*. In usual bartering, two sticks of tobacco were exchanged for one sheep. But the Damaras became confused when one trader offered four sticks at once for two sheep. The transaction had to be conducted more slowly—first two sticks of tobacco were given for one sheep, then two sticks were given again for a second sheep. When it was pointed out that the final transaction was the same as the one originally offered, the Damaras were suspicious of the trader, as though he possessed magical powers.

There are many stories like this, and they are often used to explain that a people who do not have a number system are incapable of understanding the concept of multiplication. But Galton is asking the Damaras to play a game according to his own rules, in his own language, so to speak. Unsurprisingly, they failed. It is true that the Damaras refer to all quantities above two as "many," but only in certain aspects of daily life. (Westerners do the same when they speak of disarmament as "unilateral," "bilateral," and "multilateral.") What is missing from the story is another side of the Damaras, which Howard Eves sums up nicely in his book *In Mathematical Circles*: "They [the Damaras] were not unintelligent. They knew precisely the size of a flock of sheep or a herd of oxen, and would miss an individual at once, because they knew the faces of all of the animals. To us, this form of intelligence, which is true and keen observation, would be infinitely more difficult to cultivate than that involved in counting." This sense of number is not inferior; it is only different. It served their purposes as Galton's served his. I wonder now what would have been Galton's response if, at the conclusion of the negotiations, the Damara herdsman had said, "You may take all the sheep with hooked ears." He would not have known how many to take. That must have occurred at least once, and I dearly hope that someone somewhere in Namibia is repeating intolerant stories about stupid Westerners who cannot tell one sheep from another.

The Entrance into All Obscure Secrets

WORK, MY BROTHER, REST IS NIGH—

PHARAOH LIVES FOR EVER!

BEAST AND BIRD OF EARTH AND SKY,

THINGS THAT CREEP AND THINGS THAT FLY—

ALL MUST LABOR, ALL MUST DIE;

BUT PHARAOH LIVES FOR EVER!

—*SACHEDON*, GEORGE JOHN WHYTE-MELVILLE

THERE IS A YELLOWING DOCUMENT IN THE EGYPTIAN SECTION of the British Museum that is a highly valuable manuscript to anyone interested in puzzles and their histories. The author is a scribe named A'h-mose or Ahmes, which means "A'h (the moon-god) is born." He claims to have written the document during the reign of A-user-Re, which takes it to the Egypt of 1650 B.C. Ahmes, however, tells us he is only copying a much older papyrus, which was written in the time of Ne-ma'et-Re, sometimes called Amenemhet III, a ruler of Upper and Lower Egypt, which takes the document back to almost 1850 B.C., and perhaps even earlier if that text was itself a copy of an older one.

HEAT, WIND, AND HIGH WATER

One might think that the profession of a scribe was a lowly one, but actually they were highly regarded in ancient Egypt. Their education started at an early age and continued for many years, mainly because the texts that they worked on were so highly valued, and any mistake would be transmitted to future copies. One sign of the importance of a scribe is the fact that his education was often associated with a temple. The exercises given to the apprentice scribe have been preserved in one of these temples at Thebes. They make interesting reading today; apparently they were meant to frighten the young student into working harder. The following has been freely translated into very modern-sounding English:

> You should have seen me when I was your age. Then I had to sit with my hands in manacles, and by this means, my limbs were tamed. Three months I bore them and sat locked up in the temple. My father and my mother were in the field and my brothers as well. But when I became free of the manacles, then I surpassed everything I had done before and became the best in the class and outshone the others in the art of writing. Now do as I say, and you will prosper, and soon you will find that you have no rival.

Further evidence of the high esteem given to scribes is found in the *Teachings* of someone named Tuauf. The document, now preserved in the British Museum, was probably used as a schoolbook for novice scribes. Tuauf says:

> I would have thee love books as thou lovest thy mother, and I will set their beauties before thee. The profession of the scribe is the greatest of all professions; it has no equal upon the earth. Even when the scribe is a beginner in his career his opinion is consulted. He is sent on missions of state and does not come back to place himself under the direction of another.

Then Tuauf proceeds to beat us over the head with his opinion of other professions:

The coppersmith has to work in front of his blazing furnace, his
fingers are like the crocodile's legs, and he stinks more than the
insides of fish . . . The waterman is stung to death by gnats and
mosquitoes, and the stench of the canals chokes him . . . The
weaver is worse off than a woman. His thighs are drawn up to his
body, and he cannot breathe. The day he fails to do his work he is
dragged from the hut, like a lotus from the pool, and cast aside. To
be allowed to see daylight he must give the overseer his dinner . . .
The reed-cutter's fingers stink like a fishmonger's; his eyes are dull
and lifeless, and he works naked all the day long at cutting reeds.

This tirade continues for several pages, until Tuauf finally declares,
"Every toiler curses his trade or occupation, except the scribe to whom
no one says, 'Go and work in the fields of so-and-so.' "

We can see a scribe in one of the murals excavated from the tomb of
Menna, an important scribe who died in the fourteenth century B.C. in a
city called Abd-el-Qurna. The mural portrays Menna as he estimates
the taxes of the region during a harvest. To his right a farmer is being
punished, presumably for failure to pay his share. A large figure on his
left was called a *harpedonaptai*, or rope-stretcher, the government official
who actually measured the farmer's land; one coil of rope has already
been drawn taut, and another is still wrapped around his shoulder. The
stretched rope is used as a primitive measuring tool to obtain the
straight-line distance of one side of the field. Based on these figures
Menna had to calculate the farmer's taxes. It is possible that the method
of computation had been learned from the manuscript that Ahmes had
copied.

The only title on this document is *Directions for Attaining Knowledge
into All Obscure Secrets*. Rather unfairly, it is not generally named for
Ahmes, but instead is called the Rhind Papyrus because it was purchased by A. Henry Rhind, a Scottish antiquary. Rhind came into
possession of the document in 1858 while vacationing in Egypt. He was
told that the loose pages of ancient papyrus had been found in the ruins
surrounding Thebes. Rhind himself died of tuberculosis only five years
after his return to England, far too soon for him to have witnessed the
remarkable discovery that came later. For it was nearly a half century
after his death that certain important sections of his document turned

Figure 13. "The entrance into . . . all obscure secrets . . ." (Reprinted from Chace, et al, 1927)

up, quite by accident, in the New York Historical Society. These missing fragments were mixed together with ancient medical texts that had been donated by the collector Edwin Smith. When combined with Rhind's documents, the missing fragments revealed a text that was not at all an antiquary's curiosity, but "one of the ancient monuments of learning," as it is now commonly referred to.

The manuscripts open with a beautiful little poem (see Figure 13):

Accurate reckoning. The entrance into the knowledge of all existing things and all obscure secrets.

And it ends with a curious prayer:

Catch the vermin and the mice, extinguish the noxious weeds. Pray to the God Ra for heat, wind, and high water.

Between the two, the papyrus holds what seems to be the popular puzzles of its day.

NUMBERS AND COMPUTATION

To understand the problems, we must understand the way Ahmes solved them. The numbers he used were based on ten, a fulfillment of the idea that de Heinzelin believes to have found on the Ishango bone. In many ways this number system is functionally the same as ours. There was, for example, a different symbol for each power of ten. The first eight of these are shown in Figure 14.

The numbers were repeated as necessary. Thus, the number 365 and the number 3650 were written as shown in Figure 15.

The number system does not require a separate symbol for zero. The absence of a certain power of ten is represented by the absence of the corresponding symbol. There is a psychological barrier to zero as a number symbol, a barrier felt by all ancient people and quite a few modern children. The problem lies in the logical contradiction of having something stand for nothing. The very nice, but very limiting, Egyptian answer to the problem is to have nothing stand for nothing instead.

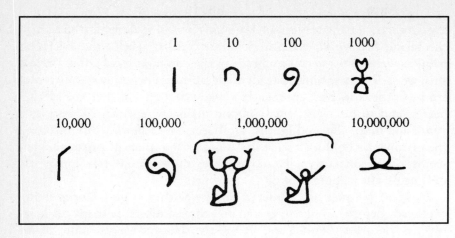

Figure 14. Egyptian numerals

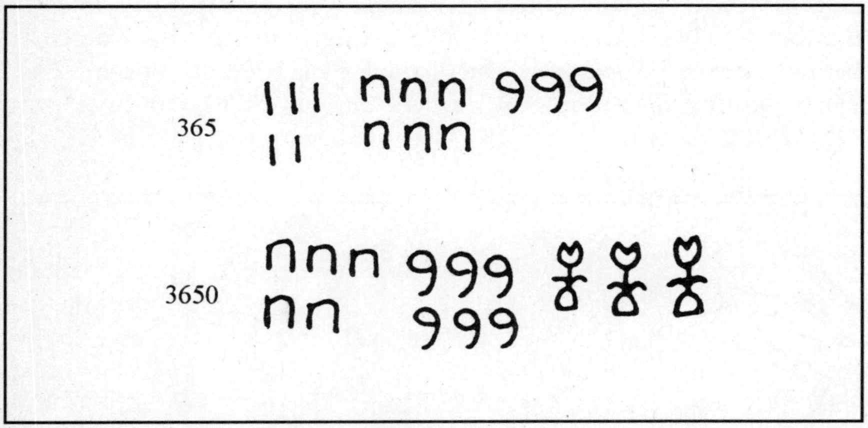

Figure 15. 365 and 3650, as Ahmes would write them

The system allows for arbitrarily large numbers, although new symbols must be invented for each new power of ten. To see how closely the system resembles our modern system, consider our trick of multiplying a number by 10: We place a 0 at the end of the number, as when we say $45 \cdot 10 = 450$. The Egyptians needed only to change each symbol in a number to the symbol for the next higher power of 10; the exact number of symbols remained the same. You can see this in the numbers for 365 and 3650 in Figure 15.

Archaeologists have often uncovered various tablets in which numbers play a prominent role. Figure 16 is a palette and a macehead of the Egyptian Pharaoh Nārmer, who once found it necessary to punish the Libyan nation for rebelling against him. In 16(b), the Pharaoh's name is written between two heads of the cow-goddess Hathor. Below this, we see Nārmer himself ready to decapitate a prisoner. Beneath him are two other captives, apparently already dead. To his left is a sandal-bearer, and to his right is a symbolic prisoner, represented only by a trunk and head. The god Horus, symbolized by a hawk, is humiliating the prisoner by holding a stick in his nose. On top of the prisoner, what seems to be six flowers is actually the number 6,000—apparently indicating the slaughter of 6,000 prisoners.

In 16(a) Nārmer sits under a canopy with the god Horus flying overhead. Before him is the Queen and three dancers, perhaps celebrating his victories. Behind and below the dancers we see more of his plunder. With a little imagination, and by using the figures above, it is easy to decode. In the bottom left corner, for example, we find the number 120,000. Above this is a squatting man with his hands tied behind his back. Apparently, the Pharaoh took 120,000 captives. Elsewhere on the macehead, the reader can find "400,000 cows" and "1,422,000 goats."

Figure 16. Reprinted from
Budge, 1985
(a)
Memorial Tablet of Nârmer

The beauty of the new numbers lies in the fact that they permit counting to continue indefinitely. (Imagine how the Bakairi would respond to this.) Almost as a direct consequence of this, the Egyptians also had a simple system of addition. They merely piled up the symbols of the two numbers into a new number. If there were ever more than 10 identical symbols, these were replaced with a single symbol for the next higher power, similar to our modern method of carrying in addition.

There was also a simple method of multiplication, used many times throughout the Rhind Papyrus. To illustrate, we will show how the Egyptians found $7 \cdot 22$. The Egyptians created two columns, placing a "1" at the top of the first, and a multiplicand (either 7 or 22) at the top of the second. Then each number was doubled repeatedly:

(b)
Great Macehead of Nârmer

$$
\begin{array}{cc}
1 & 7 \\
2\ \checkmark & 14 \\
4\ \checkmark & 28 \\
8 & 56 \\
16\ \checkmark & 112 \\
\hline
2 + 4 + 16 = 22 & 14 + 28 + 112 = 154
\end{array}
$$

We checked numbers in the first column that sum to the second multiplicand, in this case $22 = 2 + 4 + 16$. The corresponding numbers in the second column are totaled to give the final answer: $7 \cdot 22 = 154$. Essentially, the Egyptians found that $7 \cdot 22 = 7 \cdot (2+4+16) = 7 \cdot (2^1+2^2+2^4)$. Any multiple of 7 can be found in this way, since any number can be expressed as the sum of powers of two (although it is doubtful that the Egyptians knew this). Had we looked instead for $19 \cdot 7$, we would have checked the numbers 1, 2, and 16 in the first column (since $19 = 1+2+16$), and found the sum $7 + 14 + 112 = 133$.

This method is obviously the forerunner of the Ethiopian method of multiplication that we saw earlier. That the two produce identical results can be seen in the computation for 7 • 22 below, where columns 1 and 2 repeat the Egyptian method, and columns 2 and 3 repeat the Ethiopian method. Notice how the Egyptians essentially checked off what the Ethiopians called the "good houses." The correspondence between the two methods will always hold.

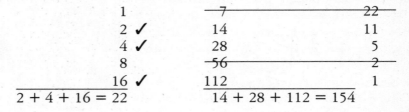

1	~~7~~	~~22~~
2 ✓	14	11
4 ✓	28	5
8	~~56~~	~~2~~
16 ✓	112	1
2 + 4 + 16 = 22	14 + 28 + 112 = 154	

That the two methods are identical is not very surprising, since both methods are based on the idea of representing a multiplicand in binary. Remember that we were able to extend the Ethiopian method by using ternary instead of binary numbers. Can you do the same for the Egyptian method? That is, instead of doubling each column, can you triple them, or quadruple them? Can you find a general method for finding the correct product?

Division was not quite as simple for the Egyptians. For example, consider this problem of the Rhind Papyrus:

> I go down 3 times; $\frac{1}{3}$ of me, $\frac{1}{5}$ of me is added to me; return I, filled am I. Who am I?

The strange phrasing is quite typical of these problems, by the way. It arises because Ahmes still does not know how to express a puzzle. It seems to be asking for the sum of $3 + \frac{1}{3} + \frac{1}{5}$—a trivial problem by today's standards, but in Figure 17 you can see what the poor scribe went through.

At the top is the original hieratic or sacred script, which should be read from right to left. A heavy horizontal line, not present in the original, divides the hieratic script from the hieroglyphic rendition with corresponding lines between the two numbered appropriately. The difference between hieratic script and hieroglyphics is a purely formal one: The first is writing, the second printing. The hieroglyphic numerals are also translated into modern notation, but these, too, must be

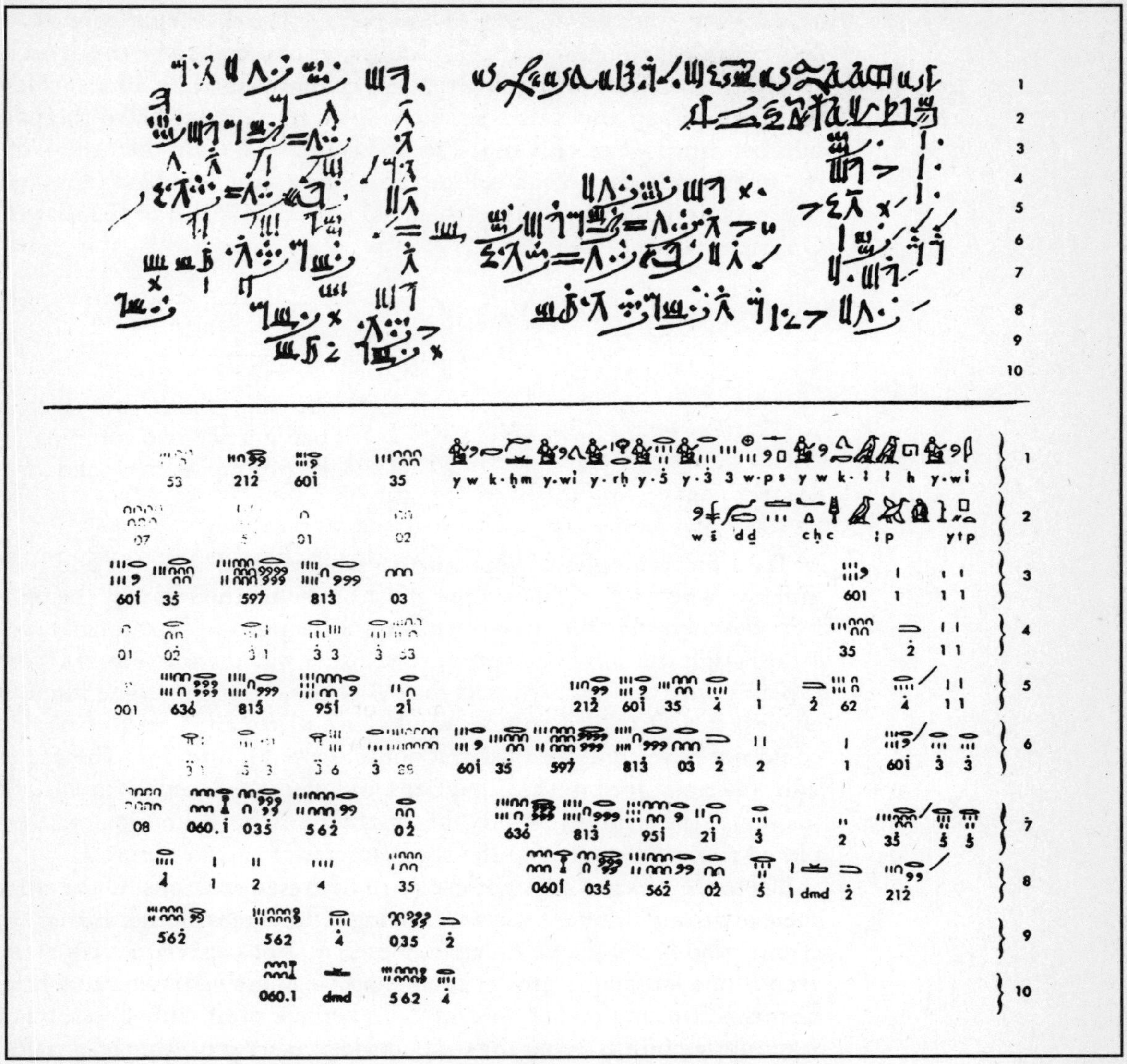

Figure 17. "... Return I, filled am I. Who am I?" (Reprinted from Chace, et al., 1927)

read from right to left; thus, where "35" is printed, 53 is meant.

The figure above has reproduced the many errors that Ahmes committed in his solution. But it is well worth looking into the Egyptian method of division and their use of fractions. Let us divide 43 by 8 exactly the way Ahmes would have done it. We begin with two columns, the first headed by a "1" and the second headed by the divisor, in this case 8. Then we double the two columns until we almost reach the dividend, in this case 43. Then we start over and halve the two numbers until we reach 1 in the second column. We can then check off the numbers in the second column that sum to the dividend (43), and the corresponding numbers in the first column will sum to the answer. On paper, we get:

1	✓	8
2		16
4	✓	32
$\frac{1}{2}$		4
$\frac{1}{4}$	✓	2
$\frac{1}{8}$	✓	1

→ At this point we start halving the two columns, beginning with 1 and 8

Total $1 + 4 + \frac{1}{4} + \frac{1}{8}$ 43

Try a few examples of your own to see how well it works and how quickly it becomes tedious. One effect of the method is that the only fractions used were the "unit fractions," or fractions with a numerator of 1 (although the single exception to the rule was the fraction $\frac{2}{3}$). This explains why the problem asks for "$\frac{1}{3}$ of me, $\frac{1}{5}$ of me." The number above is exactly the way Ahmes would have written it: $5 + \frac{1}{4} + \frac{1}{8}$. He could not have combined the fractions, as we do, into $5\frac{3}{8}$. The use of unit fractions meant the Egyptians did not need new symbols for fractions; they simply wrote the number in the denominator, then placed an oval over it. You can see examples of this in Figure 17.

There are two glaring deficiencies in Egyptian fractions. One is that there are many different ways of writing a fraction. Another is that we cannot readily see if two different representations are in fact equal, or even if one fraction is greater than another. Many commentators have dismissed this method of unit fractions because of its clumsiness, but a very subtle point is being missed. Consider another of Ahmes' puzzles, namely dividing three loaves among five people. We would answer, "Each man receives $\frac{3}{5}$ of a loaf." Ahmes would answer, "Each man receives $\frac{1}{3} + \frac{1}{5} + \frac{1}{15}$." There is a sense in which the latter answer is more complete, since it not only gives the correct answer but also shows how to cut the loaves in practice. Look at the matter in practical terms. The modern answer implies that we could give three men one whole piece of bread worth $^3/_5$ of a loaf, and then give the other two men two pieces of bread, one worth $^1/_5$ and the other worth $^2/_5$. Is this fair? If you were an Egyptian worker, perhaps unschooled in mathematics, would you not think the one large loaf is worth more than the two smaller pieces? After all, the other worker can make a nice sandwich while you are left with croutons. The Egyptian answer, far from being clumsy, is actually meant to describe how to go about cutting the bread. Thus, each person receives exactly three pieces of bread, the first is $^1/_3$ of a loaf, the second $^1/_5$ of a loaf, and the third $^1/_{15}$ of a loaf. (See Figure 18.) The answer is as fair as the modern answer, but it has the added advantage of being *obviously* fair, even to one who does not understand the arithmetic behind it. Ahmes could not understand a fraction in any other sense. It is almost as though the original problem—the only one Ahmes could ask—is, How do we divide three loaves among five men in such a way that each man receives the same quantity and the same number of pieces?

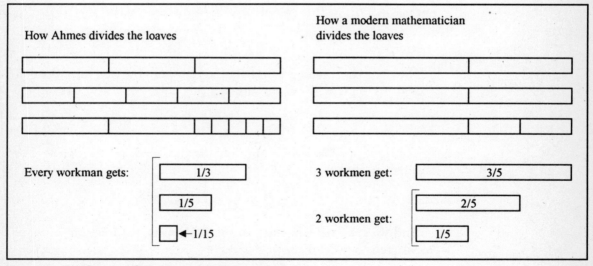

Figure 18. Dividing a loaf, ancient and modern methods

TWO MODERN PROBLEMS ARISE

Another effect of the Egyptian method of division is that no two unit fractions could have the same denominator. For example, Ahmes would not have written a number like $5 + \frac{1}{8} + \frac{1}{8} + \frac{1}{8}$, since he would have found that needlessly confusing. The question arises: Can you write *all* fractions as the sum of unit fractions, no two of which have the same denominator? If the answer is no, you can imagine what effect this would have had on Egyptian puzzles—it would have meant that certain of them would forever remain the "obscure secrets" that Ahmes wrote about in his preface.

It was only in 1880 that the matter was looked into by the British mathematician James Joseph Sylvester. The answer is yes, all rational fractions were available to Ahmes, and there is a simple technique for finding their representation. Consider the fraction $\frac{5}{11}$. How is this to be written in unit fractions? First, find the largest unit fraction that does not exceed $\frac{5}{11}$; in this case we get $\frac{1}{3}$. Now subtract it out:

$$\frac{5}{11} - \frac{1}{3} = \frac{4}{33}$$

Now we continue and find the largest unit fraction that does not exceed $\frac{4}{33}$. This is $\frac{1}{9}$, so we subtract this out:

$$\frac{4}{33} - \frac{1}{9} = \frac{3}{297}$$

Continue on. The largest unit fraction that does not exceed $\frac{3}{297}$ is $\frac{1}{99}$. Subtract it out.

$$\frac{3}{297} - \frac{1}{99} = 0.$$

And we are finished. Thus, to the Egyptians, the fraction $\frac{5}{11}$ would be written $\frac{1}{3} + \frac{1}{9} + \frac{1}{99}$.

If you look at the fractions we started with each step of the way, you'll find something interesting: The fractions were $\frac{5}{11}$, $\frac{4}{33}$, and $\frac{3}{297}$, in which the numerators (5, 4, 3) always decrease. Sylvester showed that this will always be the case, and thereby proved that the procedure always comes to an end since ultimately nothing of the fraction will be left over.

How did we find the unit fractions above? We wanted to find the largest unit fraction that did not exceed $5/11$. The unit fraction that exactly *equals* $5/11$ is

$$\frac{1}{(^{11}/_{5})}$$

Now, $^{11}/_5$ equals 2 and some little bit left over. The unit fraction that does *not* exceed $5/11$ must have a denominator just greater than this, namely $1/3$, exactly what we used. Similarly, when we wanted the unit fraction that did not exceed $4/33$, it is easiest to find the integer just greater than $^{33}/_4$, namely 9, and use the unit fraction $1/9$.

Consider the general fraction A/B, in which A does not divide B. We need to find the largest unit fraction that does not exceed A/B. Again, we know one unit fraction that is exactly equal to A/B, namely

$$\frac{1}{(B/A)}$$

Let the integer portion of B/A be N, so that $B = AN + R$, where R cannot equal zero. Now then, the unit fraction we want must be $1/(N+1)$. This gives us

$$\frac{A}{B} - \frac{1}{(N+1)} = \frac{A(N+1) - B}{B(N+1)}$$

Must this new numerator, $A(N+1) - B$, be less than the old numerator, A? Yes. Remember that $B = AN + R$, so that

$$\begin{aligned} A(N+1) - B &= A(N+1) - (AN+R) \\ &= AN + A - AN - R \\ &= A - R \end{aligned}$$

which is certainly less than A.

This is the second time the Egyptians turned out to be lucky. First, they used a method of multiplication that assumes every number can be written in binary, which they could not have proved, and second, they used a method of division that assumes every fraction can be written as the sum of unit fractions, which was not proved until 1880.

A second problem arises: Can any fraction with an *odd* denominator—such as $^2/_7$ or $^4/_9$ or $^5/_{13}$—be written as the sum of unit fractions, all of which have *odd* denominators, no two alike? For example:

$$^5/_{13} = {}^1/_3 + {}^1/_{21} + {}^1/_{273}$$

Will this, too, always work? The question was posed in 1956, and no one has yet answered it. Thousands of computer hours have been spent trying to find a contradicting example, but to no avail. It seems that the answer is yes, but no one knows for sure.

HOW TO SAVE A CAMEL'S LIFE

As a puzzle endures and travels across continents, it sometimes loses its original sensibilities. Often, new light can be thrown on a puzzle if we engage in a kind of back-formation, creating a resonable history for it. This can be done with the well-known puzzle of an Arabian merchant who willed that 17 camels were to be divided among his three sons in the proportions $^1/_2$, $^1/_3$, and $^1/_9$. One poor animal had to be drawn and quartered! Fortunately, the lawyer who carried out the decree realized that it is simpler to add a single camel to the lot, making 18 camels in all. Certainly, the sons could not argue with this, since they would each receive more than expected. In fact, the three sons get 9, 6, and 2 camels respectively. There is exactly one camel left over, which is returned to the lawyer. The puzzle works because the sum of the fractions is itself a fraction of the form $d/(d+1)$. Specifically, we get $^1/_2 + {}^1/_3 + {}^1/_9 = {}^{17}/_{18}$. Because the numerator and denominator differ by one, precisely one new camel must be added in order to effect the division.

The character of an Arabian merchant as well as the use of camels points to a Middle East origin. This may also explain the fact that the fractions are unit fractions. It is easy to vary the problem while keeping its general flavor. For example, the merchant may have 11 camels, to be divided among his three heirs in the proportions $^1/_2$, $^1/_3$, and $^1/_{12}$. Or 7 camels to be divided as $^1/_2$, $^1/_4$, and $^1/_8$. In every case, a clever lawyer supplies a single camel, makes the required divisions, then gets his camel back. The more interesting question, and perhaps the one that was asked in the Arabic countries, is, How many different puzzles of this sort are there? Expressed purely in terms of numbers, what we want are all possible sets of three numbers a, b, and c, such that $1/a + 1/b + 1/c = d/(d+1)$. But all puzzles must also obey three restrictions: First, they must be Ahmes-like in the sense that proportions must be distinct unit fractions; second, the lawyer must be required to give, and receive, exactly one camel; third, $d + 1$ must be evenly divisible by a, b, and c. This last restriction accounts for the fact that a camel cannot be divided.

At first blush, it seems there are an infinity of such numbers. We begin by setting a equal to 2, b equal to 3, and allow c to vary from 4, to 5, to 6, and so on. In each case there is a new set of fractions. Some of these sets will possess the desired properties, others will not, but we will never know until we check each one separately. Consider the first set:

$$1/2 + 1/3 + 1/4 = 13/12$$

This clearly does not fit our restrictions, since the sum of the fractions is not of the form $d/(d+1)$. At best, we can construct from this a puzzle in which a merchant, not very bright, divides his 12 camels among his sons in the proportions $1/2$, $1/3$, $1/4$. A lawyer, seeing what is happening, adds his own camel to the lot and gives the sons 6, 4, and 3 camels respectively—then gets nothing back! As puzzles go it is a letdown.

We meet similar pitfalls until c equals 7. Now we have

$$1/2 + 1/3 + 1/7 = 41/42$$

Since the sum is of the form $d/(d+1)$, we have a proper puzzle in which a merchant divides his 41 camels among his sons in the proportions $1/2$, $1/3$, and $1/7$.

If you play at this long enough you will sense that the number of fractions that work is actually limited. Fortunately, we find right away that a cannot equal anything other than 2. Assume the opposite, that a equals 3. Then the smallest value of $(d+1)$ we can get is 12, which arises when $a = 3$, $b = 4$, $c = 6$. But

$$1/3 + 1/4 + 1/6 = 9/12$$

and the sum is not of the form $d/(d+1)$. Obviously, things will get worse as b and c increase, since then the fractions get even smaller. So we restrict ourselves to $a = 2$. Similar reasoning will show that b must equal either 3 or 4. In fact, there are really only seven solutions in all, listed in Figure 19. Each line of this table is a new Arabian merchant puzzle. If we relax our "Ahmes-like" restriction, which forces each fraction to be distinct, then there are four other solutions. And if we look at the problem in strictly numerical terms, trying to find all solutions of the equation $1/a + 1/b + 1/c = d/(d+1)$, there are three more.

	Number of Camels	First Son	Second Son	Third Son
Ahmes-like solutions	41	1/2	1/3	1/7
	23	1/2	1/3	1/8
	17	1/2	1/3	1/9
	11	1/2	1/3	1/12
	19	1/2	1/4	1/5
	11	1/2	1/4	1/6
	7	1/2	1/4	1/8
Non-Ahmes-like solutions	9	1/2	1/5	1/5
	5	1/2	1/6	1/6
	12	1/3	1/3	1/4
	3	1/4	1/4	1/4
Other numerical solutions	5	1/3	1/3	1/6
	5	1/3	1/4	1/4
	14	1/2	1/3	1/10

Figure 19. How to divide camels

AS AHMES WAS GOING TO ST. IVES

Readers who enjoy a kind of "amateur Egyptology" should try to decipher Figure 20, a reproduction of problem 79 of the Rhind Papyrus. Once again, we have both the hieratic script and the hieroglyphics, with modern numbers printed under the hieroglyphics. Look at the numbers in the left-hand column first; they are a little surprising.

The numbers are 7, 49, 343, 2301, 16807, and 19607. The first five numbers are so nearly the first five powers of seven that we may assume Ahmes made a slight clerical error in his transcription and meant 2401 for the fourth number. The error, off by 100, is the type that easily

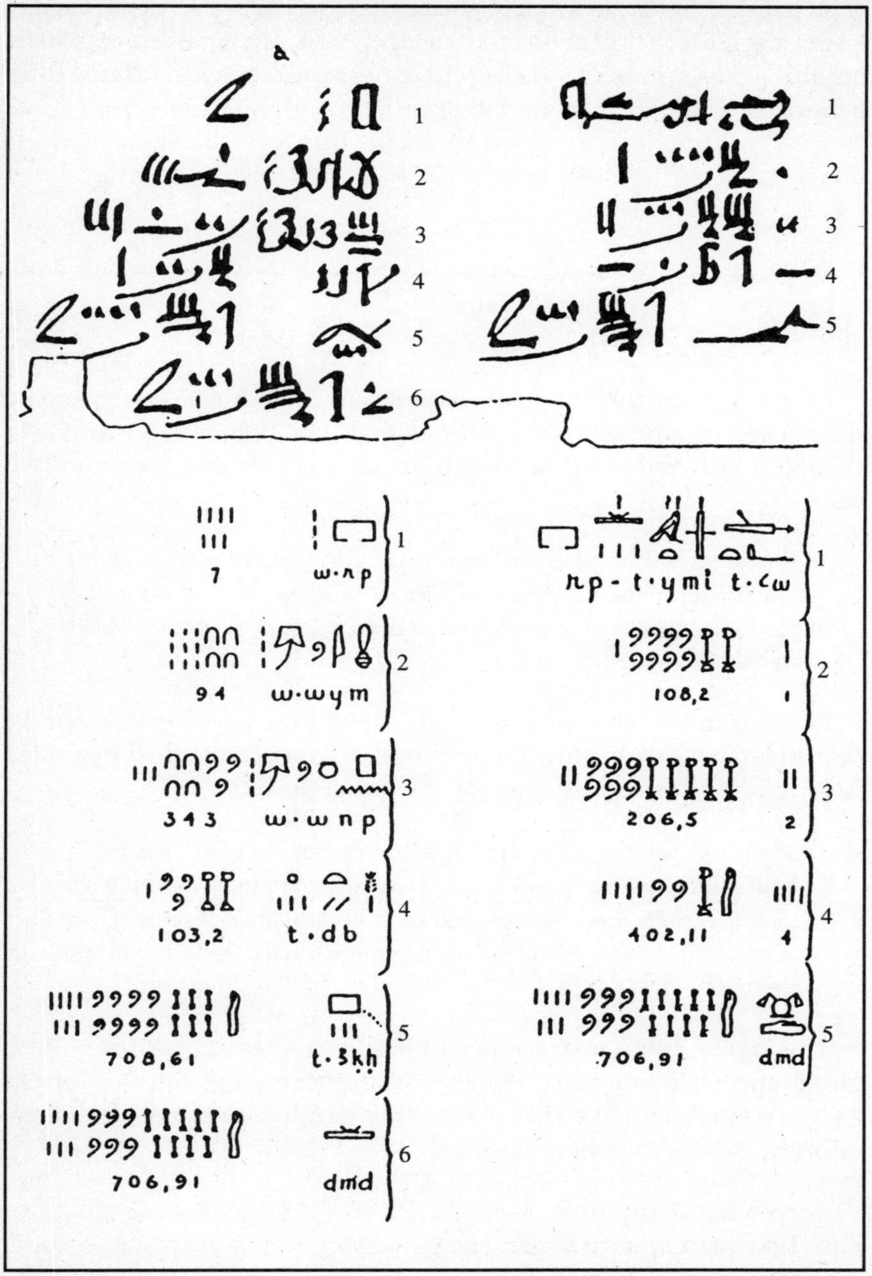

Figure 20. "As I was going to St. Ives . . ." (Reprinted from Chace, et al., 1927)

occurs in the Egyptian number system. The last number confirms our guess since, once we make the change, it is the sum of the other numbers. The numbers and the phrase next to each are translated fully below:

Houses	7
Cats	49
Mice	343
Sheaves of wheat	2401
Hekats of grain	16807
Total	19607

Does this crazy shopping list remind you of anything? It seems to be the answer to a problem that Ahmes does not bother to mention, as though it is already well known to his audience. It may have run like this:

> A man owned 7 houses. In each house, there were 7 cats. Each cat killed 7 mice. Each mouse ate 7 sheaves of wheat. Each sheaf would produce 7 hekats of grain. Grain, wheat, mice, cats, houses: What was the man's entire estate?

If this is indeed the missing puzzle, then it occurred again about 30 centuries later, with only minor variations, in Leonardo Fibonacci's *Liber Abaci*. Fibonacci's version of the puzzle reads:

> Seven old women are on the road to Rome. Each woman has 7 mules, each mule carries 7 sacks, each sack contains 7 loaves, with each loaf there are 7 knives, and each knife is in 7 sheaths. How many objects are there: women, mules, sacks, loaves, knives, sheaths?

This again asks for a geometric progression based on seven. The puzzle appeared once more in eighteenth-century England, this time as a child's nursery rhyme that is probably familiar to the reader. Interestingly, Ahmes' cats have returned:

> As I was going to St. Ives
> I met a man with seven wives.
> Each wife had seven sacks,

Each sack had seven cats,
Each cat had seven kits.
Kits, cats, sacks, wives,
How many were going to St. Ives?

Thus, a puzzle that originated in the Egypt of the pharaohs became a nursery rhyme in Victorian England, certainly the longest and most enduring word-of-mouth journey in history. A primitive kind of number mysticism, still caught in our cortex, may explain why the number seven should have remained unchanged throughout its journey.

To the right in Figure 20 is a second solution to the problem. Above the solution is the statement, "The sum according to the general rule—multiply 2801 by 7," and then comes two columns of numbers.

1	✓	2801
2	✓	5602
4	✓	11204
Total		19607

This is the method of multiplication that we saw earlier. Since the sum of the checked numbers in the first column is 7, then the sum of the corresponding numbers in the second (19607) must be 7 • 2801. (Notice that all rows are checked. Is this perhaps why the number 7 was chosen in the puzzle? And is this perhaps also the reason that this number has held mystical significance for so many different civilizations, because it is the sum of the first three powers of two?)

The example is obviously meant to provide a check on the earlier calculation, but why is 7 • 2801 taken as a check? Typically, Ahmes gives no reason, but since $2801 = (7^5-1)/(7-1)$, the method is uncomfortably close to a modern formula. To find the sum of n terms in the geometric series

$$a + ar^1 + ar^2 + ar^3 + \ldots$$

we need only find the product

$$a(r^n-1)/(r-1)$$

Ahmes was using the very same formula, setting $a = 7$, $r = 7$, and $n = 5$. Unfortunately, we have no other reason but this one solution to assume the Egyptians knew of this formula.

THINK OF A NUMBER

Often, a problem in the Rhind Papyrus is phrased so strangely that it is difficult to understand the thought behind it. Problem 28 is an example:

> Two-thirds is to be added.
> One-third is to be subtracted.
> 10 remains.
> Take one-tenth of this; there becomes 1.
> The remainder is 9.
> Two-thirds of it, namely 6, is to be added.
> The sum is 15.
> One-third of this is 5.
> Lo! 5 goes out; remainder 10.
> That is how you do it.

This may be interpreted as a very early example of a "think-of-a-number" problem, as though it actually meant:

> Think of a number. Add two-thirds of the number to itself. Subtract one-third of the sum from itself. If your final answer is 10, then the number you first thought of is 9.

That, at least, is the first part of the problem. The rest should be interpreted as a proof of the solution. Thus, begin with 9:

> Two-thirds of 9 is 6. Add the two together and get 15. One-third of 15 is 5, which we subtract out ("Lo! 5 goes out"), and the remainder is 10.

And as the scribe says, "That is how you do it." Of course, this type of problem has been very popular through the ages. A parlor game mentioned by Fibonacci in the *Liber Abaci* is actually a very clever variation of a "think-of-a-number" problem: Guests are seated in a row. One of them is wearing a ring, although the host does not know who, nor does he know which hand, which finger, or which joint the ring is on. The wearer is told to count his position in the row, double it, add 5 to the product, multiply the sum by 5, and add 10. To this figure, the wearer is told to add a number indicating the finger. (It is easiest to count the little finger on the left hand as 1 and the thumb on the right as 10.) The sum is multiplied by 10, and the wearer adds to the product a number indicating the joint of the finger. (We can count the fingertip as 1, and the farthest joint as 3.) The host is given the number, and he now knows who is wearing the ring, and on which hand, finger, and joint it is placed.

A later chapter on the *Liber Abaci* will give the solution, but for now I leave it for the reader. Hint: Subtract 350 from the final number.

THE MERCHANT'S RULE

The problems in the Rhind Papyrus that are most interesting are those that point to a general method of solution. Problem 24 is an example: "A heap and its $1/7$ part become 19. What is the heap?" (It is interesting to see that Ahmes uses the word "heap" to mean a general number, much as we today would use x.) The solution runs as follows:

> Assume 7.
> Then heap is 7
> and $1/7$ of the heap is 1
> making a total of 8.
> As many times as 8 must be multiplied to give 19, so many times 7
> must be multiplied to give the required number.

The text then finds that $7 \times 19/8 = 16^5/8$, which is the heap or the final solution.

What Ahmes has done is assume that the heap, or unknown quantity, is equal to 7, apparently because this will allow him to find the $1/7$th part very easily. He quickly discovers, however, that 7 is incorrect, since $7 + (1/7 \cdot 7)$ is only equal to 8, not 19 as called for in the problem. He then says, in essence, "in order to make 8 become 19, I must multiply it by $19/8$; therefore in order to make 7 the correct heap, I must also multiply it by $19/8$." (Ahmes' solution was much more tedious, of course, since he was restricted to unit fractions.) This is why in the last sentence he multiplies 7 by $19/8$, and arrives at the correct answer. This type of solution is sometimes called *regula falsi* or false position, a mixture of trial and error and proportional corrections. The *falsi* in *regula falsi* comes about because we need to guess an answer that we know is wrong. After that Ahmes uses a simple proportion. This is the first example of what later became invaluable to the merchants of the Middle Ages, when it was sometimes called the Merchant's Rule, or the Rule of Three, or even the Golden Rule.

You can see why the rule was so useful to merchants, who may know that, say, one pound of an item is worth a certain amount, and then need to sell a quantity that was worth a different amount. Similarly, Ahmes knew that 7 produced a certain number, namely 8, and then needed to find the number that would produce 19. Today, of course, this is a trivial matter, but not so around 1850 B.C.

A very complicated use of the *regula falsi* may be found in another of Ahmes' problems, this one interesting for its layers of convoluted arithmetic. It obviously does not relate to any practical problem of Ahmes' time, but is presented purely as entertainment:

> Loaves 100 for man 5, $\frac{1}{7}$ of the 3 above to man 2 those below. What is the difference of share?

> [Interpretation: Divide 100 loaves among 5 men in such a way that (1) the shares received are in arithmetical progression; and (2) $\frac{1}{7}$ of the largest 3 shares ("the 3 above") equals the smallest 2 shares ("to man 2 those below"). What is the arithmetical progression?]

An arithmetical progression is a sequence in which every number differs by a constant from the one before it. We know that Ahmes wants an arithmetical progression because he asks for the "difference of share." For example, 5, 9, 13, 17 is an arithmetical progression in which the "difference of share" is 4. Before reading Ahmes' solution, the reader should try it alone. It is easily solved by modern methods, but to get a better feel for the world of the ancient Egyptians, try solving it using only the method of false position. Ahmes' solution itself is typically cryptic, and gives only a hint:

> Do it thus: Make the difference of the shares $5\frac{1}{2}$. Then the amounts that the five men receive will be 23, $17\frac{1}{2}$, 12, $6\frac{1}{2}$, 1: Total 60. As many times as is necessary to multiply 60 to make 100, so many times must these terms be multiplied to make the true series.

Notice that the last sentence of the solution is a restatement of the principle behind the *regula falsi*. Ahmes begins with the assumption that the constant difference in the arithmetical progression is $5^1/2$. We do not know where this came from, but it very likely originated from a previous application of a *regula falsi* type of method.

We can recreate what might have happened. We will assume that the difference is only 1. This gives us a progression of 1, 2, 3, 4, 5. But the two smallest terms sum to 3, and $1/7$ of the three largest terms is $1^5/7$. These are supposed to be equal, but they actually differ by $3 - 1^5/7 = 1^2/7$.

So then, let us assume instead that the difference is not 1 but 2. This gives us a progression of 1, 3, 5, 7, 9. But now the two smallest terms sum to 4, and $1/7$ of the three largest terms is 3. These are still not equal, but now they differ only by $4 - 3 = 1$.

If we continue this way, we find that as we *increase* the constant of the arithmetical progression by 1, we *decrease* the difference in the two sums by $2/7$. We want the difference to go down to zero; thus, as Ahmes might say, "As many times as $2/7$ will go into $1^2/7$, that is the amount to increase 1." Now, $1^2/7$ divided by $2/7$ equals $4^1/2$. That is what we add to 1, and thus get $5^1/2$, the very number that Ahmes used in his solution. This is not quite the same as a *regula falsi*, but the idea behind it is very similar. Why did Ahmes not say he found the number this way, if in fact he did? Probably because the arithmetic would have been so difficult for him.

Now let us return to the solution. Ahmes assumes the progression should be 23, $17^1/2$, 12, $6^1/2$, 1. He notes that the total here is 60. But the problem demanded that the sum of the loaves should be 100. Thus, he uses a second application of the *regula falsi* principle. To make 60 become 100, he must multiply it by $100/60$ or $5/3$. He multiplies every figure in the progression by this number and arrives at the new progression: $38^1/3$, $29^1/6$, 20, $10^5/6$, $1^2/3$. This, finally, answers the problem: It is an arithmetical progression (the constant is $9^1/6$), it sums to 100, and the sum of the two smallest terms is equal to $1/7$ the sum of the three largest terms.

THE NUMBER PI

One section of the Rhind Papyrus is reserved for geometric problems. Egypt's fame in this area was well known to its neighbors. Long after the Greeks had surpassed the Egyptians in their solutions of mathematical problems, they continued to pay homage to what they rightly considered the birthplace of the new science. A question asked even then was: Why did geometry begin in Egypt, and not elsewhere? It was a question that concerned the Greek historian Herodotus, who records the answer that was commonly given during his time: Periodic inundations of the Nile sometimes changed the shape and size of the land along its bank, and therefore a system of measurement had to be worked out that would insure a fair means of taxation. In Herodotus' own words:

> . . . [King Sesostris] distributed the land to all the Egyptians, giving an equal quadrangle to each man, and from this he made his revenue, having appointed them to pay a certain rent [that is, tax] every year: and if the river should take away anything from any man's portion, he would come to the king and declare that which had happened, and the king used to send men to examine and to find out by measurement how much less the piece of land had become, in order that for the future the man might pay less, in proportion to the rent appointed: and I think that thus the art of geometry was found out and afterwards came in Hellas [or Greece] also.

Problem 50 is an important example of this idea of measurement, since it contains one of the first notions of pi (usually symbolized π) or the constant obtained by dividing a circle's circumference by its diameter:

> A cylindrical granary of 9 diameter and height 6. What is the amount of grain that goes into it?

> [Interpretation: What is the volume of a cylinder whose diameter is 9 units and whose altitude is 6 units?]

In his solution, Ahmes assumes that the area of the cylinder's base is equal to the area of a square with a side of 8 units. We know, of course, that the area of the circle is π times the radius-squared. By putting our formula next to Ahmes' we obtain a value for the ancient Egyptian concept of pi,

$$\pi \cdot (^9/_2)^2 = 8^2$$
$$\pi = 8^2 \cdot (^2/_9)^2 = 3.16049$$

which is a very respectable value. The true value is 3.14159 . . .

How did Ahmes arrive at this value of pi? One clue can be found in Problem 48, in which he asks for the area of a circle inscribed in a square that is 9 units on its side, or, as we would put it, the area of a circle with a 9-unit diameter. To answer this, Ahmes trisects the sides of the square to produce 9 smaller squares within it, as we have done in Figure 21. The diagonals are drawn through the corner cells to produce an (irregular) octagon, which Ahmes apparently assumes is equal in area to the circle. It is, of course, very nearly equal, and this seems to be enough to satisfy him. Now then, what is the area of the octagon? Obviously, it must be equal to the five smaller squares plus the four triangles, two of which will make another smaller square. Thus there are in all 7 smaller squares for a total of $7 \cdot 9 = 63$ square units.

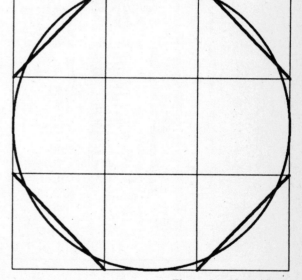

Here, Ahmes cheats. He says 63 is nearly 64, which is equal to 8^2. Thus he has proven, at least to his own satisfaction, that the area of a circle with diameter 9 is equal to the area of a square with side 8.

The problem that Ahmes posed is important not so much for its solution but because it is the first instance of a general recognition that pi is a constant. You can see in this little problem the first clear step in humanity's oldest and most tantalizing puzzle—what is the value of pi?

Figure 21. How Ahmes calculated pi

The question can only be answered approximately, of course, since pi is a transcendental number, that is, it cannot be expressed in the form:

$$a_n x^n + a_{n-1} x^{n-1} + \ldots + a_2 x^2 + a_1 x + a_0$$

where all the coefficients a_i are integers. This is true regardless of which value of x we choose. One consequence is that pi will escape notation in all possible number systems, which always seems a strange situation for a number that can be found in such a simple figure as a circle.

Ahmes' general idea is to break a circle down to approximate its area. It is interesting to see the same idea in a seventeenth-century Japanese scroll, reproduced in Figure 22. Even without translating it, one can see what is going on. A regular polygon is inscribed in a circle, then the parts of the polygon are rearranged into a figure that is close to a rectangle. The area of the rectangle is used to approximate the area of the circle.

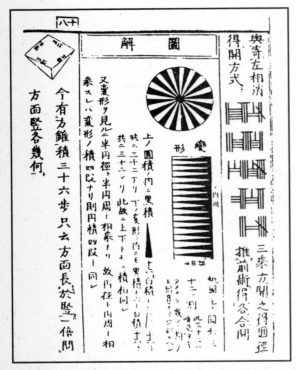

Figure 22. Ahmes' idea, used in Japan

This in turn is similar to the most direct way to calculate pi, a method first developed by one of the great mathematicians, Archimedes of Syracuse, illustrated in Figure 23.

The idea here is of particular importance because it allows us to calculate pi to any precision necessary. First, take a circle of diameter 1 and circumscribe and inscribe regular hexagons about it. The value of pi must be somewhere between the values of the perimeters of the two hexagons. The one outside is obviously too large and the one inside is obviously too small. But by doubling the number of sides on the polygons we can "close in" on the circle and obtain the value of pi to an increasingly greater precision. Archimedes used this method to end up with polygons with 96 sides and claimed correctly that pi was somewhere between $3^{10}/71$ and $3^1/7$. In decimal notation, this calculates pi to only 2 decimal places.

Here again, the same idea can be found in other cultures. In A.D. 264 the Chinese mathematician Liu Hui used polygons of 3072 sides and calculated pi to the fifth decimal place. By the fifth century Tsu Ch'ung-Chih and his son calculated pi to the tenth decimal place. The computations are lost, but the feat was repeated in A.D. 1300, using a monstrous circle a full 10 feet in diameter, and polygons of 16,384 sides. To hint at the achievement, Figure 24 contains a polygon of only 40 sides. No circle is actually drawn. It is only an optical illusion created by the fact that the 40 sides of the polygon are sitting so closely to the circumference of a circle.

The task that Ahmes set himself continues to this day. Recently, pi has been calculated to a precision of 480 million digits, and no doubt there are more to follow. Computing pi with such precision is useful as a method of making computers "burp" to find any fault in the wiring, but as a practical enterprise it is utterly without worth. Hermann Schubert, a German mathematics professor, once explained why in an often-quoted passage that is startling in its images:

> Conceive a sphere constructed with the earth at its center, and imagine its surface to pass through Sirius, which is [8.8 light-years] distant from the earth. Then imagine this enormous sphere to be so packed with microbes that in every cubic millimeter millions of millions of these diminutive animalcula are present. Now conceive these microbes to be unpacked and so distributed singly along a straight line that every two microbes are as far distant from each other as Sirius from us, 8.8 light-years. Conceive the long line thus fixed by all the microbes as the diameter of a circle, and imagine its circumference to be calculated by multiplying its diameter by pi to 100 decimal places. Then, even in the case of a circle of this enormous magnitude, the circumference so calculated would not vary from the real circumference by a millionth part of a millimeter.

Still, finding pi to ever more precision is a puzzle that has mirrored every step and fumble in human development. No matter which culture you choose you will always find an attempt to calculate pi.

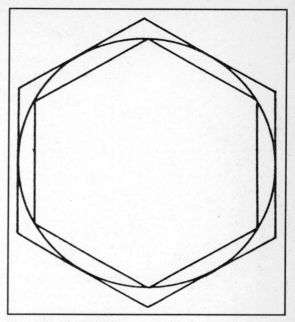

Figure 23. Archimedes' method of calculating pi

Figure 24. There is no circle within this figure (Reprinted from Beckmann, 1971)

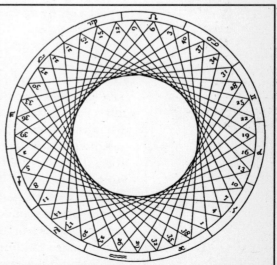

A NEEDLE DROPPING AT RANDOM

The classic problem associated with pi is Buffon's Needle Problem, in which we calculate pi in a purely probabilistic way.

> A needle of length L falls through the air, flutters about in random winds, then falls on a board with horizontal lines separated by a distance d, where d is greater than L. What is the probability that the needle will fall on a line?

On the face of the problem there seems little reason to mention pi at all. But oddly, the answer is $P = 2L/(\pi)d$. If we rearrange the equation, we get $\pi = 2L/(P)d$. The value of P can be estimated by actually dropping the needle a number of times. This means that if you drop the needle often enough you should arrive at a fairly accurate calculation of pi, without ever once trying to measure the diameter or circumference of a circle. The puzzle is a great favorite because of its beguiling ability to associate a constant of the universe with a purely chance event.

The problem was first posed by Georges-Louis Leclerc, Comte de Buffon, in the eighteenth century. Buffon himself was an interesting character. It was he who first tested a feat that was commonly attributed to Archimedes. The feat, as originally described by Plutarch, was a plausible enough story concerning Archimedes defending his native Syracuse by using cranes and missiles. Sometime in the twelfth century, John Tzetzes had distorted the original story into a comical tale of mirrors that focused the sun's rays on the invading ships, ultimately burning them to ashes. Surprisingly, it is Tzetzes's embellishments that are often repeated in our own history books. We do not know if Buffon believed the fable, but we do know that he attempted to duplicate it, and succeeded! He used 168 mirrors, and ignited wooden planks from a distance of about 150 feet.

Buffon's Needle Problem may seem a little difficult at first, but to understand the idea behind it we will look first at something simpler. In Figure 25, we have drawn a circle with a radius of 1, and we circumscribe it with a square with a side of 2.

If we toss a coin onto the square, assuming that the coin touches the figure at only a single point, what is the probability that it will also land in the circle? Finding the probability of anything is generally a matter of counting the number of favorable events and the number of all

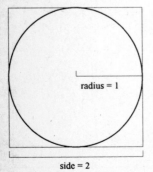

Figure 25. What is the probability that a tossed coin will land in the circle?

radius = 1

side = 2

possible events. In the same way, this problem calls for us to find the number of points in the circle and the number of points in the square. (That is not exactly correct, but we do much the same thing by taking the area of the circle and square respectively.) The probability in question is found by dividing the two areas. The area of the circle—the area of *any* circle—is πr^2, which in this case simply equals pi, since the radius was set at 1. The area of the square is 4. Therefore the probability in question is $P = \pi/4$. Again, this means pi $= 4P$. Theoretically, it should be possible to toss several coins onto the figure and keep track of the number that fall anywhere on the square (which we will call s) and the number of these that also fall on the circle (called c). Now the ratio c/s is our approximation of the value of P. Plugging this into the formula above we can compute $4(c/s)$, which should give us a good approximation of pi.

Of course, there is nothing magical about Figure 25. We could easily have used Figure 26 instead.

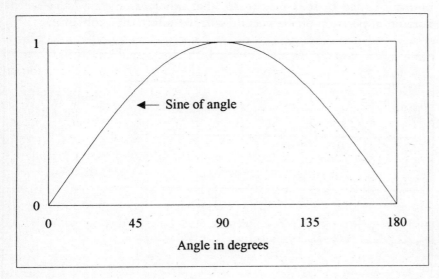

1

← Sine of angle

0

0   45   90   135   180

Angle in degrees

Figure 26. What is the probability that a tossed coin will land under the sine curve?

Once again, if a coin is tossed at random onto the figure, what is the probability that it will fall under the curve? The solution this time requires mathematics that is somewhat difficult, but it is well worth the effort to follow along. Parts that appear strained can be worked out at a more intuitive level.

The solution, in principle, is the same as for the circle-in-a-square figure seen earlier. We need the area of the figure as a whole, and the area of the section under the curve. Now, the curve in the figure plots two values, x and an angle θ; it is determined by the formula $x = \frac{1}{2}L\sin\theta$, where $\frac{1}{2}L$ can be taken as any constant (although later, of course, it will be half the length of the needle). The area of the figure under the curve is found by integration; doing this, we find the probability must be $2L/\pi d$. Granted, this was not as straightforward as the previous figure, since it involved calculus, but the principle behind it is the same. It has the added advantage of helping us solve Buffon's Needle Problem, as we will soon see.

Figure 27 is an illustration of a needle of length L falling at random on a plane with horizontal lines, each line separated by a distance d. There are only two parameters of interest here. One is the distance of the center of the needle from the horizontal line, which in the figure is called x. The other is the angle the needle makes with the perpendicular drawn from the center of the needle to the horizontal, which in the figure is called θ. It is easy to see that other parameters, such as the horizontal position of the needle, will not affect the problem.

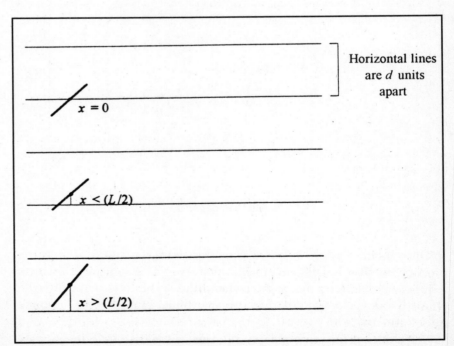

Figure 27. What is the probability that a tossed pin, L units long, will land on a line?

Whether or not the needle touches a horizontal is determined by these two parameters. In the top of the figure, x has been reduced to zero; that is, the center of the needle touches the horizontal. In this case, the angle θ can be anything whatsoever, and the needle will always touch.

In the middle of the figure, x has been increased a little; that is, the center of the needle is removed somewhat from the horizontal, but still x is less than $\frac{1}{2}L$. In this case, certain angles will force the needle to touch the horizontal, while others will not. More specifically, the needle will touch if x is less than $\sin\theta$.

Finally, at the bottom of the figure, x has been increased to such an extent that it is now greater than $\frac{1}{2}L$. Obviously, in this case the needle will never touch a horizontal, no matter how it is twirled about its center.

In order to summarize everything, we need to chart x against θ in such a way that for any given value of x, we can find the values of θ that will cause the needle to touch a horizontal. If we had such a figure, we would have the answer to Buffon's problem, since the probability in question could be read directly from the chart. But such a graph was already presented in Figure 26. The area under the curve in this figure represents all the positions and orientations of the needle that will cross one of the horizontals.

Thus, we have already solved Buffon's Needle Problem. The probability that a needle will cross a vertical is $P = 2L/\pi d$.

This was Buffon's solution. We know that he tested it experimentally, but we do not know that he ever changed the equation around in order to use his experiment to calculate pi. That was first done by Pierre-Simon Laplace, one of the great French mathematicians and an important figure in the development of probability theory. It was Laplace who first noticed that Buffon's problem, originally intended as a mere diversion, also gives a remarkable way of approximating pi. We have in the solution pi $= 2L/P(d)$. The values of L (the length of the needle) and d (the distance between two vertical stripes) are known beforehand. We approximate P by simply tossing a needle onto the appropriate board. Then—let wholly random forces act as they will—we will always arrive at a fair estimate of pi.

Many have been captivated by the magic of the puzzle. One such was a Captain Fox, who engaged in the pastime of tossing a needle onto a striped board while idling away his time recuperating from injuries during the American Civil War. Another was an Italian mathematician, Mario Lazzarini. In 1901 he claimed to have tossed a needle that was 2.5 cm on a board with parallels that were 3.0 cm apart. He found that of 3408 tosses, exactly 1808 of them had touched a line. According to Laplace's formula, this estimates pi as (2 • 2.5 • 3408)/ (3.0 • 1808) = 3.1415929, which is pi correct to 6 decimal places.

But Lazzarini obviously faked his data. Buffon's problem is a nice diversion, but as a practical method of calculating pi it is wholly inappropriate. It is possible to show, in fact, that even with 3400 tosses the estimate of pi that it produces will probably not be correct to more than the fourth decimal place. Lazzarini's hoax has been reported by so many otherwise careful authors that very few care to notice that his eccentric figures—why stop at 3408 trials?—are almost certainly chosen to disguise the famous fraction $^{355}/_{113}$, first found in the fifth century by the Chinese, which gives a fairly precise value of pi, as was well known to Europeans of Lazzarini's time. Lazzarini's hoax was first uncovered by N. T. Gridgeman in 1960, but I still find it repeated, even by authors who should know better.

Petr Beckmann has run a computerized simulation of a tossed needle. His results are shown in Figure 28. Scanning down the right column, one can almost see the needle edging closer and closer to pi. But notice that even after 12,000 tosses, we only get a value of 3.1417725.

"MORE PRECIOUS THAN THE TREASURES OF EGYPT . . ."

Long after its glory had faded, the "treasures of Egypt" remained something of a legend. The phrase was used that way by the Hebrews, even in the time of St. Paul. The Greeks also customarily paid homage to the Egyptians, long after their own civilization had far eclipsed all of their neighbors. Even Archimedes did not consider himself well-schooled until he first studied in Egypt, although it is doubtful that he learned anything original there.

We may think that we have come very far from "the treasures of Egypt," but it is always shocking to find how close we really still are. The closeness does not lie in anything specific; it lies more in the myths, or consciousness, that define our times.

Consider the quaint story of King Seneferu. Finding himself dispirited one day, he asked the priest Tchatcha-em-ankh to arrange a boating expedition for him. So the priest gathered together twenty beautiful women, arrayed them in jewels, and commanded them to row and sing for the king. "For the heart of thy majesty will rejoice and be glad when thou sailest about hither and thither, and dost see the beautiful thickets that are on the lake." But while rowing, one of the women dropped a prized jewel of new turquoise, and she and the other women stopped rowing. In order not to displease the king, Tchatcha-em-ankh spoke certain words of power, which caused the waters of the lake to part, so that he could easily reclaim the jewel. Then he returned the waters to their previous state, and the rowing continued, to the pleasure of the king.

Or consider another story, about the prophet Zaclas. At the funeral of a young man who had died from an unexplained illness, the man's elderly uncle threw himself on the bier and accused the man's widow of poisoning his nephew in order to inherit his property. The widow denied this, but some at the procession were so outraged that they plotted to set fire to her house. The uncle cried out, "Let, then, Divine Providence decide the truth." Just then, Zaclas emerged from the crowd, and he used a magic plant to touch three times the mouth and breast of the dead man. Then he turned to the East and prayed. The lungs of the corpse were filled with breath, and when questioned by Zaclas he declared that, indeed, his wife had poisoned him.

Number of tossed needles	Pi
500	3.2154341
1000	3.2414911
1500	3.1645569
2000	3.1620553
2500	3.1407035
3000	3.1430068
3500	3.1460674
4000	3.1421838
4500	3.1435557
5000	3.1446541
5500	3.1401656
6000	3.1217482
6500	3.1175060
7000	3.1354983
7500	3.1453135
8000	3.1452722
8500	3.1493145
9000	3.1441048
9500	3.1384209
10000	3.1392246
10500	3.1493701
11000	3.1527658
11500	3.1485284
12000	3.1417725

Figure 28. Calculation of pi (Reprinted from Beckmann, 1971)

It would be too coy to pretend that we have not seen these stories before. They were used much later by the Hebrews and the early Christians to capture a sense of a spirit much higher than earthly powers. Although we may not say that either story was usurped directly from Egypt, nevertheless it is obvious that the original intuition of this spirit existed before either the Christians or the Hebrews had put it to such abiding effect. That is the most precious of the Egyptian treasures—their intuitions.

They were the proper inheritors of whatever mind-set had originated among the Ishango. They went quite far with it, and more importantly, they gave what they could to others around them.

WORK, MY BROTHER, WHILE 'TIS DAY—

PHARAOH LIVES FOR EVER!

RIVERS WASTE AND WANE AWAY,

MARBLE CRUMBLES DOWN LIKE CLAY,

NATIONS DWINDLE TO DECAY;

BUT PHARAOH LIVES FOR EVER!

—*SACHEDON*, GEORGE JOHN WHYTE-MELVILLE

On a Temple Roof

MAKING NINE-HOLES WITH THEIR KNIVES

AFTER EVENING PRAYERS

—RECORD OF A PUNISHMENT GIVEN TO TWO MEN,
IN A MANX ECCLESIASTICAL COURT, 1699

O N THE SIDE OF THE NILE NEAR THE CITY OF THEBES, THERE sits one of the great monuments of the world, the temple at Kurna. Its construction was started by Ramses I around the year 1400 B.C. and finished by his successor, Seti I, about 50 years later. The slabs on the roof of the temple have a few curious etches, some of which are reproduced in Figure 29.

These figures were most likely cut by the masons who were working on the temple. The sketch in Figure 29(a) seems to be left unfinished and even partially crossed out; perhaps a mistake had been made. The other sketches, however, were very obviously used as game boards of some sort, as though the masons were getting in some quick entertainment to pass the time.

PENTALPHA

Can we discover how the games were played? Concerning the game sketched in the pentagram in Figure 29(b), something similar to it is mentioned by Pollux in *Onamasticon*: "Each of the players has five men on five lines, so that Sophocles naturally says 'five-lined boards and the

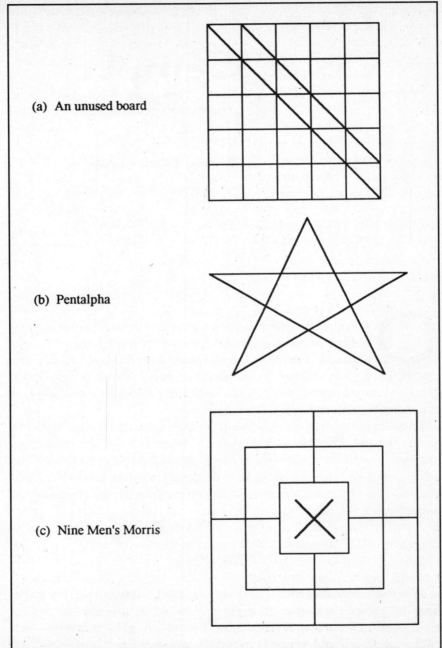

(a) An unused board

(b) Pentalpha

(c) Nine Men's Morris

Figure 29. Etchings on a
temple roof

throws of the dice.' " The original quote from Sophocles cannot be found. The statement, as it appears in Pollux, is hopelessly cryptic, but we should remember that the Greeks took many of their games from Egypt, so it is quite possible that the "five lines" mentioned here is the same as the game in Figure 29(b).

Fortunately, a pentagram is still used in a game played in Greece today, where it is called Pentalpha, and something similar to it is played by the Spanish. The latter may have brought it to Mexico and from there it spread to Native Americans throughout North America. It is very likely descended from the game mentioned by Pollux, and that in turn is probably the game etched for all eternity on the roof at the temple at Kurna. The rules are quite simple. The diagram has ten points of intersection among the five lines, and in Figure 30 we have labeled all ten. The points on the outside are the "A" points, and those on the inside are the "B" points.

As played today, it is a one-person game. The player takes a marker, such as a checker piece, and places it on one of the unoccupied points, then moves it to a second point, which may or may not be unoccupied, and finally lands it on a third point which, like the first, must be unoccupied. The three points must be consecutive and lie on a straight line. For example, a proper move would be A1-B5-B4. But one could not go A1-B5-A2, since this does not lie on a straight line. Having placed a marker on B4, the move B4-B3-A4 is now prohibited, since you are starting on an occupied point. The move A4-B3-B4 is similarly prohibited, since you are now landing on an occupied point. However, the move A3-B4-B5 is quite legal since this only takes you through an occupied point. This is continued until all of nine markers have been placed, but if before then the player is blocked from making a legal move, the game is lost.

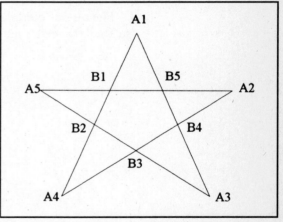

Figure 30. Pentalpha

Pollux describes a game that is played by two people, not one, and that involves the use of dice. This may describe a two-handed version of the same game in which each player uses dice to win or lose a turn. In any case there are many complications like this to consider.

The reader should try the game a few times to test its level of difficulty. It is not at all as simple as it may seem. More challenging is to find a general rule for its solution, and not just a step-by-step diagram.

The easiest procedure is this: The first move may be made anywhere at all on the board. Every subsequent move should take you to the first point made in the previous move. There will always be exactly one way of doing this. Furthermore, since the first move is legal, then the second move must also be legal, since it will always begin and end at an unoccupied point. For example, assume the first move is A1-B5-B4. Then you want the second move to end at A1 (that is, the first point of the previous move). There is only one way of doing this: B2-B1-A1. You are certain that A1 is unoccupied since it was a legal beginning for the previous move. Also, B2 must be unoccupied since it was not used up to this point. Now the next move must end at B2 (the first point of the previous move). Again, there is only one way of doing this: A3-B3-B2. The next move must end at A3, and so on through the board.

Here is one complete game. Notice how the moves chain up together, so that the first point of one move is the last point of the next move:

                (1) A1-B5-B4
                (2) B2-B1-A1
                (3) A3-B3-B2
                (4) B5-B4-A3
                (5) A5-B1-B5
                (6) B3-B2-A5
                (7) A2-B4-B3
                (8) B1-B5-A2
                (9) A4-B2-B1

Of course, the above rule will always work, but it by no means exhausts other possible games. The following, for example, is a valid game, but it breaks the chaining rule in two places:

                (1) B2-B3-A3
                (2) A1-B1-B2
                (3) A5-B1-B5
                (4) B4-B5-A1
                (5) A4-B3-B4
                (6) B1-B2-A4
                (7) A2-B5-B1
                (8) B3-B4-A2
                (9) B3-B2-A5

It is reasonable to extend the game to boards of different configurations. In Figure 31 we try using a hexagram in a game that might be called Hexalpha. Once again there are 4 points on a line, but this time there are 6 lines and 12 points in all, so we will consider the game complete when 11 markers have been placed on the figure according to Pentalpha's rules. The outside points are labeled A and the inside points are labeled B.

Can the game be played here? No. Not only will the chaining rule not work, but all possible strategies to place 11 markers on the figure will fail. The problem is in the nature of the hexagram. Consider points A1 and A4. From either of these points you can get to B2, and from either of them you can get to B5. You might say that B2 and B5 are "siblings," in the sense that they can be gotten to from the same nodes. The presence of siblings makes the game impossible. If you look at a pentagram, you will find that there are no siblings.

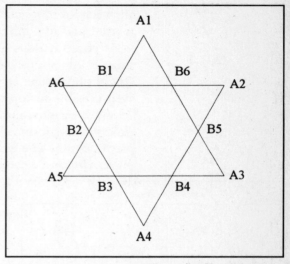

Figure 31. Hexalpha

An interesting exercise for the reader is to extend the game to higher orders, into games of "*n*-alpha," consisting of *n* lines each with four points of intersection. For which values of *n* is the game possible?

THE MORRIS BOARD

The final game etched into the temple roof is played on a board that has three concentric squares, Figure 29(c). Once again, we can obtain some idea of the original game by looking at similar games played today in Greece, and as far away as England and the Scandinavian countries. The game is usually called the Mill, or Nine Men's Morris. The shepherds in Warwickshire passed their long hours by tracing a Morris board in the soil. When the rains fell, the soil would become soggy, leaving a gloomy sight that Shakespeare describes in *A Midsummer Night's Dream*:

> And crows are fatted with the murrion flock;
> The nine men's morris is filled up with mud.

The game is played by two players, each with nine markers. Play proceeds in two stages. In the first stage, each player takes turns placing a marker on one of the twenty-four points on the board formed by the intersection of two lines. The object of the placement is to form a mill, or three markers on a straight line. Having formed a mill, a player is allowed to remove one of the opponent's markers, although not one that is itself part of a mill.

After all markers have been played, the game shifts into its second stage. Now the players take turns moving their markers along the straight lines, again trying to form a mill or three markers in a row. It is even possible to "open" a mill by moving a marker from it, and then "close" it by moving the same marker back to its original location. Each time a mill is formed, the player takes an opponent's marker that is not part of a mill. The game is over when a player cannot move, or when a player is reduced to only two markers.

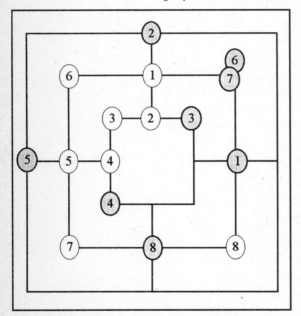

Figure 32. Nine Men's Morris (Reprinted from Mott-Smith, 1978)

There are many levels of strategy in the game, and the constraints of the board are such that a game that seems to be going to one player can suddenly turn to the other player with even a single bad move. Geoffrey Mott-Smith gives a wonderful example of this. In Figure 32 we have a game played between White and Black. The order in which the markers were played is noted on the marker itself. Follow the game and you'll see how White, by far the superior player, actually ends up losing the game.

White has made the obvious first move by placing a marker on a four-way intersection, allowing for many future mills. Black has already made a foolish move by not blocking at least one of these mills. After White plays the second marker, Black is forced to block. In fact, in moves 2 through 5, Black does nothing but react to White's moves by blocking mills.

When White plays the sixth marker, he has established a fork, that is, he has two possible mills: White can complete the mill of 6-1 or the mill of 6-5. Black, of course, can only block the first of these, which he does by playing the sixth marker. White completes the 6-5 mill by playing the seventh marker. He now takes away Black's sixth marker, and Black replaces it with the seventh. This is the first time that Black comes close to forming a mill with the 7-1 markers, and that happens by accident. White blocks it easily with the eighth marker, and once again Black must respond by blocking a mill with his eighth marker.

Try to finish the game for White. He is obviously winning, in that he has one more marker than Black. But with a little foresight you can see that the game is already over and it is Black, not White, who has won. After the two players play their last marker, White will be able to make at most one more move. Black has all the others cornered.

It is not possible to state a general rule for winning in this game, as we did in Pentalpha, since there is too much give-and-take among the opposing strategies.

OVID'S GAME AND MODERN VARIATIONS

This ancient Egyptian game is the grandfather of alignment games, or games in which players try to get a certain number of markers in a row, and to stop the other player from doing so at the same time. The basic board sketched into the temple at Kurna underwent several changes as it traveled into different cultures. A reduced version of the game, a kind of Three Men's Morris, became popular among the Romans. This is the *Ludis terni lapilli* that Ovid encourages young girls to learn in *Ars Amatoria*, or *The Art of Love*:

> Chess is a game to beware: Your Queen is apt to be taken,
> Castles and Knights undone, King in a corner, and mate!
> Try something simpler, with marbles, or balls in a net or a
>   pocket.
> Try Tic-Tac-Toe, where you get three-in-a-row.

Ovid's Game was played with what is now called a typical 3 × 3 Tic-Tac-Toe board (see Figure 33). Each player had three markers. As in Nine Men's Morris, a player placed a marker trying to achieve a mill of three. If neither side did this, they took turns moving the markers to an adjacent cell (although not diagonally adjacent), again with the intention of achieving a mill. It is easy to see that an opening move in the center will guarantee a win for the first player. Assume White chooses *e*. Then Black has only two responses: To play in a corner cell (such as *a*), or an off-corner cell (such as *b*). Assume Black takes *a*. Then White should take *h*, forcing Black into *b*, and White into *c*, and Black into *g*. All the markers are played now. In the next moves, White has only to move the marker in *e* into *f*, and the marker in *h* into *i* for a win.

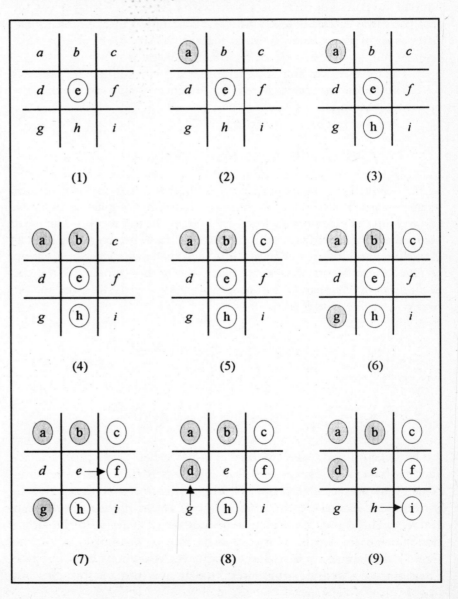

Figure 33. How to win Ovid's game

If Black instead takes the off-corner cell *b*, then White should respond in *g*. All the moves will be forced once again, leading to a win for White. These two responses cover all possible moves for Black, since other cells are simple rotations of the board.

At some point, the idea of moving the markers was dropped and the new game was called in English-speaking countries by a variation of the first words of a common nursery rhyme:

> Tit-Tat-Toe, my first go,
> Three jolly butcher boys all in a row.
> Stick one up, stick one down,
> Stick one in the old man's crown.

The words "Tit-Tat-Toe" are nonsense syllables that have a nice mill-forming 1-2-3 sound about them. The rhyme was recited while playing a number of different games. It contains a rule for keeping score. A point was given either "up" or "down," that is, to the player sitting on the "upside" or "downside" of the board, depending on who won. The "old man" was sometimes called "Old Nick," a constant figure in early British games who received the point in case of a tie. A winning player received not only his own points but also all those that Old Nick had accumulated. There are allusions to Old Nick even in England's adult lotteries, such as the method of allotting unsold property in the Common Field System. "The land is going to Old Nick" meant the land will continue to lie fallow since no one won the lottery. The association with decay may have contributed to Old Nick's later reincarnation as Satan.

The basic theme of alignment games—to get a certain number of markers in a row, while blocking the opponent from doing the same—is quickly exhausted in most versions, but this is deceiving. Even the simplest alignment game—the standard version of Tic-Tac-Toe—offers extraordinary possibilities to anyone interested in the analysis of games. You cannot hope to win at Tic-Tac-Toe by sneaking in a three-in-a-row construction while your opponent is occupied elsewhere. Instead, you must create a "critical path" on the board. A critical path consists of at least three intersecting lines drawn through a Tic-Tac-Toe board, each line cutting across three cells and therefore representing a possible win. Each point of intersection on the critical path lies on two lines. This is the secret of its success, since by following the critical path you can present your opponent with two distinct ways of winning. The opponent, of course, cannot block both ways at the same time.

Any cell on a Tic-Tac-Toe board can generate critical paths in which that cell is a point of intersection. Figure 34 has the one critical path of an off-corner cell, the three paths of a corner cell, and the one path for the center cell. Other critical paths are rotations and reflections of these. One look at these paths and you can see why the off-corner cell is the weakest opening, the corner cell is much stronger, and the center cell is the strongest of all.

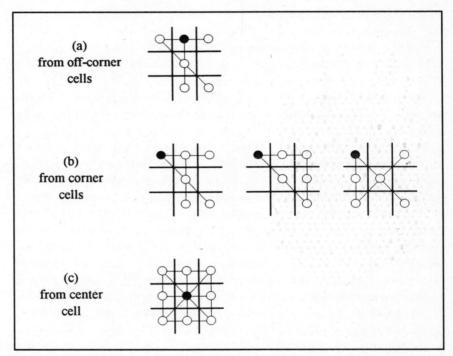

(a)
from off-corner
cells

(b)
from corner
cells

(c)
from center
cell

Figure 34. Critical Paths

If you are the first player, your strategy should be to place your marker on any cell, and in your mind generate one of the critical paths associated with it. If your opponent places a marker off the critical path, the game is already yours. If your opponent plays on the path, remember you can switch to one of the other paths. Now on your next turn, place your marker on one of the other points of intersection. Assuming your opponent plays rationally, his second move is forced. Now play on the third point of intersection and you'll find you have two possible ways to win, and your opponent must forfeit.

If you are the second player, you should form a counter strategy. Generate for yourself all the critical paths that the opponent must be working with after his first move. Then play a cell that lies on a point of intersection. If, from this point on, you do nothing but block your opponent's possible wins, the game will end in a draw. The situation is more complicated if your opponent opens with the center cell, since there is no move that trespasses on all paths generated from there. But by taking a corner cell it is possible to force the opponent, at the risk of losing the game, to abandon his strategy in mid-play. This, too, will end in a draw.

It is easy to see that the best the second player can do is tie, never win. This is because the first player can always engage in strategy-stealing behavior. Assume the second player has a strategy of winning. The first player can place the first marker at random, and then essentially become the second player. So any strategy that favors the second player can be stolen by the first, but not vice versa.

The critical-path analysis is nice because it captures in a single picture both the essence of the game and the strategy for winning. What once seemed like a game in which you might blunder mindlessly to a win now turns out to be something quite concrete and lawful.

The game can be varied in ways that will make the critical path useless. An example that is at once simple but remarkably tricky was invented by Ronald Graham of Bell Laboratories. In this game, the two players are not called X and O, but Odd and Even. The first uses the numbers 1, 3, 5, 7, 9; and the second uses the numbers 2, 4, 6, 8. Odd moves first by placing one of his numbers in the standard Tic-Tac-Toe grid. Then Even moves. And so on. Once a number has been played, it cannot be replayed. The object of the game is to place a number that creates a straight line of three numbers that sum to 15. The player who places the last number wins, even if the other two numbers were placed by the opponent. For example, if 2 and 8 occupy the two corner cells of the grid, and I (Odd) place a 5 between them, then I win the game, even though my opponent (Even) played the first two numbers.

The game takes on a certain wild quality, since the numbers I play may later become exactly the numbers that my opponent needs. George Markowsky at the University of Maine, performed an exhaustive computer search of all possible moves and discovered that the first player can always win, although there is no easy strategy similar to a critical path. The reader should play it a few times to test its level of difficulty.

Independently of Graham, P. H. Nygaard invented a very similar game. Once again, the two players are called Odd and Even, and once again they are armed with the same set of numbers, but this time one can win not only by getting three numbers in a row that sum to 15, but also by getting three numbers in a row of the same parity. In other words, I can win by playing a 5 between 2 and 8 (since this gives me 15 in a row) or by playing a 5 between 3 and 9 (since this gives me three odd numbers in a row). Nygaard's game is similar to playing Graham's game and Tic-Tac-Toe simultaneously.

Nygaard's rules place enough of a restriction on the game that some general principles can be found. For example, if Odd plays 5 for the first move, he has lost the game, and it does not matter where it has been placed. (See Figure 35.) Even's response should always be to play a 2 next to it. Odd sees that Even will sooner or later play an eight to create $5 + 2 + 8 = 15$, and so must block immediately. Assume he plays a nine. Even should now play a 4 in such a cell that 5 and 4 lie in a straight line and 2 and 4 lie in a straight line. Even has essentially created a fork, since he can play a 6 to create 5, 4, 6 (which is a straight line that sums to 15), or to create 2, 4, 6 (which is a straight line of even numbers).

We had to assume that Odd blocks with 9, since as Figure 35 shows, when Even played 4, Odd could have completed the line with 4, 2, 9 (which sums to 15) and essentially stolen Even's strategy. But if Odd does not block with 9, Even can still win. Can you find how?

Another variation is called Meta Tic-Tac-Toe, played on the board in Figure 36. Notice that the board is a kind of meta Tic-Tac-Toe board. It is a standard 3-by-3 square, but the nine cells are not empty; instead each is filled with a smaller Tic-Tac-Toe square. The player who wins three games that lie in a row is the meta-winner. The first player marks only one cell, thereafter the two players alternately mark two cells. A mark may be played in any one of the nine games.

I'm afraid that this time there is no solution to be given. This intriguing game is guaranteed to capture and hold your imagination for countless hours. If you believe it is only nine Tic-Tac-Toe games, and therefore only nine times as difficult to play, you will be shocked to find whole new considerations arise out of nowhere. Meta Tic-Tac-Toe was first discussed in the *Journal of Mathematical Recreations*, which means the best amateur and professional mathematicians from around the world have worked on it. The time is ripe for a novice's fresh insight.

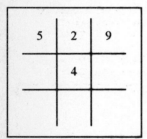

Figure 35. How to lose Nygaard's game

HIGHER ORDERS AND HIGHER DIMENSIONS

The obvious variation is to extend the Tic-Tac-Toe to higher orders. For example, consider the six-in-a-row game, played on an order-6 board. This game was analyzed by Hales and Jewitt in *Transactions of the American Mathematical Society*. Figure 37 is an analysis of the game accomplished by "pairing" the cells in such a way that a player following the pairs will always land in a cell that blocks a critical path, even though it may be difficult to see the critical path itself. Notice that the figure is symmetrical around the two double lines that divide the figure into 4 quadrants. I only needed to give you one quadrant; the other three could have been recreated by reflecting everything across the lines. When your opponent plays a cell, take the closest one that has the same marking and that lies in the direction of the line in the cell. For example, if your opponent plays the second cell in the top row, which in this case has a horizontal marking, you would move horizontally to the next cell with the same marking; this would be the fifth cell in the top row. If instead your opponent took the third cell, which has a vertical marking, you would move vertically to the third cell of the bottom row. If at any point the cell you require is taken, or if your opponent chooses the center, then take a cell at random. Your opponent cannot win.

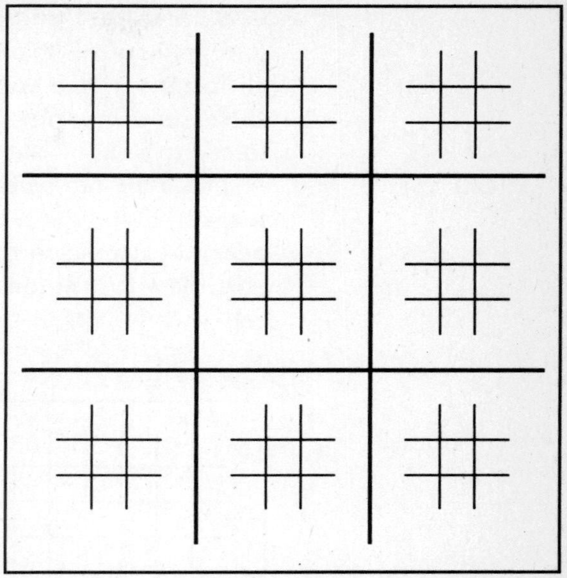

Figure 36. A Meta Tic-Tac-Toe board

Figure 37. How to win order-6 Tic-Tac-Toe

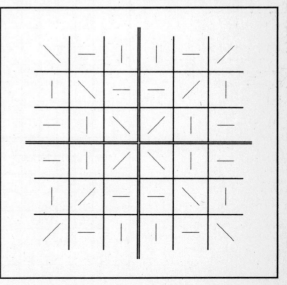

The secret behind Figure 37 is really quite simple: Each row has two horizontal lines, and each column has two vertical lines. Thus, if you follow the rules, no one will ever get six in a row. This may be taken as an intuitive, bare-bones proof that for any *n* equal to or greater than three, an *n*-in-a-row game played on an order-*n* board can always be forced to a tie by the second player.

This type of "pairings" analysis can be extended to unimaginable lengths. Figure 38 is a Hales-Jewitt diagram on an infinite board. (The general patterns on the board can be extended in any direction.) Is it possible to win at nine-in-a-row on this infinite board? No. Whichever cell your opponent takes, take the cell that is paired with it by the

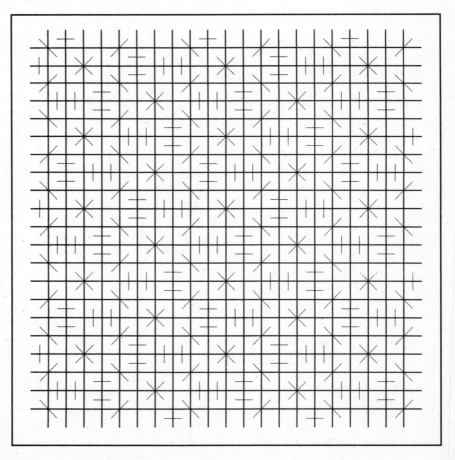

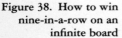
Figure 38. How to win nine-in-a-row on an infinite board

straight lines. Once again, you will block all possible critical paths, and the game will end in a draw. It is possible to create an infinite board similar to this that will allow the second player to force a tie in all n-in-a-row games, as long as n is equal to or greater than 9.

To give one final twist, we will look at a game of three-dimensional Tic-Tac-Toe as analyzed by Solomon W. Golomb, played on an 8-by-8-by-8 cube. Figure 39 is one octant of the cube made up of four order-4 planes lined up in back of each other. You must reflect this octant to the left to obtain a second octant, then reflect both below to obtain the other two octants, then reflect everything behind to obtain the entire cube. In the figure, of course, three of the four planes are hidden from view, so they have been repeated below.

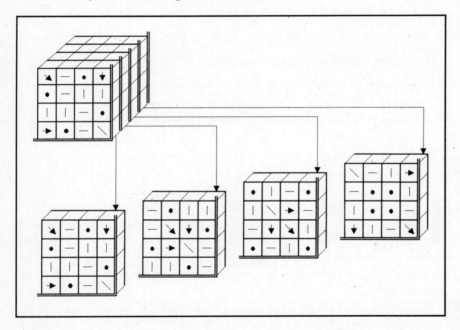

Figure 39. Three-dimensional Tic-Tac-Toe

The markings may seem unusual, but that is only because the three-dimensional figure has been flattened on the page. The marks $(-)$, $(\backslash)$, and $(|)$ are the usual ones on the planes. The bullet $(\bullet)$ represents a horizontal going right through a cubette from front to back. The arrows $(\searcharrow)$ are diagonal lines also going through a cubette. You can follow these markings just as you would the original Hales-Jewitt pairings and never lose in a game of three-dimensional Tic-Tac-Toe.

To Measure the Heavens

JOHN GUTENBERG DID *NOT* INVENT MOVABLE TYPE. IT WAS INVENTED IN CHINA. WILLIAM HARVEY DID *NOT* DISCOVER THE CIRCULATION OF THE BLOOD IN THE BODY. IT WAS DISCOVERED—OR RATHER, ALWAYS ASSUMED—IN CHINA. ISAAC NEWTON WAS *NOT* THE FIRST TO DISCOVER HIS FIRST LAW OF MOTION. IT WAS DISCOVERED IN CHINA.

—*THE GENIUS OF CHINA*, ROBERT TEMPLE

I T IS SAFE TO SAY THAT VIRTUALLY ALL HISTORIES OF ANCIENT people were incomplete until 1954, the year that Joseph Needham published the first volume of his monumental study, *Science and Civilization in China*. From that point on, the "origin" of one or another idea was pushed further back in time, and was generally found to be located in China.

One evidence of the genius of China may be found in a simple inscription that dates back to the thirteenth century B.C.—Greek civilization did not even exist then, and Moses was still to lead the Hebrews out of Egypt. It may seem like a simple inscription at first, but it is actually quite extraordinary. It refers to 547 days as "Five hundreds plus four decades plus seven days." Why is this extraordinary? It is the first example of a decimal number system, the one that is now fundamental to all of modern science, and the one that is found virtually throughout the world. Its first appearance in Europe is in a Spanish manuscript of A.D. 976, approximately 2,300 years after the Chinese inscription, but even so its use did not flourish in Europe until after the publication in 1202 of *Liber Abaci* (*The Book of the Abacus*), by Leonardo Pisano (or Fibonacci). A later chapter will have many of Fibonacci's puzzles.

There is an interesting theory behind the early development of the decimal system in China. Nearly all people first used alphabetic characters to symbolize numbers. Such an easily available system may have hidden the possibilities of a decimal notation. The ancient Greeks, for example, were very advanced in all areas of mathematics, but they used "alpha," the first letter of their alphabet, to symbolize "one," and "beta," the second letter, to symbolize "two." There was therefore no need to stop at nine, as is usually done in a decimal notation. Instead, they went past "theta," the ninth letter, to symbolize "ten" as "iota," and so on.

The Chinese, however, did not possess an ordered alphabet, in which one symbol was recognizably the first, another the second, another the third, and so on, like our *ABC*'s. They wrote instead in word-characters,

Figure 40. Master and pupil at a counting board (Reprinted from Temple, 1987)

so a number notation had to be invented from scratch. From earliest time, the Chinese "wrote" their numbers by placing rods in the pockets of a wooden counting board, probably the fore-runner of an abacus. (Figure 40 is a woodcut illustrating a master patiently instructing a pu-pil on the use of a counting board.) The number "ten" was represented by a single rod in the second pocket, and nothing in the first pocket. The Chinese number system—indeed, even our own number system—is simply a way of doing the same thing on paper.

Similar devices were known in Greece proba-bly by the seventh century B.C. It was typical in the West, however, to find a decimal *machine* such as this existing side by side with a de-cidedly nondecimal (even nonpositional) *number system*. The problem seems to be a reluctance to accept that a single symbol may mean some-thing different depending on how it is used. A machine was somewhat more acceptable to some, because of its physical presence. Even so, Roman authors often used counting boards, which were functionally similar to the Chinese versions pictured in Figure 40, in allusions to airy insubstantiality. Polybius writes of political influence peddlers:

> These men who surround the King are really like the pebbles on a counting board. The pebbles, according to the pleasure of the reckoner, may be valued at one moment as little as a chalkous [small currency, such as a penny] or at the next moment as much as a talent [larger currency].

This is like saying of a sycophant: "He is as changeable as a number!" The allusion is lost on us, but at one time it was easily understood by much of the world. Centuries later Martin Luther made a similar allusion:

> To the counting master all counters are equal, and their worth depends on where he places them. Just so are men equal before God, but they are unequal according to the station in which God has placed them.

Such allusions are noticeably absent among the Chinese, which is a good indication of exactly what they accomplished.

WAS PASCAL CHINESE?

The original Chinese numbers looked very much like the counting rods that were used on the wooden boards. Figure 41 is a fairly complete list. A rod laid horizontally was a unit. Five rods can be piled one on top of the other this way, but the number "6" was symbolized with a vertical rod on the left, and a unit (or horizontal) rod next to it. Ten was

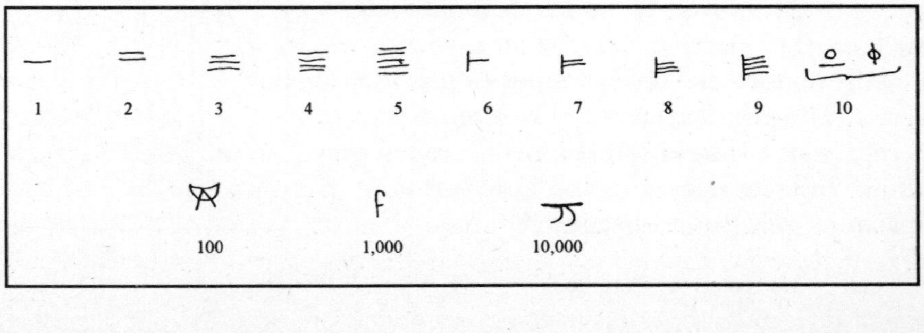

Figure 41. Chinese numerals

a horizontal rod with a "0" above it, somewhat like our number 10 lying on its side. Thus, the "0" was used for the same reason we use ours, to distinguish a "1" from a "10." With enough practice, it is possible to get a very good feel for the logic of Chinese notation.

One way to do this is to decipher the triangle of numbers illustrated in Figure 42, taken from *The Precious Mirror of the Four Elements*, written in 1303 by Chu Shih-chieh. Can you translate the numbers and find a pattern in the triangle? The circles along the left and right sides all contain the number 1. The circles within the triangle are the sum of the two circles connected to it from above. Thus, the number 35, along the eighth row, is the sum of the 15 and 20 above it. The method can be followed throughout the triangle, down to symbols for the numbers 56 and 70.

This triangle, by the way, is particularly interesting because it is one example—there are many others—of a "European" idea that actually originated in China. Some readers may recognize

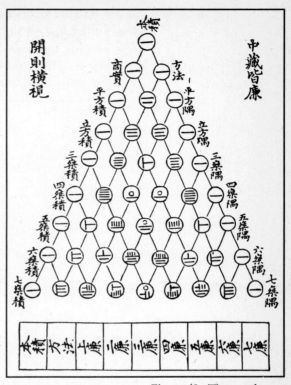

Figure 42. The number triangle of *The Precious Mirror of the Four Elements* (Reprinted from Temple, 1987)

it as "Pascal's triangle," a simple method of finding the coefficients when a binomial (or the sum of two numbers) is raised to higher powers. This was Pascal's purpose, as well as Chu Shih-chieh's. To illustrate its use, assume you wish to raise $(a+b)$ to the power of 2. You will get

$$(a+b)^2 = (1 \cdot a^2) + (2 \cdot ab) + (1 \cdot b^2)$$

The numbers 1, 2, 1 are the coefficients; they appear as the second line—notice we raised the binomial to the second power—in Chu Shih-chieh's triangle. If you raise $(a+b)$ to the third power, the coefficients will be the third line of the triangle. And so on. The triangle is a great time-saver, since it is possible to find solutions to problems with very little work.

There are actually many more relations packed into this seemingly simple triangle than the Chinese (or Pascal, for that matter) ever realized. Its simple additive generating formula—in which each number is the sum of the two numbers above it—can be used in reverse to create the "other half" of the triangle sitting above it, as is illustrated in Figure 43. Every line in this hidden half can be found by a corresponding subtractive formula, or simply by imagining the numbers needed to find the row beneath it. Thus, the 1 that Chu Shih-chieh placed at the top of his triangle must have been generated by a 1 and 0 on either side of it.

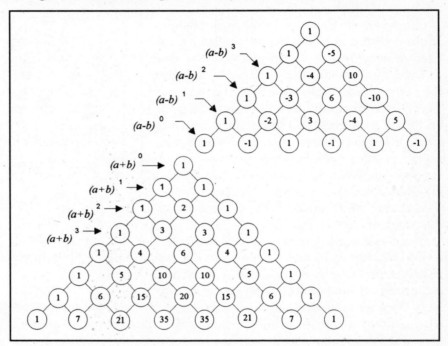

Figure 43. Chu Shih-chieh's triangle, and its negative upper half

Just as the *n*th row of the original triangle gives the coefficients of $(a+b)$ raised to the *n*th power, so does the *n*th row of the hidden triangle give the coefficients of $(a-b)$ raised to the *n*th power. The rows of the two parts of the triangles meet at a 45° angle. For example, let us find $(a-b)^3$.

$$(a-b)^3 = (1 \cdot a^3) + (-3a^2b) + (3 \cdot ab^2) + (1 \cdot b^3)$$

The numbers 1, -3, 3, 1 are found in the third row of the triangle. We will see that this beautiful triangle of the Chinese also contains in it some of the figurate numbers as well as the Fibonacci sequence. It is always fascinating to see that so much can be packed into such a simple array.

The caption beneath the triangle in Figure 42 reads "the Old Methods." And in fact the author of *The Precious Mirror* tells us that he has taken the triangle from an earlier text, one written in 1100, where the triangle is called *Piling-up Powers and Unlocking Coefficients*. It is now lost, but its mention serves to remind us that Pascal was over 400 years late with his "invention."

. . . -3, -2, -1, 0

Unfortunately, although the full measure of China's glory is impressive, we may never realize all of what was actually accomplished. Sometime in the second century B.C. the Emperor Shih Huang-ti burned most of the books of Chinese scholars. For the next four hundred years, scholars were forced to transcribe the entire lexicon of traditional knowledge, and to do so largely from memory or from fragments of charred scroll. We may never know how much was lost, but we do know that in the act of transcribing, work was often attributed to an ancient sage in order to increase its prestige. Thus, even the work that remains cannot be correctly dated.

One such work is the *Chiu-chang suan-shu*, or *Nine Chapters on the Mathematical Art*. It is usually thought to have been written sometime between the third and first century B.C., so when the author of *The Precious Mirror* writes about "the Old Methods," he very likely means methods in *Nine Chapters*. It is a marvelous summary of, perhaps, all mathematical knowledge to be found in ancient China, most of it set forth as a series of often quaint, and always intriguing, puzzles. Its likely author is a man named Chang Tshang, but future generations copied the book and generally added their own commentaries, so the earliest version remaining to us was prepared by Liu Hui in the third century A.D., an author we met previously for his work on calculating pi. Only portions of the book have been translated into English, but what we have is remarkable indeed.

Consider for example this puzzle from the eighth chapter, titled *"Fang ch'eng,"* or "The Way of Calculating by Tabulation":

> There are three grades of corn. Neither two baskets of the first grade, three baskets of the second grade, nor four baskets of the third grade taken separately comprise a full required measure. If, however, one basket of the second-grade were added to the [two measures of the] first-grade corn, [or] one basket of the third-grade corn were added to the [three measures of the] second-grade corn,

[or] one basket of the first grade were added to the [four measures of the] third-grade baskets, then the grain would comprise one required measure in each case. How many measures of the various grades does each mixed basket contain?

The puzzle is simple by today's standards, but its purpose was to reveal two quite remarkable discoveries. You can see both of them in Figure 44, which is not from *Nine Chapters* but which still gives a detailed account of "calculating by tabulation."

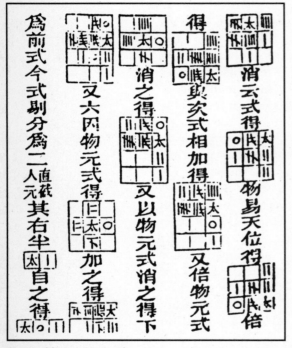

Figure 44. Calculation by Tabulation (Reprinted from Temple, 1987)

First, you can clearly see the symbol for zero, 0. Quite likely its form was meant to represent an empty compartment on the counting board. The figure was used in China long before it ever entered the West. Second, and more startling, is the presence of negative values! On the counting board, a negative number was denoted by red rods, as opposed to the usual black rods used for positive quantities. In print, the negative number was denoted by a line crossing the usual symbol for the positive number. You can see some of these negative numbers in Figure 44. Both zero and negative quantities are natural concepts to people who possess a number system; other people meet such concepts with a kind of horror.

The "tables" in Figure 44 are exactly what we today would call matrices, used by the Chinese, then as today, to represent a system of equations. Each cell of the matrix or table is an unknown; for example, the first cell might be the first grade of corn, and so on. Today we are inclined to use symbols instead, but the idea is identical to what the author of *Nine Chapters* had in mind. The problem above would be represented by the following table, in which x, y, and z are the measures respectively of the first-, second-, and third-grade corn:

$$2x + y \qquad = 1$$
$$3y + z = 1$$
$$x \qquad + 4z = 1$$

We may multiply a row by a constant, add or subtract one row from another, and so on until we can solve for one of the unknowns. For the problem above, we multiply the last row by 2, to obtain the new equation:

$$2x + 8z = 2$$

Now subtract this new equation from the first, to get:

$$y - 8z = -1, \text{ or}$$
$$y = -1 + 8z$$

If we replace this value of y in the second equation, we get:

$$-3 + 24z + z = 1$$

This will give us all the solutions:

$$x = {}^9/_{25} \text{ of the required measure}$$
$$y = {}^7/_{25} \text{ of the required measure}$$
$$z = {}^4/_{25} \text{ of the required measure}$$

Throughout the problem we were forced to use both 0 and negative numbers, a fine example of how puzzles are invented to force us to use new tools—in this case the decimal number system.

WAS MORRIS WIKENFELD CHINESE?

It is interesting to compare *Nine Chapters* with other ancient works, such as the Ahmes (or Rhind) Papyrus. Very often the two books develop the same line of thought even though there was no commerce between the two cultures. We see, for example, the very useful principle of the *regula falsi* again, although in China it was called the Method of Excess and Deficiency, because it involved two guesses that were usually greater and less than the correct answer. Here is one such problem, which the reader will find simple:

A certain number of people are buying some chickens. If each person pays 9 *wen* there is a surplus of 11 *wen*, and if each person pays 6 *wen* there is a deficiency of 16 *wen*. Find the number of people and the cost of the chickens.

Considering how early the Chinese had adopted a decimal number system, it is not surprising to find in *Nine Chapters* many of the puzzles that, centuries later, would intrigue so many people so far from China. For example, there is the famous "dog and hare" problem:

A hare runs 50 *pu* ahead of a dog. The latter catches the former after running for 125 *pu*. When the two are 30 *pu* apart, in how many *pu* will the dog overtake the hare?

A similar problem was sent by Alcuin of York to the Emperor Charlemagne in the early ninth century. (We will see other of Alcuin's puzzles in a later chapter.):

A dog and a hare are 150 feet apart. The dog follows when the hare runs. The dog leaps 9 feet at a time, while the hare travels 7 feet [in the same amount of time]. How many feet will be travelled by the pursuing dog, and the fleeing hare, before it is seized?

Both puzzles are simple enough for the reader to solve, but it is interesting to note that the Chinese, equipped with a positional number system, possessed a general proof for all such "pursuit" problems, while Alcuin, having nothing better than Roman numerals, gave only the answer to this one specific problem. His answer reads in part: "The distance between the dog and hare is 150 feet, half of which is 75. The dog goes 9 feet at a time, and 75 times 9 is 675. This is the number of feet the chasing dog runs." This answer is useless if a few parameters of the problem are changed. Looking at the general principles behind a puzzle is a trait that generally accompanies the positional number system.

Perhaps the most startling example of the way the puzzles of *Nine Chapters* consistently reappear in later times is the following:

Given a right triangle with one leg 5 units long and the other leg 12 units long, what is the length of the side of the largest square that can be inscribed in the triangle?

The identical problem reappeared in 1985 in the "Reader's Reflections" section of *Mathematics Teacher*, submitted by Morris Wikenfeld:

> Given a right triangle with legs of length *a* and *b* and hypotenuse of length *c*, what is the length of *x*, the side of the largest inscribed square having the right angle as one of its vertices?

Figure 45 shows the original illustration as it appeared in *Nine Chapters*. It is not very different than the one that appeared more recently in *Mathematics Teacher*, although, out of respect for the originator, I have kept the Chinese terms *ku* and *kou* for the legs of the triangle, and *hsien* for the hypotenuse. That the two problems are identical was first noticed by Frank J. Swetz, a consistently entertaining author on the history of mathematics.

The problem is interesting now for the same reason it was interesting over two thousand years ago: It poses a beautiful relationship in a remarkably simple design. The figure shows that there are actually two right triangles. The larger has legs of length ku and kou, and the smaller has legs of length *s* and (ku−*s*). Obviously, the two triangles are similar since their respective angles are equal. Therefore, the following relation holds: ku/kou = (ku−*s*)/*s*, whereupon *s* = ku • kou/(ku+kou). Thus, the sides of an inscribed square are equal to the product of the triangle's legs divided by the sum of its legs—a strikingly elegant solution. Keep in mind that the triangle can be any size whatsoever. As it shrinks or grows, so does the square inside it, and the side of the square will always bear the same relationship to the legs of the triangle.

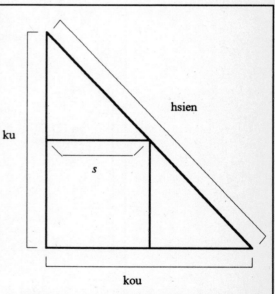

Figure 45. What is the value of *s*?

With a very modern attitude, the author of *Nine Chapters* creates a variation of the problem. This time we inscribe a circle, and not a square, in the right triangle. What is the length of its radius?

The solution is typically cryptic but we can get a good feel for the spirit behind it in Figure 46. Only part (a) appears in the original manuscript. Notice that the author has enclosed the triangle inside a

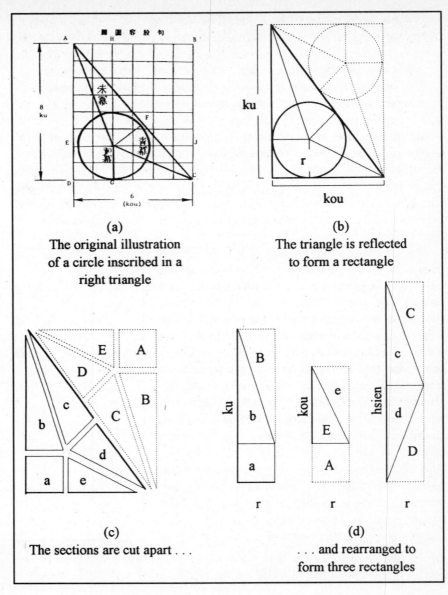

(a)

The original illustration
of a circle inscribed in a
right triangle

(b)

The triangle is reflected
to form a rectangle

(c)

The sections are cut apart . . .

(d)

. . . and rearranged to
form three rectangles

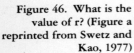

Figure 46. What is the
value of r? (Figure a
reprinted from Swetz and
Kao, 1977)

rectangle, the sides of which are the two legs of the triangle. Three radii
are dropped, each one perpendicular to one side of the triangle. Then
lines are drawn from two vertices to the center of the circle. In all, the

author has divided the triangle into four smaller triangles and a square. In (b) we have reflected these smaller figures in the other part of the large rectangle. Of course, a figure and its reflection are exactly equal. In (c) we "explode" the figures apart.

Finally, in (d) we reassemble everything into three very manageable rectangles, just as though it were a jigsaw puzzle. Nothing has been lost in the exploding and reassembling, so the area of the rectangle in (b), which is ku • kou, must equal the sum of the areas of the three rectangles in (d), which are (ku•r) + (kou•r) + (hsien•r). This gives us:

$$ku \bullet kou = (ku \bullet r) + (kou \bullet r) + (hsien \bullet r), \text{ or}$$

$$r = \frac{ku \bullet kou}{(ku + kou + hsien)}$$

which answers the problem. Once again, the relationship is stunning and simple.

We might call the general approach above the "jigsaw approach." As a method of solving geometric problems it is somewhat limited, but where it is appropriate it brings a remarkable concreteness to what may otherwise appear too abstract. Perhaps most intriguing, however, is the fact that it may be based on a simple children's game that was popular among the prostitutes of China! The game is now called Tangrams, and we will see several of its puzzles in a later section.

WAS PYTHAGORAS CHINESE?[1]

The two puzzles above were taken from the last of *Nine Chapters*, which concerns itself entirely with the right triangle. The chapter is titled "Kou-Ku" or "Leg-Thigh," apparently because of the "right angle" shape of the leg when the knee is bent. Kou and ku were the names given to the two sides of a right triangle, always illustrated with

---

[1] The question was taken from the title of a book by Frank J. Swetz and T. I. Kao: *Was Pythagoras Chinese? An Examination of Right-Triangle Theory in Ancient China.* The book contains a translation of part of *Nine Chapters*. Obviously, I have paraphrased the title to head previous sections as well. Other books and articles by Swetz, each one a fascinating look at the history of mathematics, may be found in the bibliography.

the kou lying horizontally. Of course, there is no real need to give these two legs different names. The third side, what we call the hypotenuse, was called hsien, or stretched string.

The principle behind the puzzles of the chapter is well known: Given any right triangle, the square built on the hsien is equal in area to the squares built on the kou and the ku. It is appropriate to describe the theorem in these Chinese terms, because *Nine Chapters* shows, beyond a doubt, that the theorem, usually credited to Pythagoras of Greece, is actually of independent Chinese origin.

Before the full principle of right triangles was known, the Chinese had examined the 3-4-5 triangle—that is, a triangle that has legs of 3 and 4 units, and a hypotenuse of 5 units. This is the smallest, or most primitive, of all right triangles with integer sides. The 3-4-5 triangle was so common, in fact, that it was given a special name, *Hsuan-thu*. You can see the *Hsuan-thu* below in Figure 47. It was used to illustrate the following dialogue in the *Chou Pei Suan Ching*, or *The Arithmetical Classic of the Gnomon and the Circular Paths of Heaven*, possibly written in the time of Confucius in the sixth century B.C. The dialogue shows a sense of awe for the triangle, as though its uncanny necessity of forming a right angle somehow revealed a secret plan of the Deity. Despite the mysticism, however, it still contains a very nice proof that the 3-4-5 triangle is indeed a right triangle, although it is by no means general enough to be called a proof of the right-angle theorem:

> Of old, Chou Kung addressed Shang Kao, saying, "I have heard that the Grand Prefect (that is, Shang Kao himself) is versed in the art of numbering. May I venture to inquire how Fu-Hsi anciently established the degrees of the celestial sphere? There are no steps by which one may ascend the heavens, and the earth is not measurable with a footrule. I should like to ask you what was the origin of these numbers?"
>
> Shang Kao replied, "The art of numbering proceeds from the circle and the square. The circle is derived from the square and the square from the rectangle. The rectangle originates from the fact that $9 \cdot 9 = 81$. Thus, let us cut a rectangle (diagonally), and make the width 3 units wide, and the length 4 units long. The diagonal between the two corners will then be 5 units long. Now after drawing a square on this diagonal, circumscribe it by half-rectangles like that which has been left outside, so as to form a

square plate. Thus, the four outer half-rectangles of width 3, length 4, and diagonal 5, together make two rectangles of area 24; then, when this is subtracted from the square plate of area 49, the remainder is of area 25. This process is called 'piling up the rectangles.' The methods used by Yü the Great in governing the world were derived from these numbers."

Chou Kung exclaimed, "Great indeed is the art of numbering. I would like to ask about the Tao of the use of the right-angled triangle."

Shang Kao replied, "The plane right-angled triangle laid on the ground serves to lay out straight and square by the aid of cords. The recumbent right-angled triangle serves to observe heights. The reverse right-angled triangle is used for ascertaining distances. By the revolution of a right-angled triangle [that is, compasses] a circle may be formed. By uniting right-angled triangles, squares and oblongs are formed. The square pertains to earth, the circle belongs to heaven, heaven being round and the earth square. The numbers of the square being the standard, the dimensions of the circle are deduced from those of the square. Heaven is like a conical sun-hat. Heaven's colors are blue and black, earth's colors are yellow and red. A circular plate is employed to represent heaven, formed according to the celestial numbers; above, like an outer garment, it is blue and black, beneath, like an inner one, it is red and yellow. Thus is represented the figure of heaven and earth. He who understands the earth is wise, and he who understands the heavens is a sage. Knowledge is derived from the straight line. The straight line is derived from the right angle. And the combination of the right angle with numbers is what guides and rules the ten thousand things."

Chou Kung exclaimed, "Excellent indeed."

(One look at Figure 47 will show that we have here essentially the same jigsaw approach that we saw previously.)

It is sometimes suggested that this same 3-4-5 triangle was also known among the Egyptian *harpedonaptai*, or rope-stretchers, who surveyed the areas around the Nile after its inundation. According to this theory, the rope was knotted in two places, forming three lengths of 3, 4, and 5 units. When the rope was stretched tight so that the lengths formed the three sides of a triangle, the angle between the 3-side and

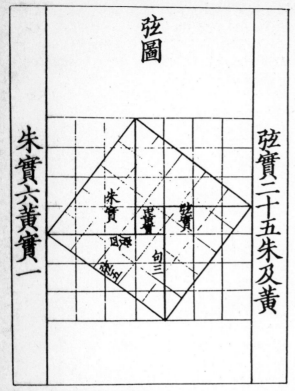

弦圖

朱實六黃實一

弦實二十五朱又黃

朱實

黃實

弦實

句三

Figure 47. The Hsuan-thu of the *Circular Paths of Heaven* (Reprinted from Swetz and Kao, 1977)

the 4-side would be a right angle, since $3^2 + 4^2 = 5^2$. Such a device, it was said, may have been used in the construction of pyramids and other sacred sites. We know that, for religious reasons, the Egyptians were very particular about the orientation of these buildings. Perhaps by sighting a star as it rises and sets on the horizon, they were able to find the North-South line. The rope-stretchers then could have used their triangles to find the East-West line lying perpendicular to this. The theory is so nice that we almost wish it were true. Unfortunately, there is nothing to support it. We assume Ahmes had no general understanding of right triangles, because no problems concerning them appear in his papyrus, even though it is a rich source of puzzles. The earliest mention of right triangles in Egyptian literature appears in 300 B.C. in a Cairo papyrus: "A ladder 10 cubits has its foot 6 cubits from a wall; to what height will it reach?" Even then, the Egyptians endowed the 3-4-5 triangle itself—not the right triangle in general—with near mystical properties: The leg of length 4 represented Osiris; the leg of length 3 represented Isis; and the hypotenuse of length 5 represented Horus, the son of Osiris and Isis. The mysticism is not very different from that found in China in the *Arithmetical Classic*, but in Egypt the mysticism was undoubtedly due to the use of the triangle among the priesthood; in China it is more a human response of humility before the unfolding laws of nature. In Egypt, the sacred triangle remained just that; in China, it became a law of geometry.

We really do not know what the first proof of the general right-angle theorem looked like, but if it originated in China we should expect it to follow along the lines of the jigsaw approach. Such a proof appears in India, which inherited much of China's original discoveries. It was published first in *The Lilavati* by the mathematician Bhaskara. There are many stories surrounding this book, but most claim that while working on an astrological chart—those were the days that respected mathematicians did such things—Bhaskara discovered that his daughter, Lilavati, was destined to marry a man who would later take his, Bhaskara's, life. For this reason, Bhaskara forbade his daughter to leave his presence unchaperoned; and to relieve her boredom, which must have been considerable, he presented her with the mathematical text that now bears her name. I doubt that the book was sufficient recompense for such cruel loneliness, despite the father's attempt to direct the lessons to "lovely and dear Lilavati, whose eyes are like a fawn's." For one thing, the poor child was made to solve fairly obnoxious problems about the relative worth of sixteen-year-old female slaves. (If you're curious, they were worth only about eight oxen that have worked for two years, and their value decreases rapidly with age.) One puzzle is more interesting. It consists entirely of the diagram in Figure 48, and beneath it is the single word "Behold!"

Figure 48. Behold!

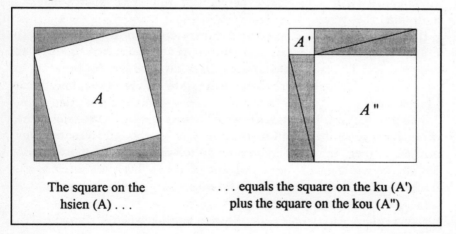

The square on the
hsien (A) . . .

. . . equals the square on the ku (A')
plus the square on the kou (A")

Figure 48. Behold!

Behold, indeed. The four identical right triangles in the first illustration are rearranged in the second. The space A in the first illustration, which is the square on the hypotenuse, must equal the space A' and A'' in the second, which is the sum of the squares built on the other two sides. The "jigsaw" method of rearranging the figures is very much in the Chinese spirit. Could this be the missing proof?

BEHOLD! ... BUT I DON'T KNOW WHY!

Look again at Figure 48. If I gave you a sheet of gold equal in area to A, or two sheets of gold equal in area to A' and A'', which would you take? Obviously, the answer is "It doesn't matter; they are equal." In fact, what we have done in the right-angle theorem is to take a square (the one on the *hsien*) and divide it into two smaller squares (the ones on the *ku* and the *kou*). How many squares can we divide this way? It is useful in answering this to restrict ourselves to squares with integer sides, otherwise the question becomes needlessly unwieldy. Now, each right-triangle corresponds to a square that can be divided. In fact, the triangle itself tells us how to go about the division. For example, there exists a right-triangle with sides of 3, 4, and 5 units. So obviously, a square with side 5 can be divided into two squares with sides of 3 and 4. This simply means that $5^2 = 3^2 + 4^2$. We know that there are an infinity of right-triangles with integer sides, so there are an infinity of squares that can be divided this way.

But now let us move to higher dimensions. Are there cubes with integer sides that can be divided into two smaller cubes, again with integer sides? The two smaller cubes must have the same volume as the first? Can we divided a hypercube in this way? How about still higher dimensions?

The problem was first stated over 300 years ago by Pierre de Fermat, a French lawyer and amateur mathematician—although you should not let the qualifier "amateur" mislead you; he was one of the most important mathematicians of the seventeenth century. Fermat's interest was in numbers pure and simple, so he actually stated the problem like this:

> Does the equation $x^n + y^n = z^n$ have a solution when x, y, z and n are all positive integers?

He gave an answer in two parts: When n equals 2, there are an infinity of solutions; but when n is greater than 2, there are no solutions. In the first case, when n equals 2, we are restricted to squares; and in the second case, when n is greater than 2, we are dealing with higher dimensions, cubes, hypercubes, and so on. It is a very pretty answer, and it reveals a great deal about integers. But in keeping with his irritating habits, Fermat did not bother to provide a proof, and this time he made a further pest of himself by writing in the margin of a book, as though it were a mere afterthought, "I have found a truly wonderful proof which this margin is too small to contain."

During the ensuing 300 years, countless mathematicians have tried to find the "truly wonderful proof" to what is now called Fermat's Last Theorem, but all have failed. It was extraordinary to watch this quintessentially simple puzzle, so easy to state, defeating the world's most brilliant mathematicians. Proposed by an amateur, it stymied the professionals. Alive and kicking after 300 years, it was a constant reminder that there are some obscure secrets that the human mind may not enter. Many wanted to see the puzzle disappear as quickly as possible. The German Academy of Science even offered a prize to anyone who could solve it. There were no takers.

As I write, however, Dr. Andrew Wiles of Princeton University has what many believe to be the ultimate proof, devoid of any errors whatsoever, although of course a final judgement must wait for a number of years. If he is correct, then we may be witnessing the conquest of one of the world's great and most long-lived puzzles of all time. But Dr. Wiles has given us a two-sided sword. In the opinion of many who have seen his proof, it is so arcane and technical that less than 1 percent of even serious mathematicians can comprehend it. He himself required three lectures, delivered across three days, just to explain it. So, does the equation $x^n + y^n = z^n$ have a solution in positive integers when n is greater than 2? Yesterday, my smug answer was, "We do not know." Tomorrow, my more humble answer might be, "Definitely not, but I don't know why."

THE PROSTITUTES' PUZZLE

If this book were written before 1965, I would have been able to present a truly remarkable theory concerning the origins of the *Hsuan-thu* and more generally what we have called the "jigsaw approach" used to solve some geometric problems. This theory holds that the origins may be found in an ancient Chinese game called the Clever Puzzle of Seven-Pieces, or Tangrams, as it is known in the West. The name "Tangram" may have been given to the puzzle by American sailors who customarily referred to all things Chinese as Tang, from the Cantonese word mean-

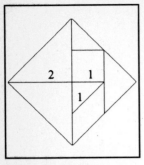

Figure 49. The Tans at rest

ing China. More colorful etymology has it that the game was played by Chinese prostitutes, or Tan, while waiting for their johns; the familiar suffix "gram" was added later.

The seven Tans are pictured in their "resting position" in Figure 49: The large square is cut into a smaller square, two large triangles, two small triangles, one medium triangle, and a rhomboid. The object of the game is to rearrange these seven pieces in order to produce other figures. The Tans may seem limiting at first, because there are so few pieces, but it is altogether astonishing to find what a little imagination can do. This possibly accounts for the long-standing fascination with the game—a great deal comes from a very little. You may like to cut out the seven Tan pieces in order to try some of the constructions that follow.

Figure 50 presents five typical configurations: a swan, a stork, a dog, and a cat in two poses. In each case, the internal lines of the configurations are given so the reader can see how it is made. Notice some of the impossible effects, such as the pencil-thin leg of the stork. Notice, too, how a simple tilt of a Tan is sufficient to convey the arching muscles of the second cat's back, or the steely, unblinking gaze of the first cat. You can see here an element that is found in much of Chinese art, where a simple curved line is sometimes used to convey a whole world of meaning, such as supreme gracefulness. The viewer must use his imagination to supply the rest.

If you look very quickly at Figures 46 and 50, you cannot miss the fact that the same creative energies lie behind both. In fact, if you follow the proof in Figure 46 and then try to create the stork in Figure 50, you will notice that in some sense you are tapping into the same mental resources. Is it possible that the origins of China's geometry lay in a game played by prostitutes? After all, Figure 46 explodes a rectangle into ten pieces and produces three separate rectangles, and Figure 50 explodes a square into seven pieces and produces a lovely stork. Chinese prostitutes invented geometry, or Chinese mathematicians invented a jigsaw puzzle. At some level, the game and the science become one and the same.

Is that not a wonderful theory? Alas, it is very likely wrong. In 1965 Ronald C. Read of the University of Waterloo showed that the clever Puzzle of Seven-Pieces probably originated in China around 1800, long after *The Arithmetical Classic*. The idea that it is much older seems to

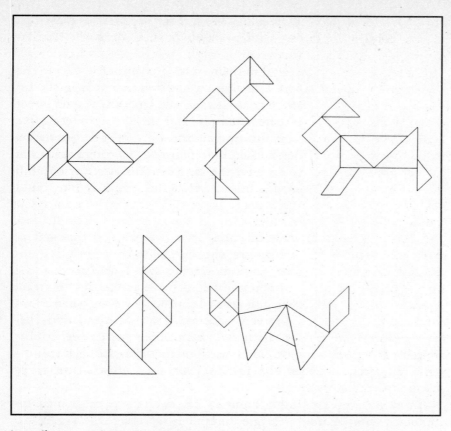

Figure 50. Five Tangram animals

have been nothing more than a hoax perpetrated by Sam Loyd, an American puzzlist. The hoax was so believable that it was accepted by other authorities, including Martin Gardner, who later did much to clear the air by popularizing Read's findings.

Despite Loyd, however, there are some who believe that the puzzle existed as early as the Chou dynasty, in which case it would predate *Nine Chapters*, if not the *Hsuan-thu* itself. Whatever the case, we have here simply a case of the chicken and the egg. It is obvious that the same visual and spatial talents for shifting about geometric figures led to both the Tangram and the first proof of the right-angle theorem—we just do not know which one that talent created first.

The nature of the talent can be seen more clearly the deeper we delve into Tangram constructions. We very quickly develop a sense of the

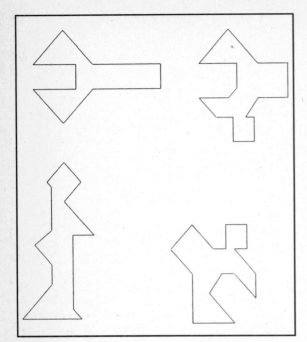

Figure 51. A Tan illusion

geometry of things that is often at odds with our usual way of looking at the world. A startling example of this was created by Read. Look at the Tangram constructions in Figure 51. The first is a wrench and next to it is a shorter wrench. The second is a Japanese woman in her ceremonial dress, and next to it is the same woman bowing at the waist, her bustle showing behind her. I do not give the internal lines of these four constructions because, for the full effect, it is necessary for the reader to build them alone.

Now then, did you notice, after all that work, that the short wrench and the bowing woman are actually the same figure? The answer is probably no, and I confess that the bowing woman took me far longer to create than the short wrench, and even when I was finished with both I saw no similarities between them. The problem, of course, is that we look at figures wrongly. Tangram constructions can help create a sense of figures as a set of lines and angles, the same sense that can be found in the *Hsuan-thu*.

An even more startling example is the Tangram paradox, first invented by Sam Loyd himself. An example is reproduced in Figure 52. The two upper figures seem to be identical in all details, but the second has a foot, which the first does not. The relative sizes of the figures have not been altered, so surely a Tan is missing in the first. But no, both figures use all seven pieces. You can see the paradox in the line drawings.

A similar paradox also appears in the two lower figures of Figure 52, this time without the line drawings. Once again, the second triangle is identical to the first, but there is a hole in it. Can you show how it is done?

Look again at the two triangles. The first, without the hole, is a convex figure, while the second is not. One way to see if a figure is convex is to take any two points within the figure and draw a line between them. If the line lies wholly within the figure, and if this can be done with any two points whatsoever, then the figure is convex. A modern question to ask about Tangrams is, How many convex figures are possible using all seven Tans?

This question was asked and answered in the 1940s. Oddly enough, there are only thirteen convex figures, not counting, of course, rotations and reflections. One of these is the square in Figure 49; another is the triangle in Figure 52. Nine more are shown in Figure 53, and of these only six are presented with line drawings. The other two are left for the reader who, as a final, rather difficult puzzle, may try to find the missing convex figures that are known to exist.

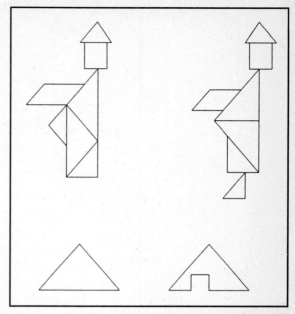

Figure 52. A Tan paradox

THE FIRST TURTLE?

A story is often told of a scientist who gave a lecture on the orbiting of the planets around the sun. At the end of the lecture, an old lady proclaimed: "What you have told us is rubbish. The earth is really a plate standing on the back of a giant turtle." But, the scientist demanded, what is the turtle standing on? "You're a very clever young man," said the old lady, "but it's turtles all the way down."

There is a sense in which historians would like to see turtles all the way down. To understand our own numbers, we must go back to the Egyptians, who gave us decimals, and then to the Ishango, who gave us ones. Where did these ones come from? What is *that* turtle standing on? We don't know, but in this case we are not disappointed in leaving off, since, after all, they are only etches carved into a bone.

What is surprising about China is that here, too, we are standing on the first turtle, but this time we have far more than just bone etches. We have full-blown mathematics, and all that this implies, including a haughty understanding of nature's logic. Where did it all come from? It came from China. And beyond that, we have no turtle to stand on.

"To measure the heavens," it is said in *The Arithmetical Classic of the Gnomon*, "one inch is like a thousand miles." It strikes me as unimaginably disrespectful to say this, but I am certain that most readers think that sounds like a fortune cookie. You must read deeper into it. The

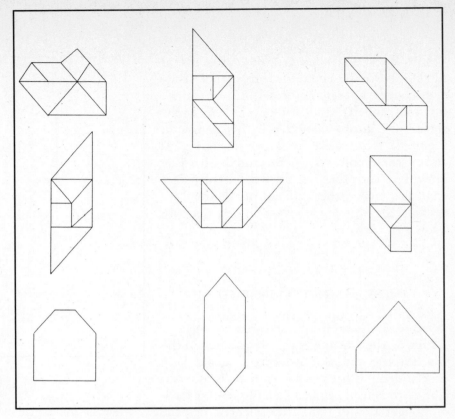

Figure 53. Some convex Tangram figures. What are the other two?

chilling fact is that the Chinese *wanted* to measure the heavens, and they did so at a time when most people could barely manage measurements on earth.

WHEN ASIA STARVES, THE WEST SENDS GRAIN. WE ASSUME THAT WESTERN AGRICULTURE IS THE VERY PINNACLE OF WHAT IS POSSIBLE IN THE PRODUCTIVE USE OF SOIL FOR THE GROWTH OF FOOD. BUT WE SHOULD TAKE TO HEART THE ASTONISHING AND DISTURBING FACT THAT THE EUROPEAN AGRICULTURAL REVOLUTION, WHICH LAID THE BASIS FOR THE INDUSTRIAL REVOLUTION, CAME ABOUT ONLY BECAUSE OF THE IMPORTATION OF CHINESE IDEAS AND INVENTIONS.

—*THE GENIUS OF CHINA*, ROBERT TEMPLE

On a Turtle Shell

SOME HARMONIZE YIN AND YANG, THE GROWTH AND DECAY OF

THE SEASONS, THE FIVE NOTES OF THE SCALE, THE PITCH

PIPES USED IN DIVINATION. . . . BUT THIS ESOTERIC

MATHEMATICS (AS IT IS CALLED) CANNOT BE SEPARATED FROM

THE MINOR ART OF EARTHLY CALCULATION.

—CHIN CHIU-SHAO, WRITING OF MAGIC SQUARES IN
MATHEMATICAL TREATISE IN NINE SECTIONS

O F CHINA'S MANY ACHIEVEMENTS THERE IS ONE THAT SEEMS strangely insignificant but that has actually succeeded in conquering the attention of most of the world's puzzle enthusiasts. This is the magic square, an array of numbers from 1 to n^2 configured in an order-n square in such a way that the rows, columns, and diagonals all sum to the same magic constant. It is easier to understand the magic square by looking at the original one from China, reproduced in Figure 54. On top is the usual depiction of the figure using knotted cords, and on the bottom is the same square with modern numbers. The reader can see that the numbers along the three horizontal, three vertical, and two diagonal lines all sum to the same magic constant, 15.

This square is called an order-3 square, since it has 3 cells on a side. In general, the magic constant of an order-n square will always be $\frac{1}{2}n(n^2+1)$; when $n = 3$, this gives us 15. Also, there will be $2n + 2$ straight lines that sum to the constant.

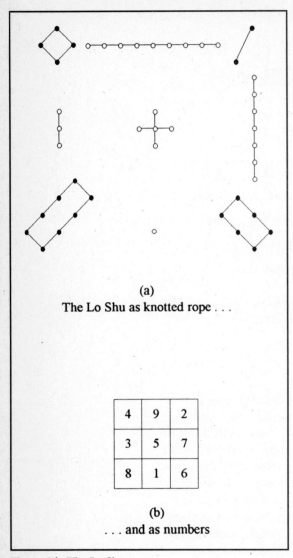

(a)

The Lo Shu as knotted rope . . .

4	9	2
3	5	7
8	1	6

(b)

. . . and as numbers

Figure 54. The Lo Shu square

According to legend, the square was found by the Emperor Yü the Great, whose name is also associated with the right-angle theorem, as we saw previously. The legend holds that Yü found the square on the shell of a turtle as it emerged from the River Lo, and for this reason it is sometimes called the *Lo Shu* square. In later years it also came to be associated with the *I Ching*, an ancient Chinese work of numerological superstitions. The legend claims that the *Lo Shu* originated in the twenty-third century B.C., but, like many "folk histories" in China, this legend exaggerates the antiquity of an invention in order to bring it a higher dignity. If nothing else, the exaggeration reveals the significance that was placed on the square. Modern Chinese scholars claim the *Lo Shu* originated no earlier than the fourth century B.C., certainly ancient enough. And from the beginning it has been the obsession of nearly everyone who has ever dabbled in mathematics.

Notice that the corner cells of the *Lo Shu* contain even numbers, and the off-corner cells form a T of odd numbers. The T was called in China the *Ho-T'u* and it was sometimes regarded as a talisman in its own right. At the center of the square is 5, the center of the sequence of numbers. Diametrically opposite cells, such as $4 + 6$ or $3 + 7$, will always sum to 10, twice the center cell. Since the *Lo Shu* is the only possible order-3 magic square, and since trivial variations made by rotations and reflections will not disturb the basic arrangement, all of this is an inescapable feature of the square itself. From the earliest years, this beautiful, uncanny symmetry conveyed to many the same yin-yang motif that is found throughout Asian philosophy, symbolizing here, as elsewhere, a harmonizing of opposites in the universe. For this reason, the square was sometimes given to the ill as a kind of mystical medicine, to bring their bodily elements back into balance.

A dramatic way to see the orderliness of a magic square is to draw a straight line through the cells in sequence beginning at "1." Such a line is called a sequence pattern. The American architect Claude Brogden was so taken by these sequence patterns that he began every chapter of his autobiography with a different one. He even built the sequence pattern of the *Lo Shu* into the ventilation grill of his most distinguished work, the Chamber of Commerce in Rochester, New York.

THE MEANING OF THE MAGIC

Magic squares often arrive on the heels of the positional number system, like lost baggage. They serve, perhaps, to soak up the initial mysticism that surrounds the number system itself, the sense that there is something unknown out there that only numbers can reveal. (There is; it's called logic.) Magic squares are also "out there," explainable only by the numbers that compose them, although it is never quite certain what exactly is being explained. Magic squares are perfect, but their perfection is wholly self-contained; they refer to nothing outside themselves. Every country and every period gave the magic square a new meaning.

The most common interpretation was spiritual. Actually, any object that provides a sense of order can be endowed with mystical connotations. We can take a little break here to relate the interesting story of another orderly matrix called the Sator stone, which is something like an alphabetical magic square. See Figure 55(a). The stone was found in Cirencester, England, in 1868, but it is believed to be much older, because an identical stone was excavated from the ruins of Pompeii. Begin at the top left corner and read left to right or top to bottom. Now begin at the bottom right corner and read right to left or bottom to top. The message is always the same: "Sator Arepo tenet opera rotas," meaning loosely, "The sower Arepo holds the works in motion." Of course, it is nothing more than five unconnected words, and the second one, "Arepo," is not a word at all but five letters designed to make the square work. But its translation has a faintly religious sound, as though it meant "God is watching the universe." With enough work it is possible to find theological significance in all its aspects. For example, it was common in England to rearrange the letters in the shape of a cross, as in Figure 55(b). The message now reads "our father" and the leftover "a" and "o" at the ends seem to signify the alpha and omega. Similarly, the letters can be anagrammatized into "Oro te, pater; oro te, pater; sanas," meaning "I pray to you, father; I pray to you, father; thou healest."

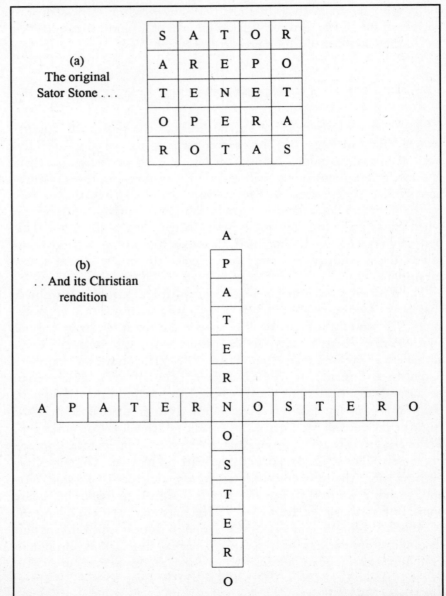

(a)
The original
Sator Stone . . .

(b)
. . And its Christian
rendition

Figure 55. "The sower Arepo holds the works in motion."

Magic squares are like this in that they evoke a feeling that there must be a meaning to them. Looking hard enough, a meaning is easy to find. Ancient Jews, especially in the East, often used the *Lo Shu* to represent the Deity whose image and name they could not denote in more direct ways. The constant of the *Lo Shu*, 15, is written in the Hebrew number system with the first two letters of Jahveh. The uniqueness of the *Lo Shu* seemed to indicate that when all things came together in a logical whole, the name of Jahveh would always reveal itself.

In Islam, too, the *Lo Shu*, undoubtedly obtained from China, was given a spiritual meaning. The knotted rope of the original Chinese square was by coincidence an ancient curse among Semitic people of the Middle East. It is used this way in the Koran:

I take refuge with the Lord of Daybreak
From the evil of all He hath made,
From the evil of darkness when it gathers
From the evil of women who blow upon knots
And the evil of the envious when he envies.

By placing the knotted ropes inside a square with its orderly rows and columns, the *Lo Shu* seemed to counter the threat of a curse, as though it represented blessed events that were necessarily painful. In *The Deliverance from Error*, Al-Ghazalli, an Arab scholar who held an enormous influence over medieval Europe, encourages the use of the *Lo Shu* during pregnancy: "[The square] is written on two pieces of cloth never touched by water. The pregnant woman keeps her eyes fixed on them and puts them under her feet and forthwith the child hastens to come out." This power of the magic square is said to be an example of wisdom that cannot be attained through reasoning alone, a popular notion throughout the Middle Ages, due largely to Al-Ghazalli. The idea is fundamental to understanding Dante's *Divine Comedy*, as is Al-Ghazalli's description of Mohammed ascending into heaven.

Undoubtedly, the most significant square to arise in the Middle East is the order-5 square in Figure 56. Like the *Lo Shu*, this square was often used to represent the Deity. To make the magic work, the reader must supply the missing number in the center, which of course is "1." Thus, neither the Deity nor the oneness of the Deity—at the center of all things, bringing order and meaning to everything around it—was directly represented.

15	16	22	3	9
2	8	14	20	21
19	25		7	13
6	12	18	24	5
23	4	10	11	17

Figure 56. An Islamic magic square

The Islamic use of the *Lo Shu* was the origin of a curious symbol used by the early Freemasons in Europe. You can find the symbol etched into the walls of most buildings that date back to the twelfth century, looking like the stylized "41" in Figure 57. When written like this over the *Lo Shu*, the "41" covers eight of the nine squares, and leaves only the "8" itself untouched. The significance of the "8" in Freemason numerology is no longer known, but it is a prominent symbol throughout freemasonry.

The magic square was given a whole new meaning several centuries later by the German artist/mathematician Albrecht Dürer. By this time no one would take seriously the claims to spiritualism that others had given it, but Dürer was still able to capitalize on the square's ability to beguile us with its meaningless perfection. Figure 58 is a copy of Dürer's most famous etching, "Melancholia I." To Dürer, the melancholy of the title did not mean the kind of soft sadness that it means today, but a kind of emotional listlessness that overcomes one who is obsessed by thoughts that do not lead to immediate action. In Dürer's time, it was commonly thought to be an affliction of mathematicians, forever fussing with concepts of logic and necessity but never actually changing the world.

The large, heavyset woman in the foreground symbolizes this kind of heavy, sterile thinking. She is pondering the strange polyhedron to her right that distorts our vision of the ladder behind it. In his sketchbook, Dürer called it a "truncated cube on a pedestal." The trappings of mathematics are strewn all around her, but meanwhile the poor bony dog at her feet remains unfed. On the wall behind her is a magic square, which we reproduce in Figure 59.

Many authors have noted that the year of the engraving, 1514, is in the middle cells of the bottom row. But there are many other surprises. Change the numbers to squares; then the sum of the first two rows (or columns) is equal to the sum of the last two rows (or columns). Similarly, still using squares, the sum of the odd rows (or columns) is equal to the even rows (or columns). Most surprising is the fact that the sum of the numbers on the diagonals is equal to the sum of the numbers on the off-diagonals. This is true if we use either the squares or the cubes of these numbers instead.

This is the square that hangs over Adrian's piano in *Doktor Faustus* by Thomas Mann. "What the principle was upon which this magic uniformity rested I never made out," says Serenus Zeitblom, Mann's narrator,

Figure 57. The Freemason symbol

Figure 58. Albrecht Dürer's "Melancholia I"

"but by virtue of the prominent place Adrian had given it over the piano, it always attracted the eye, and I believe I never visited his room without giving a quick glance, slanting up or straight down, testing once more the invariable, incredible result." Mann, too, used the magic square as a fitting symbol of the melancholic spirit, the kind of self-possessed thinking that leads ultimately to a pact with the devil.

Figure 59. The Dürer square

16	3	2	13
5	10	11	8
9	6	7	12
4	15	14	1

PANDIAGONAL SQUARES

The Islamic square in Figure 56 is said to be pandiagonal, since not only the two main diagonals, but also all the broken diagonals, such as $(2+16+10+24+13)$, or $(22+20+13+6+4)$, will sum to the magic constant of $\frac{1}{2} \cdot 5(5^2+1) = 65$. These pandiagonal squares were popular throughout the Middle East and elsewhere because they bring a higher meaning to what is already a beguiling pastime. The easiest way to see the broken diagonals is to roll the magic square into a cylinder by joining the right and left edges, as is done in Figure 60(a). Now begin at any cell along the base of the cylinder and draw a line spiraling upward, like the line on a barbershop pole, either clockwise or counterclockwise. The broken diagonals are the numbers along the line. We can go one step further. Join the top and bottom bases of the cylinder, forming what mathematicians call a torus—it is simply a doughnut-shaped surface—as is done in Figure 60(b). Now all rows, columns, main and broken diagonals (either clockwise or counterclockwise) will form a closed loop. All such loops will sum to 65. One property of a pandiagonal square is that if you unfold the doughnut anywhere at all—not necessarily along the original seams—the new square will still be magic and pandiagonal. In Figure 60(c) we unfold the same square along arbitrary seams in order to show the magic pandiagonal result. If you compare this square with the original, you will notice that all we have actually done is rotate some of the rows and columns.

An old trick for showing essentially the same thing is to tile together four copies of a pandiagonal square. This is done in Figure 61, using the same Islamic square. Now every order-5 subsquare within it—you will find 5^2 in all—will be magic and pandiagonal. And these are all distinct squares; that is, they are not ones that can be obtained through rotation and reflection. In the figure we have outlined one subsquare that is more interesting than the others: It is not only pandiagonal, but associative; that is, diametrically opposite cells such as 24 and 2, or 14 and 12, will always sum to twice the center cell.

There is a remarkably graphic way to represent pandiagonal squares of order-4 that use, appropriately enough, a tesseract, or four-dimensional cube. You may have difficulty visualizing a four-dimensional cube, but if you stare at Figure 62 long enough you will see in it several ordinary cubes (of three dimensions) which have been joined together at their faces to form a tesseract, just as squares are

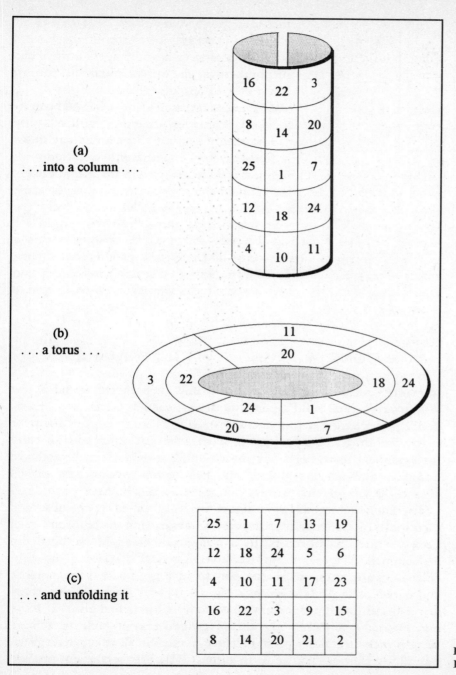

(a)
. . . into a column . . .

(b)
. . . a torus . . .

(c)
. . . and unfolding it

Figure 60. Folding the Islamic square . . .

15	16	22	3	9	15	16	22	3	9
2	8	14	20	21	2	8	14	20	21
19	25	1	7	13	19	25	1	7	13
6	12	18	24	5	6	12	18	24	5
23	4	10	11	17	23	4	10	11	17
15	16	22	3	9	15	16	22	3	9
2	8	14	20	21	2	8	14	20	21
19	25	1	7	13	19	25	1	7	13
6	12	18	24	5	6	12	18	24	5
23	4	10	11	17	23	4	10	11	17

Figure 61. Tesselating the plane with a pandiagonal square

joined together at their edges to form a cube. Each vertex of the tesseract has a number associated with it between 1 and 16. The sum of the four numbers on any quadrilateral will sum to 34, the magic constant.

But the tesseract is made up of several pandiagonal magic squares. To find them, start at any quadrilateral of a given shape and write down the four numbers, moving either clockwise or counterclockwise, as a row in the magic square. Move around the tesseract to faces of the same shape—these are parallel faces in the tesseract—to find the other rows. Figure 62 lists just two of these, the first of which is believed to be the earliest pandiagonal square, found in an eleventh-century Jaina inscription at Khajuraho, India; the others I leave for you to find.

CONSTRUCTING A MAGIC SQUARE

If magic squares look like simple things, you might spend a few minutes trying to build a fairly small one, such as an order-6 square. You'll find that a few minutes will quickly change to a few hours or more. Building a magic square of an arbitrary order was an early mathematical recreation. The most popular method was brought to Europe by Simon de la Loubère, Louis XIV's envoy to Siam, who learned of it in the seventeenth century during his travels in Asia.

The Loubère Method, as it is now (wrongly) called, is one of several mentioned in a rare manuscript titled "A Treatise on the Magical Use of Letters" (meaning numbers) by a Nigerian scholar, Mohammed ibn Mohammed. The manuscript has a vivid way of describing the difficulty of constructing a square: "Do not give up, for that is ignorance and not according to the rules of this art. Those who know the arts of war and killing cannot imagine the agony and pain of a practitioner of this honorable science. Like the lover, you cannot hope to achieve success without infinite perseverance." And again there is the idea that something quite profound is underfoot: "Work in secret and privacy.

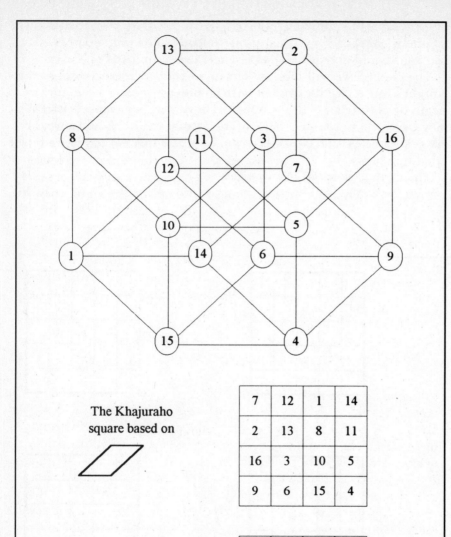

The Khajuraho
square based on

7	12	1	14
2	13	8	11
16	3	10	5
9	6	15	4

A pandiagonal
square based on

13	2	7	12
3	16	9	6
10	5	4	15
8	11	14	1

Figure 62. A tesseract

The [numbers] are in God's safekeeping. God's power is in his names and his secrets, and if you enter his treasury you are in God's privacy, and you should not spread God's secrets indiscriminately."

The method we will look at, similar to Loubère's, can be called the Knight's Move. We illustrate it with an order-5 square. See Figure 63. Begin by placing a "1" in the upper right corner. Now make a knight's move, as in chess, to place the "2." This knight's move should always be one cell to the left and two cells down. Continue this way to place all the other numbers.

The method may fail in two ways:

First, you may land outside the grid into one of the ghost cells. In

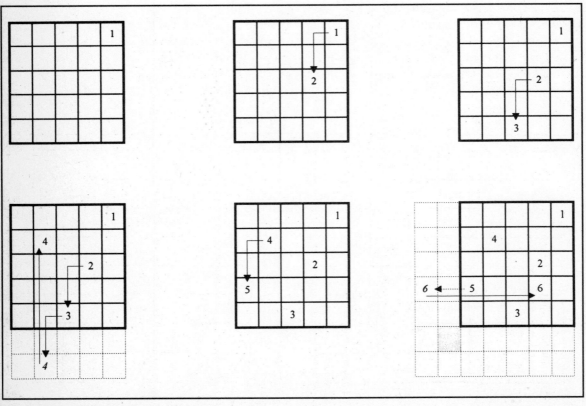

Figure 63. Creating an odd-order magic square

this case always move 5 cells (or *n* cells in the general case of an order-*n* square) either upward or rightward or conceivably both, whichever you need to take you back into the square. This is done with the "4" in Figure 63.

Second, you may land in a cell that is already occupied, including the shaded area of the ghost cells. In this case, instead of making the knight's move, simply move two cells to the left. Proceed as above if this takes you into a ghost cell. This is done with the "6" in Figure 63. If you complete the square, the result will be an order-5 square, and, like all Knight's Move squares, it will also be pandiagonal.

The Knight's Move method will only work for odd-order squares. It would be nice to have a corresponding method that works for even-order squares, but alas none exists. Order-*n* squares in which *n* is doubly even—that is, divisible by four—have a very simple method, illustrated for an order-8 square in Figure 64.

We divide the square into smaller subsquares of order-4 and we draw the two main diagonals through each of these. Now begin in the upper left cell and insert numbers sequentially beginning with "1" by moving left to right, but only insert a number if it is not crossed by a diagonal.

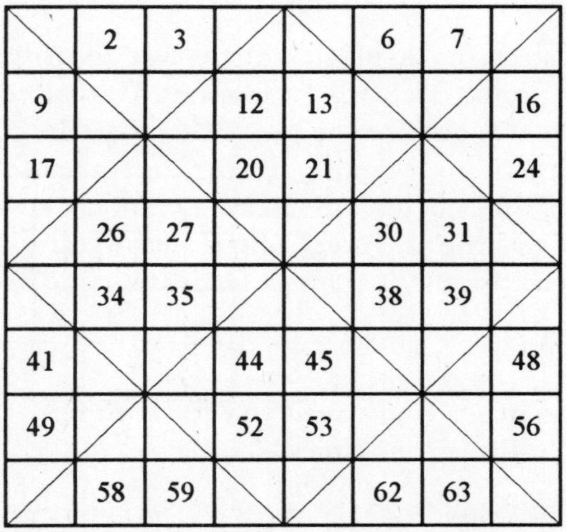

64	2	3	61	60	6	7	57
9	55	54	12	13	51	50	16
17	47	46	20	21	43	42	24
40	26	27	37	36	30	31	33
32	34	35	29	28	38	39	25
41	23	22	44	45	19	18	48
49	15	14	52	53	11	10	56
8	58	59	5	4	62	63	1

Figure 64. Creating a doubly-even order magic square

When that is finished, begin in the lower right cell and repeat the process, again beginning with "1," this time moving right to left. Of course, this time you insert a number only if it *is* crossed by a diagonal. The result is magic.

The interesting aspect of these two methods is that we must assume they were achieved strictly through trial and error. The method of multiplying two squares together to obtain a third larger square has a more modern feel to it. As an illustration, we will multiply the *Lo Shu* square of order-3 and the Khajuraho square of order-4 to produce a new square of order 3 • 4 = 12. We will take the *Lo Shu* as our blueprint— we change it into a very large order-3 square, in which each "cell" is actually a complete order-4 Khajuraho square. Notice this gives us $(3 • 4)^2 = 144$ cells altogether. The first set of numbers, 1 through 16, we place just as they appear in the Khajuraho in the subsquare that corresponds to the position "1" in the *Lo Shu* square. The next set of numbers, 17 through 32, we place in the subsquare that corresponds to the cell "2" in the *Lo Shu* square. We order these numbers as they appear in the Khajuraho; that is, putting 17 where "1" appears, 18 where "2" appears, and so on, just as though we were adding 16 to each Khajuraho cell. Figure 65 begins the process for the reader. The finished square will be magic.

BENJAMIN FRANKLIN'S MAGIC

Once the method of constructing a magic square was formalized, attention turned to creating some fascinating variations. Undoubtedly the most interesting of these was invented by none other than the great Benjamin Franklin, an American Founding Father and renaissance figure whose popular history does not do him justice. One of his squares appears in a letter he wrote to a friend, Peter Collins, in the year 1750. It is worth quoting at length because it shows a fascinating and witty mind:

> Sir,
> According to your request, I now send you the arithmetical curiosity, of which this is the history.
>
> Being one day in the country, at the house of our common friend, the late learned Mr. Logan, he shewed me a folio French book, filled with magic squares . . . in which

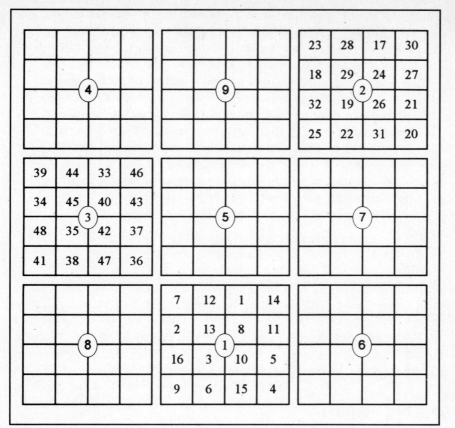

Figure 65. Multiplying
two magic squares

he said, the author had discovered great ingenuity and dex-
terity in the management of numbers; and, though several
other foreigners had distinguished themselves in the same
way, he did not recollect that any one Englishman had
done anything of the kind remarkable.

. . . I then confessed to him, that in my younger days,
having some leisure (which I still think I might have employed more usefully), I had amused myself in making
these kind of magic squares, and, at length, had acquired
such a knack at it, that I could fill the cells of any magic
square, of reasonable size, with a series of numbers as fast
as I could write them, disposed in such a manner, as that

the sums of every row, horizontal, perpendicular, or diagonal, should be equal; but not being satisfied with these,
which I looked on as common and easy things, I had im-
posed on myself more difficult tasks, and succeeded in
making other magic squares, with a variety of properties,
and much more curious. He then shewed me several in the
same book, of an uncommon and more curious kind; but,
as I thought none of them equal to some I remembered to
have made, he desired me to let him see them; and accord-
ingly, the next time I visited him, I carried him a square of
8, which I found among my old papers, and which I will
now give you, with an account of its properties.

The square that Franklin sent is reproduced in Figure 66. Although
its rows and columns will all add to the magic constant of 260, its
diagonals do not.

But as Franklin said, it has many other unusual properties. One of
these is that every half-row and half-column, and every order-2 subsquare, will sum to half the magic constant, 130. To see the other
curious properties, consider the diagrams in Figure 67. If you cut these
out and poke holes through the cells, you can slide them anywhere in
the figure and the numbers peeking through will all sum to 260.

We will never know exactly how Franklin
achieved his square; his one boast is that he
could arrange numbers magically "as fast as I
could write them." That this was not an idle
boast can be seen in the next square that he sent
to Collins. His letter continues:

I went home and made, that evening,
the following magical square of 16,
which, besides having all the properties of the foregoing square of eight,
i.e. it would make the 2056 in all the
same rows and diagonals, had this
added, that a four square hole being
cut in a piece of paper of such a size as
to take in and shew through it, just

Figure 66. Benjamin
Franklin's order-8 square

52	61	4	13	20	29	36	45
14	3	62	51	46	35	30	19
53	60	5	12	21	28	37	44
11	6	59	54	43	38	27	22
55	58	7	10	23	26	39	42
9	8	57	56	41	40	25	24
50	63	2	15	18	31	34	47
16	1	64	49	48	33	32	17

16 of the little squares, when laid on the greater square, the sum of the 16 numbers so appearing through the hole, wherever it was placed on the greater square, should likewise make 2056. This I sent to our friend the next morning, who, after some days, sent it back in a letter with these words: "I return to thee thy astonishing or most stupendous piece of the magical square, in which"—but the compliment is too extravagant, and therefore, for his sake, as well as my own, I ought not to repeat it. Nor is it necessary; for I make no question but you will readily allow this square of 16 to be the most magically magical of any magic square ever made by any magician.

A meaningless brag? Not at all. The square is shown in Figure 68. One subsquare of 16 cells has been highlighted, to show that the numbers do in fact sum to 2056. Remember, you can get any square window of 16 cells and find the same sum. Once again, the secret of its creation died with Franklin. His expertise grew so enormous—he practiced during windy political debates in Congress—that the Academy of Rouen in France presented him with a square that was supposed to represent his name. "I have perused it since but I do not comprehend it," he once confided. Unfortunately, I am unable to locate the square.

Figure 67. The constant patterns in Franklin's square

MAGIC GRAPHS

$\mathcal{T}$here are obvious questions to ask of magic squares. For example, can numbers be arranged magically in any size square? Yes, for any $n > 2$, an order-n square is possible. In fact the Knight's Move method amounts to a constructive proof of this fact for all odd n. Another question is, how many distinct squares are possible for each size? This is actually a question for computers, because the number of squares multiplies rapidly. It was last found that, for order-5, there are 68,826,306 distinct squares in all, and for higher orders the numbers can be higher

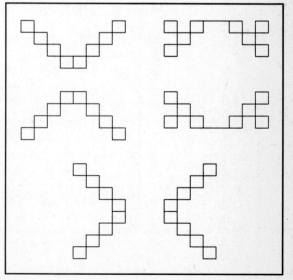

still. The most important question, of course, is, Can a magic array of numbers exist in higher dimensions? Are there magic cubes? If so, then the constant would be found in all the rows, columns, and diagonals of

200	217	232	249	8	25	40	57	72	89	104	121	136	153	168	185
58	39	26	7	250	231	218	199	186	167	154	135	122	103	90	71
198	219	230	251	6	27	38	59	70	91	102	123	134	155	166	187
60	37	28	5	252	229	230	197	188	165	156	133	124	101	92	69
201	216	233	248	9	24	41	56	73	88	105	120	137	152	169	184
55	42	23	10	247	234	215	202	183	170	151	138	119	106	87	74
203	214	235	246	11	22	43	54	75	86	107	118	139	150	171	182
53	44	21	12	245	236	213	204	181	172	149	140	117	108	85	76
205	212	237	244	13	20	45	52	77	84	109	116	141	148	173	180
51	46	19	14	243	238	211	206	179	174	147	142	115	110	83	78
207	210	239	242	15	18	47	50	79	82	111	114	143	146	175	178
49	48	17	16	241	240	209	208	177	176	145	144	113	112	81	80
196	221	228	253	4	29	36	61	68	93	100	125	132	157	164	189
62	35	30	3	254	227	222	195	190	163	158	131	126	99	94	67
194	223	226	251	2	31	34	63	66	95	98	127	130	159	162	191
64	33	32	1	256	225	224	193	192	161	160	129	128	97	96	65

Figure 68. "The most magically magical of any magic square"

each plane parallel to one of the three dimensions, and also in the "triagonals," or the two straight lines that slice through three dimensions simultaneously. Richard Lewis Myers, then a sixteen-year-old high school student, was one of the first to find a general method for finding an order-8 magic cube. No one has yet found a magic tesseract.

These are old questions. A different approach is possible. The top drawing in Figure 69 is called a magic graph. Like all graphs, it consists of nodes and edges, but in this graph we have given each of the nine edges a unique value from 1 to 9. If you sum the values of the edges that meet at each node, you will see that the nodes all have the constant 15—hence the title "magic."

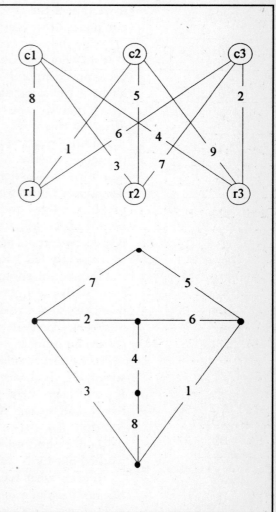

Figure 69. Two magic graphs

The idea of a magic graph represents a uniquely modern contribution to this ancient recreation, but it is wrong to think that the difference between a magic *graph* and a magic *square* is a purely formal one. Injecting the idea of a graph into a magical array of numbers opens up whole new areas of interest. And, most fascinating of all, many of these are still unanswered. The most natural question to ask is, What properties of a graph make it susceptible to a magical numbering of its edges?

The top graph in Figure 69 is sometimes called complete bipartite. Its nodes can be segregated into two groups; in our figure, these are the *r* nodes and the *c* nodes. Now, if all the nodes of one group are joined to all the nodes of the other group, and nodes within a group are never connected, then the graph is called complete bipartite. Such graphs are usually given the abbreviation $K_{r,c}$, where *r* and *c* are the number of nodes in the two groups. Our example shows $K_{3,3}$.

$K_{n,n}$ has a special magical quality, because really it is nothing more than a graphical picture of an order-*n* magic square. The top graph in Figure 69, in fact, is the *Lo Shu* graph. Look again at Figure 54. The cell that sits on row-1/column-2 has been placed on the edge that joins the nodes $r1$ and $c2$. A similar assignment was used to transfer the other cells to corresponding edges. Thus, when we sum the edges that meet at the six nodes, we are really looking at the six rows and columns of the *Lo Shu*. It is a little curious to find that Mohammed ibn Mohammed may have been the first to prove that all $K_{n,n}$ is magical for odd $n > 2$—although he never knew it.

The second graph in Figure 69, which looks like a kite, is not complete bipartite, but it is still magic. It is the smallest magic graph, if we ignore the trivial cases of a single node, or a single edge joining two nodes. It was actually created from the *Lo Shu* graph by deleting the "1" edge and then decrementing the numbers of the remaining edges by 1. It may not look like its parent graph, but only because the nodes have been moved around to avoid intersections. If the nodes of a magic graph all have the same number of edges—that is, if the graph is regular, which is always the case for $K_{n,n}$—then we can always produce a magic offspring this way.

Another example of how very specific qualities of a graph can be used to predict whether or not they are magic can be seen in Figure 70. This graph has two distinctive qualities. First, it is regular. Second, it can be decomposed into two separate cycles that each covers all the nodes of the graph, the light and dark edges in the figure. These are the so-called Hamilton cycles, which we will see in a later chapter. Graphs that possess both traits are always magic, like the one in Figure 70. It is easy to magically label such graphs. Assume there are q edges, then divide the numbers 1 through q into odd and even groups. Now look at the cycle with the light edges. Every other edge has the first of the odd numbers, and the edges that we skipped have the last of the odd numbers. The cycle with the dark edges is similarly labeled, but with the even numbers.

An important class of graph is the complete graph of order-n, or simply K_n. It consists of n nodes each connected to all the other nodes. K_n will have $\frac{1}{2}n(n-1)$ edges in all. Thus, K_3 has 3 edges, K_4 has 6 edges, and so on. We can show that for all n that is 2 more than a multiple of 4—such as 6, 10, 14, 2743770348, etc.—K_n is magic. The method of finding these graphs, illustrated in Figure 71, was first worked out by Nora Hartsfield and Gerhard Ringel.

To keep what follows concrete, we will construct the magic graph K_6, but keep in mind that the demonstration can be extended to higher n. First we place one node in the center and arrange the other nodes

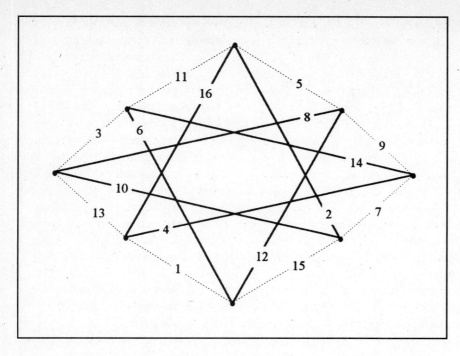

Figure 70. Two Hamilton cycles on a regular graph

around it in a regular polygon. Now we draw one edge from the center node to any one of the outer nodes, and then we draw all other edges that are perpendicular to this. This gives us a set of edges, which we label "1."

To obtain the set of edges labeled "2," we rotate everything. The easiest way to do this is by thinking of the edge extending from the center as a clock hand, and we move it by "one hour." Then we again find all the edges that are perpendicular to this one. We rotate this way again to find the "3" edges, and so on, up to the "$n - 1$" edges (in our example, the "5" edges). This is done in the upper section of Figure 71.

It is possible to think of these sets as consisting of edges of different types. Thus, each set has an "hour hand" type of edge, extending from the center to the outer edge, and a short edge, connecting two adjacent nodes, and a long edge, joining two nonadjacent nodes. In the second step, we reassemble all the edges of a given type into a subset of K_n. This is done in the middle of Figure 71. For example, in the first figure, which looks like a pentagon, we combine all short edges. In the second, we combine all the "hour hand" edges, and in the third, we combine all

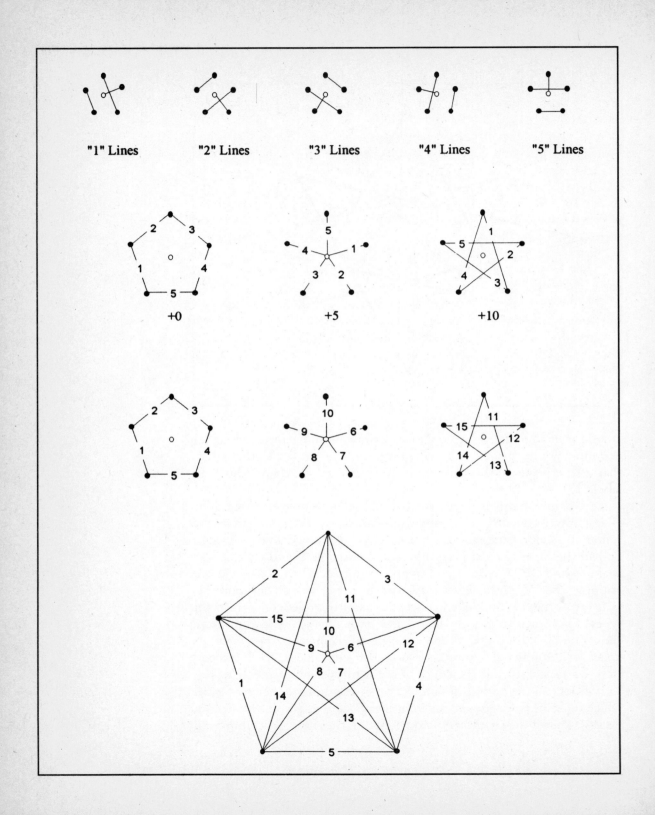

"1" Lines   "2" Lines   "3" Lines   "4" Lines   "5" Lines

+0   +5   +10

the long edges. In every case, we keep the original edge-labeling. The result is three separate subgraphs, in which all the edges are labeled 1 through 5.

It is very important to give the graph of "hour hands" a special position in the center, because we will now add an appropriate constant to each subgraph. The constant is a multiple of $n - 1$ (in our example, 5). The edges of the first are incremented by $0 \cdot (n-1)$, the edges of the second by $1 \cdot (n-1)$, and so on. The result is a new set of subgraphs in which the edge-numberings do not collide. This is done in the third section of Figure 71.

Now all of K_n can be built up. We simply merge the subgraphs together, keeping the edge-numbers as they stand. The result, found in the bottom of Figure 71, is the complete magic graph K_6.

Of course, in this demonstration, the exact value of n was not important, only that it was 2 more than a multiple of 4. Repeat it a few times with larger values in order to grasp exactly how it works. There is almost something magical in the method itself. One wonders what the ancient Chinese might have said of it.

Figure 71. Constructing a complete magic graph

Speak, Who Can

AFTER THE TREASURES OF CHINA, IT IS A LITTLE DISAPPOINT-
ing to arrive in Europe around the turn of the first millennium. The time and place, usually called the Dark Ages, was
uncommonly stagnant. The centers of learning, if any existed, were the
monasteries, where scholarship often mixed with theology to the former's detriment. An idea of the general state of affairs may be found in a
poem dedicated to the attempts of King Aethelstan to reintroduce
Euclid and the study of geometry to his native England during the early
part of the tenth century:

> Thys grete clerkys name wes clept Euclyde,
> Hys name hyt spradde ful wondur wide . . .
> The clerk Euclyde on thys wyse hyt fonde,
> Thys crafte of gemetry yn Egypte londe;
> Yn Egypte he tawzhte hyt ful wyde,
> Yn dyvers londe on every syde . . .
> Thys craft com ynto Englond as y zow say
> Yn tyme of good kynge Adelstonus day.

It must be remembered that this poem was written a full four
hundred years *after* the death of Aethelston. The clumsy sentiment

behind it should be compared to what China had already accomplished several centuries earlier.

The number system in common use in those days was the Roman numerals, a holdover from the days when Rome ruled much of the world. The Chinese, as we have seen, were already using a positional notation, and this was starting to spread through India and the Middle East, but the system would not enter Europe until the thirteenth century.

To see how primitive the system is, we need only note that it is really not very removed from the notches the Ishango etched into their bone. A stick figure is used for each quantity—I, II, III, IIII, and so on for 1, 2, 3, 4. . .[1] To make things simple, a few abbreviated symbols are also used—V for 5, X for 10, L for 50, C for 100, D for 500, and M for 1000, where each symbol is alternately twice or five times the previous symbol. (This may be because we each have two hands, and each hand has five fingers.) The sum of the first 6 Roman numerals is 666, a good-luck number for the Romans, and later the "number of the Beast" for the Christians they persecuted.

To form a number using Roman numerals, one need only pile up as many "sticks" as needed in the quantity, using an abbreviated number when possible. To aid in counting the whole quantity, the "sticks" are usually arranged from greatest to least, just as we arrange our currency by placing higher denominations above lower ones. When this order is not used, then the lesser number should be subtracted from the larger, for example, XL is 40, not 60. Despite its backwardness, the Roman numerals actually afford a very direct form of computation, as long as the computation is simple. The addition of two numbers is merely a matter of combining the symbols in the two numbers. For example:

	M	CC	XXX	III		1,233
plus	M	C	XX	I		+ 1,121
	MM	CCC	XXXXX	IIII		2,354

---

[1] Incidentally, Roman numeral 4 is not IV, as many people think, but IIII. The Romans reserved IV as Jupiter's symbol. The constitution of the Clock-maker's Guild insists on using IIII, as you can see on any watch. To my knowledge, the only exception is Big Ben in London.

Sometimes it is necessary to clean up the result. For example, the sequence XXXXX can be changed to L. Subtracting two numbers also very directly mimics the act of taking one quantity from another:

	M	CC	L	XX		III		1,273
minus		C		XXX		II		132
	M	C		XXXX		I		1,141

In this example the only real complication is that we had to "borrow" 5 X's from the L in order to complete the subtraction. Multiplication and division have no real application in Roman numerals, and for the most part these were not considered arithmetic operations at all.

What is most surprising is that any complicated work with numbers was always performed on an abacus, a device that is based almost entirely on a positional number system. There is no obvious reason why the transition to such a number system was not made more easily throughout Europe. Possibly, in other parts of the world, the abacus grew out of the number system, whereas in Europe the two came from different currents. The average individual first learned Roman numerals and only later learned the abacus, as though one were not even distantly related to the other. The situation is similar to, say, a people who have a finely nuanced language, but use it only for writing; for speaking (and thinking) they continue to grunt like cavemen.

THE EMPEROR'S PUZZLES

Although it was something of a wasteland, there was one book of puzzles that seems to have captured the imagination of a large number of people many years later. This was the *Propositiones ad Acuendos Juvenes*, or *Problems for Quickening a Young Mind*.[2] The author of the puzzles is unknown, although it is generally thought to have been written, or at least compiled, by Alcuin of York, the Abbot of St. Martin of Tours.

---

[2] Much of the information in this chapter comes from a single author: Dr. David Singmaster of the South Bank Polytechnic in England. Dr. Singmaster has kindly supplied me with the only translation of the *Propositiones* in English, which he commissioned from Fr. John Hadley. Two articles by Dr. Singmaster are particularly useful, both dealing with problems from the *Propositiones*: "Triangles with Integer Sides and Sharing Barrels," from *The College Mathematics Journal*, September 1990, and "The Jealous Husbands," from *The Mathematical Gazette*, June 1989.

Very likely, the puzzles were originally intended as a kind of diversion for the Emperor Charlemagne! The evidence of this is a letter that Alcuin sent to Charlemagne, whom he was tutoring, in 799. The letter reads, in part: "I have sent to your excellency . . . some figures of arithmetical subtlety for your amusement, on the blank part of the paper which you have sent to us; in order that what offered itself to our eye naked may come back to you clothed." Unfortunately, the copy of the letter does not include the problems. But there is another manuscript that dates to about the same time, and that opens with the greeting: "From Alcuin to his most beloved brother, Father Sigulf," who was a close companion of Alcuin. This last manuscipt is a collection of puzzles that seems to be what Alcuin had in mind in his first letter. We assume it is the collection sent to Charlemagne. We do not know how the emperor responded to the puzzles, but it is likely that he found them difficult if he paid attention to them at all.

Many of the puzzles were once associated with medieval versions of Aesop's fables, especially as they were amended by Babrius in the third century. This may explain why some of the puzzles have titles that seem to be distantly related to a typical fable. For no apparent reason, the titles sometimes appear in a cryptic form in which a letter is occasionally changed to the one following it in the alphabet. For example, "The Hare and the Hound" appears as:

"De cursu cbnks bc fugb lepprks," meaning
"De cursu canis ac fuga leporis."

We will follow the custom of assigning the book to Alcuin. The abbot is today justly remembered for his hauntingly beautiful Latin poetry, most notably this *Epitaph*:

Here halt, I pray you, make a little stay,
O wayfarer, to read what I have writ,
And know by my fate what thy fate shall be.
What thou art now, wayfarer, world-renowned,
I was: what I am now, so shalt thou be.
The world's delight I followed with a heart
Unsatisfied: ashes am I, and dust.

Wherefore bethink thee rather of thy soul
Than of thy flesh;—this dieth, that abides.

Dost thou make wide thy fields? In this small house
Peace holds me now: no greater house for thee.
Wouldst have thy body clothed in royal red?
The worm is hungry for that body's meat.
Even as the flowers die in a cruel wind,
Even so, O flesh, shall perish all thy pride.

Now in thy turn, wayfarer, for this song
that I have made for thee, I pray you, say:
"Lord Christ, have mercy on Thy servant here,"
And may no hand disturb this sepulchre,
Until the trumpet rings from heaven's height,
"O thou that liest in the dust, arise,
The Judge of the unnumbered hosts is here!"

Alcuin was my name: learning I loved.
O thou that readest this, pray for my soul.

Less well known are Alcuin's riddles, although he himself was mildly proud of them. A typical example, sent to Damoeta, the nickname of the Archbishop of Mainz, is this:

A beast has sudden come to this my house,
A beast of wonder, who two heads has got,
And yet the beast has only one jaw-bone.
Twice three times ten of horrid teeth it has.

Its food grows on this body of mine,
Not flesh, not fruit. It eats not with its teeth,
Drinks not. Its open mouth shows no decay.
Tell me, Damoeta dear, what beast is this?

It is a little disappointing to reveal that the answer is "a comb." The specific comb in question was probably the finely carved ivory comb with sixty teeth and a lion's head on either end, which Alcuin counted among his most prized possessions. Many of his followers, probably conscious of the flimflam, tried to endow it with preposterous miraculous qualities after his death. The most horrifying story in this regard was told about the same Father Sigulf who received the *Propositiones*:

Father Sigulf, with certain others, washed the body of [Alcuin] with all honour, and placed it on a bier. Now Sigulf had at the time a great pain in the head, but by faith sound in mind, he found a ready cure for his head. Raising his eyes above the couch of the master, he saw the comb with which he was wont to comb his head. Taking it in his hands he said, "I believe, Lord Jesus, that if I combed my head with this my master's comb, my head would at once be cured by his merits." The moment he drew the comb across his head, that part of the head which it touched was immediately cured, and thus by combing his head all round he lost the pain completely.

The Dark Ages, indeed.

PUZZLES FROM A DISTANT PLANET

In many cases, Alcuin's problems are quite obviously too difficult for the author. Some puzzles are even answered wrongly, such as Puzzle 52:

A certain gentleman ordered that ninety measures of grain were to be moved from one of his houses to another, thirty half-leagues away. One camel was to transport the grain in three journeys, carrying thirty measures on each journey. A camel eats one measure each half-league. How many measures will be left, when all has been transported?

This is an early example of transportation puzzles, which are still very popular. Alcuin's answer (with a few notes interpolated) is this:

In the first journey, the camel takes 30 measures 10 half-leagues, and eats 20 measures, leaving 10. [The camel eats 10 measures going and 10 more coming back for the next load.] In the second journey similarly he carries 30 measures, and eats 20 of these, leaving 10; and on the third journey he does similarly, carrying 30 measures, eating 20, leaving 10. [Actually, on the third journey, the camel should eat only 10 measures going, since there is no need to go back.] There then remain 30 measures [actually 40], and 10 half-leagues to go. [No, there are 20 half-leagues to go.] In the fourth journey [but only three journeys are allowed by the puzzle!] he reaches the house and has eaten 10 [20] measures of the 30 on the journey, and there remain of the whole sum just 20 measures. [But only 10 measures make it to the destination; the other 10 were abandoned.]

The correct answer is not really very complicated, but it is sketched out in Figure 72, using only three journeys, as the problem demands. In all, the camel must travel $52\frac{1}{2}$ half-leagues to reach the destination, and $22\frac{1}{2}$ half-leagues to return, or 75 half-leagues in all. Therefore, of the 90 measures, only 15 remain at the end of the journey.

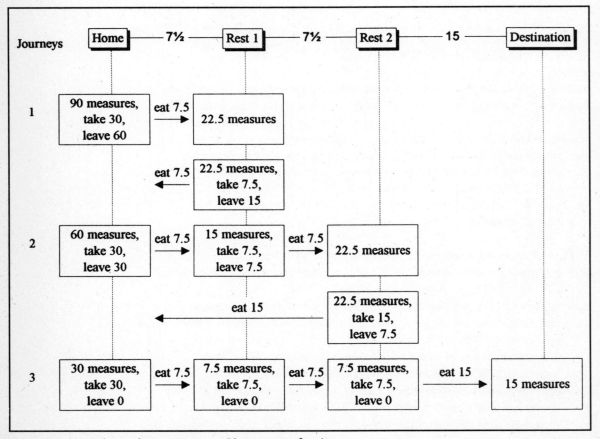

Figure 72. A certain gentleman transports 90 measures of grain . . .

Camels appear often enough in these puzzles to raise a few suspicions. For example:

> A merchant in the East wanted to buy a hundred animals for a hundred shillings. He ordered his servant to pay five shillings for a camel, one shilling for an ass, and to buy twenty sheep for a shilling. How many camels, asses, and sheep were involved in the deal?

This is an example of a linear indeterminate problem, which we will solve in a later chapter. For now, I leave the solution for you. At the moment, the interesting feature is the mention of a camel once again. Why would an English monk frame his puzzles in terms of an animal he probably never saw? The answer is that the puzzle, like many in the *Propositiones*, originated in the Middle East. The Arabs had already learned of the positional number system from the Indians, who in turn may have received it from the Chinese. The puzzles are from a very talented people; the solutions are not. To the Europeans, the puzzles must have seemed like they fell from a distant planet, contrived by a people who saw the world though different eyes, and who breathed a different type of oxygen. Rarely does Alcuin rise to the occasion. He gives the wrong answers, or misunderstands the problems, or fails to find the general principle behind them. The problems that were to quicken the mind only fell on deaf ears.

TWO MORE TRANSPORTATION PROBLEMS

In the transportation problem above, Alcuin fixes the number of journeys at three. An obvious variation is to allow the number of journeys to vary but to limit the amount of fuel. For example, here is a version that is obviously related to Alcuin's problem but that probably first arose in the twentieth century:

> A man living in the desert sends his servant to plant a flag four miles away from this home base. To survive, the servant must consume a quart of water every mile, but he can only carry five quarts with him at any time. Because they live in the desert, it is necessary to conserve water. How can the servant travel four miles, plant the flag, and return home, consuming as little water as possible?

Below in Figure 73 is a description of a solution that requires only 11½ quarts of water, which is the minimum necessary. We divide the full journey into three sections. Rest 1 is a depot ¼ mile away from the home base, rest 2 is 1¼ further still, and the destination is 4 miles from home.

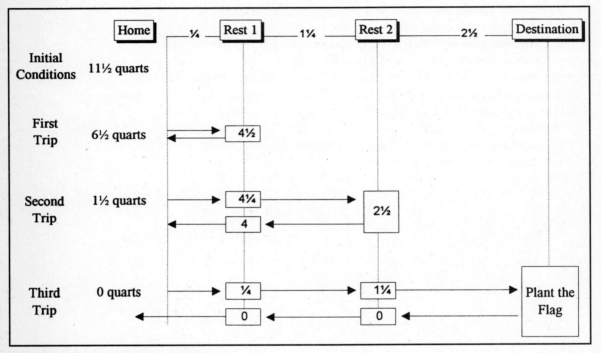

Figure 73. Planting a flag four miles from home

In the first journey, the servant takes 5 quarts of water, the most that he can carry, leaving 6½ quarts behind. He walks to the first rest, drops off 4½ quarts and returns home. The other ½ quart was consumed coming and going.

In the second journey, the servant takes another 5 quarts, leaving 1½. He walks to the first rest, replenishes his supply by taking ¼ quart, then continues to the second rest. He drops off 2½ quarts, returns to the first rest, takes another ¼ quart, and returns home.

In the third and final journey, the servant takes the remaining 1½ quarts and travels to the first rest, taking 3¾ quarts so that he now has the 5 quarts that he can carry. He proceeds to the second rest, re-plenishing the $1\frac{1}{4}$ quarts he has just used to get there, and goes to the destination where he plants the flag. He has $2\frac{1}{2}$ quarts left, which he uses to return to the second rest. There, he picks up the $1\frac{1}{4}$ quarts to return to the first rest, picks up the $\frac{1}{4}$ quart, and returns home.

The general version of the problem is to ask for the minimum amount of water needed to plant a flag n miles from home, but I do not know of any formula for answering this.

In yet another type of transportation problem, we fix the amount of fuel and ask for the longest journey possible:

> A patrol vehicle has a fuel tank that holds 10 gallons of gas. Its tank is filled from 1 of 2 50-gallon drums stored at the home base. The vehicle can carry only 1 drum at a time and it gets 10 miles to the gallon whether it carries a drum or not. How far can it go before running out of gas?

The vehicle first tanks up from drum 1, loads drum 2, travels 50 miles, drops off drum 2, then returns home. It again tanks up from drum 1, loads drum 1, travels 100 miles and unloads the drum, tanks up from it (it now has 30 gallons of gas), and returns 50 miles to drum 2. The vehicle loads drum 2, travels forward 50 miles to drum 1.

Both drums are now 100 miles from home base; the first has 20 gallons of gas left, the second still has 50 gallons of gas, and the vehicle is empty. The vehicle tanks up from drum 1, loads drum 2, travels forward $33\frac{1}{3}$ miles, drops off drum 2, and returns to drum 1. It loads the drum, and travels forward again $33\frac{1}{3}$ miles, where it meets drum 2. It tanks up on the remaining 10 gallons of gas from drum 1, loads drum 2 (which is still full with 50 gallons of gas), and travels forward 600 miles with the gas in its tank and drum. In all it travels $733\frac{1}{3}$ miles, which is the maximum possible.

The obvious general question is, "How far can a vehicle travel with n drums of gas?" This question was nicely handled as recently as 1990 by D. R. Westbrook of the University of Calgary. If n is between 2 and 6, then the answer is:

$$\frac{600}{1} + \frac{600}{3} + \frac{600}{5} + \cdots + \frac{600}{2n-3} + \frac{600 - 100n}{2n-1}$$

If *n* is 7 or greater, the answer is:

$$\frac{600}{1} + \frac{600}{3} + \frac{600}{5} + \frac{600}{7} + \frac{600}{9} + \frac{500}{11} + \cdots + \frac{500}{2n-3}$$

Notice that when *n* is 2, the first formula gives us $733\frac{1}{3}$, as we saw. And when *n* is 3, the formula gives us 860. Can the reader discover the actual steps traveling this distance with 3 drums of gas?

BROTHERS, SISTERS, CANNIBALS . . .

There is a logical problem in the *Propositiones* that has become a classic of sorts. This is Problem 17:

> Three men, each with a sister, needed to cross a river. Each one of them coveted the sister of another. At the river, they found only a small boat, in which only two of them could cross at a time. How did they cross the river, without any of the women being defiled by the men?

The usual interpretation of the problem is that a woman cannot be with another man on either bank or in the boat unless her brother is also present. (An interesting cultural note: Italian mathematicians always assumed it was acceptable to leave a woman with a man if the man's sister was also present, as a kind of chaperon. They apparently believed no man would defile a woman in front of his own family!) A necessary but not sufficient condition is that the women can never outnumber the men on a bank. The condition is weakened in a later version of the problem in which there are 3 missionaries and 3 cannibals who wish to cross the river in a 2-person boat—but at any time in the journey, the cannibals may never outnumber the missionaries on either bank. Although this version is "weaker," it is by no means simpler, and the reader may enjoy solving it.

Alcuin sketches his answer, which I give verbatim below.

> First of all, I and my sister would go into the boat and travel across;
> then I'd send my sister out of the boat and cross the river again.
> Then the sisters, who had stayed on the bank, would get into the

boat. These having reached the other bank and disembarked, my sister would get into the boat and bring it back to us. She having got out of the boat, the other two men would board and go across. Then one of them with his sister would cross back to us in the boat. Then I, and the man who had just crossed, would go over again, leaving our sisters behind. Having reached the other side, one of the two women would take the boat across, and having picked up my sister would come across to us. Then he, whose sister remained on the other side, would cross in the boat and bring her back with him. And that would complete the crossing without anything untoward happening.

This completes the maneuver in eleven one-way crossings, which is known to be minimal. A Latin couplet was sometimes used to memorize an answer that is only slightly different from Alcuin's:

Binae, sola, duae, mulier, duo, vir mulierque.
Bini, sola, duae, dolus, vir cum mulier

[Women, woman, women, wife, men, man, and wife.
Men, woman, women, man, man, and wife.]

One solution, more convenient than Alcuin's, is sketched in Figure 74. If there were no conditions of jealousy, but we only wanted to ferry the six people across the river in a two-person boat, then nine one-way crossings would be necessary: One man would ferry four people across in 4 round-trips (making eight crossings) and then ferry himself and the last person in the last crossing. The conditions of the puzzle are such that one extra crossing in each direction is necessary, as can be seen in Figure 74. The figure also gives an easy proof that the solution is minimal. Look at journey 6 in the middle. It is the position of symmetry: One couple is on each bank, and one is stuck in the boat. All that is needed to complete the journey is the reverse of the first five steps. To prove that the entire solution is minimal, therefore, we need only look at the first 5 steps; and it is easy to find all possible trips to see that these five are indeed the bare minimum.

Alcuin also includes two problems that are obviously early versions of this one. Both of these are warm-up problems, but surprisingly Alcuin gives both after the brother and sister problem, as though once again he does not see an obvious connection. The first of these is number 18:

Figure 74. Three couples
crossing a river

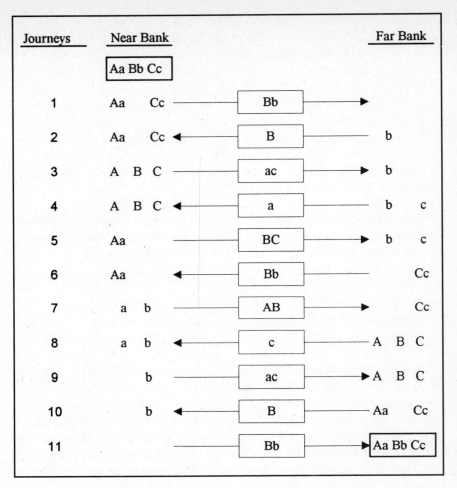

Journeys	Near Bank				Far Bank	
	Aa Bb Cc					
1	Aa	Cc		Bb →		
2	Aa	Cc	←	B	b	
3	A	B	C	ac →	b	
4	A	B	C	← a	b	c
5	Aa			BC →	b	c
6	Aa			← Bb		Cc
7	a	b		AB →		Cc
8	a	b		← c	A B C	
9	b			ac →	A B C	
10	b			← B	Aa	Cc
11				Bb →	**Aa Bb Cc**	

A man had to take a wolf, a goat, and a cabbage across the river.
The only boat he could find could take only two of them at a time.
But he had been ordered to transfer all of these to the other side in
good condition. How could this be done?

Presumably, the wolf would eat the goat, and the goat would eat the
cabbage, if left alone. The reader may enjoy rediscovering Alcuin's
procedure that would "allow for some healthy rowing, but without any
lacerating catastrophe." This same puzzle appeared in a French folktale

about the simpleminded peasant Jean L'Hébété. In a curious twist on sexism, L'Hébété is given more brains when his *wife* solves the problem.

The second problem is number 19:

> A man and a woman, each the weight of a loaded cart, with two children who between them weigh as much as a loaded cart, have to cross a river. They find a boat which can only take one cartload. Make the transfer, if you can, without sinking the boat.

Again, find Alcuin's "ingenious rowing," by means of which "the sailing may be completed without shipwreck."

These simpler variations can be found in several African folktales, where they are taken not to be difficult problems but only pleasant stories. In the Swahili tradition, a visitor from another region visits a sultan but refuses to pay tribute. He is confronted with a challenge: He must carry a leopard, a goat, and some tree leaves to the sultan's son who lives across a river, and he must use a boat that will hold only the visitor and two other items. The problem, of course, is that no two items can be left on the shore together. (This is different from the version mentioned by Alcuin, which gave the option of leaving at least the wolf and cabbage on the shore together.) The visitor, after mulling over the problem, decides to carry first the leaves and goat, return with the goat, and then carry the goat and leopard together to the son.

A similar idea is found in Zambia. This time there are four items to transport: a leopard, a goat, a rat, and a basket of corn, where each is likely to eat the one following it. The boat can hold only the man and one item. The story tells us that the man considers leaving behind the rat or the leopard, and thus reducing the problem to the one of the Swahili tradition, but, the story goes, the man finally realizes that all animals are his brothers—so he decides not to make the trip at all!

These folktales were the original clay from which Alcuin's Brother and Sister puzzle was ultimately molded. The molding continued long after Alcuin. The obvious variation is to increase the number of couples, but it will become obvious that the puzzle cannot be solved with any number of couples greater than three. Assume there are four couples. Then at some point in the journey there must be exactly five people on the far bank. The only combinations of five people are listed below, along with the necessary combinations on the near bank:

NEAR BANK		FAR BANK	
Men	Women	Men	Women
3	0	1	4
2	1	2	3
1	2	3	2
0	3	4	1

The only acceptable combination is the last, since the others have more women than men on one or the other bank, which would make some man jealous.

So far so good. But now the question is, What was the crossing immediately before this stage? The boat that arrived at the far bank could have carried either one woman and one man, or two men. (It could not have carried two women, because only one is on the far bank.) In the first case, the near bank would have had one man and four women, which is not allowed, and in the second case, it would have had two men and three women, which is also not allowed.

To expand the original problem we place an island in the middle of the river, which can be used as a temporary stopping ground for the women, who are thus protected from the men on either shore. If we do not allow bank-to-bank crossings, but force each trip to make a stop on the island, then the best solution is the one outlined in Figure 75, in which Xx represents a couple, with X the man and x the woman:

This is one of many versions looked at in detail by David Singmaster of the South Bank Polytechnic in England. Following his method, we have divided the crossings into three stages because it will help to show a more general solution. In Stage I we bring across 1 couple, and in Stage III we bring across the last two couples. The 8 crossings of Stage II bring across exactly one couple, and these crossings can be repeated as many times as necessary if we increase the number of couples. Thus, if we had 5 couples, we would need: 9 crossings of Stage I for the first couple, plus 8 crossings of Stage II repeated twice for the next two couples, plus the 9 crossings of Stage III for the remaining two couples. In general, we need, for n couples

$$9 + 8(n-3) + 9 = 8n - 6 \text{ crossings}$$

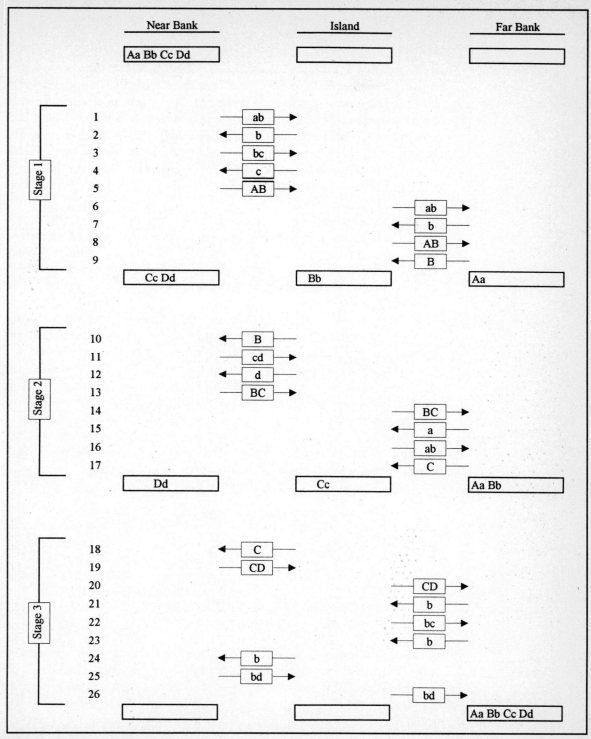

Figure 75. Four couples crossing a river

It is a simple matter to show that this solution is indeed the minimum number of crossings. Each time the boat leaves the left bank, there must be two people in it. Also, that boat must return with one person in it. Thus, a round trip will reduce the number of people on the left bank by only one, except of course the last trip, which will take two and not return at all. Therefore, if there are n couples (or $2n$ people) there must be at least $2(2n-2) + 1 = 4n - 3$ departures from the left bank to the island. Similarly, there must be $4n - 3$ departures from the island to the right bank, giving us at least $8n - 6$ crossings, exactly the number sketched in Figure 75.

The prohibition against bank-to-bank crossings is certainly arbitrary. For decades it was believed that allowing bank-to-bank crossings would require $6n - 7$ crossings, until Ian Pressman, working with David Singmaster, discovered a way to do it in only $4n + 1$. Their method is increasingly superior as the number of couples increases. It is presented in Figure 76.

Here again, the solution is marked off in stages. The four crossings in Stage II, which result in one couple being taken across, must be repeated $n - 2$ times. (In our example, it is repeated two times; we have Stage 2' and Stage 2''.) Thus, in general we will need $4 + 4(n-2) + 5 = 4n + 1$ crossings for n couples. Noting that the puzzle had been around for at least a hundred years before anyone discovered this solution, Pressman and Singmaster wrote: "The simplicity of this method startled us and we were quite surprised that no one found it sooner. One simply parks two [women] on the island and uses the two unaccompanied men to ferry couples across."

A STAIRWAY OF 100 STEPS

Problem 42 of the *Propositiones* reads:

> A stairway consists of 100 steps. On the first step sits 1 pigeon; on the second, 2 pigeons; on the third, 3; and so on up to the hundredth. How many pigeons are there in all?

This problem was given to the 7-year-old Gauss, who apparently solved it in a few minutes. What the child prodigy discovered so quickly is probably the best method of solution, and one that is similar

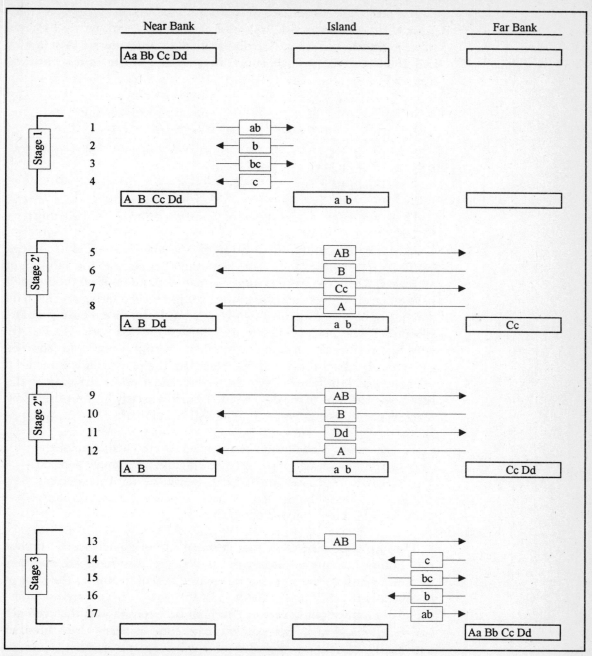

Figure 76. A better way for four couples to cross a river

to Alcuin's. It is illustrated below for an arbitrarily long series. We write down the series one way, and then under it we write the same series going the other way. Obviously, the vertical sums are each $(n+1)$, and there will be n such sums, so that the entire series must be $\frac{1}{2}n(n+1)$.

$$
\begin{array}{llllll}
S = & 1 + & 2 + & 3 + & 4 + \ldots + n \\
S = & n + & (n-1) + & (n-2) + & (n-3) + \ldots + 1 \\
\hline
2S = & (n+1) + & (n+1) + & (n+1) + & (n+1) + \ldots + (n+1) \\
2S = & n(n+1) \\
S = & \frac{1}{2}n(n+1)
\end{array}
$$

Thus, the sum of the series of numbers from 1 to 100 must be $\frac{1}{2}(100)(101) = 5050$.

As was noted by Martin D. Stern of The Manchester Polytechnic, a similar puzzle—if it can be called a puzzle—appears in the Talmud, of all places, where the story is told of a man with an unusual problem: "I have taken on myself the obligation to bring a meal offering and fixed its amount to be that contained in a vessel, but I cannot remember what I specified." The maximum offering allowed on this feast day was 61 vessels, but since the man volunteered an offering it was assumed to be some number between 1 and 60. Therefore the poor man was made to offer one vessel the first day, two the second, and so on for sixty days—the idea being that one of the days would certainly satisfy his promise. How many vessels does this come to? The Talmud explains:

> Take in your hand the numbers from one to sixty and combine the first with the last until you get to the middle, for example 1 and 60 make 61, 2 and 59 make 61, 3 and 58 make 61, until you reach 30 and 31 which also make 61. Thus, you have calculated 61 thirty times, making a total of 1,830.

The formula can be made more general, although neither Alcuin nor the Talmud attempted to do so. If you are summing all numbers between a and b, you get $\frac{1}{2}(b+a)(b-a+1)$. For example, the sum of numbers between 7 and 31 is $\frac{1}{2}(38)(25) = 475$. If you are not summing all numbers, but every nth number between a and b, then you get $\frac{1}{2}(b+a)[(b+a)/n+1]$. For example, the sum of every third number between 2 and 26 $(2 + 5 + 8 + \ldots)$ is $\frac{1}{2}(28)(9) = 126$.

The sum of the series from 1 to n is usually called the nth triangular number, abbreviated T_n. For example, $T_1 = 1$, $T_2 = 1 + 2 = 3$, $T_3 = 1 + 2 + 3 = 6$, $T_4 = 1 + 2 + 3 + 4 = 10$, and $T_{100} = 5050$, the answer to Alcuin's puzzle. The amount of fish the Apostle Peter took from the sea was $T_{17} = 156$, one of many figurate numbers found in the Bible. These numbers are called triangular because they represent the number of objects that can be placed within successively larger triangles. The middle portion of Figure 77 illustrates the first of these.

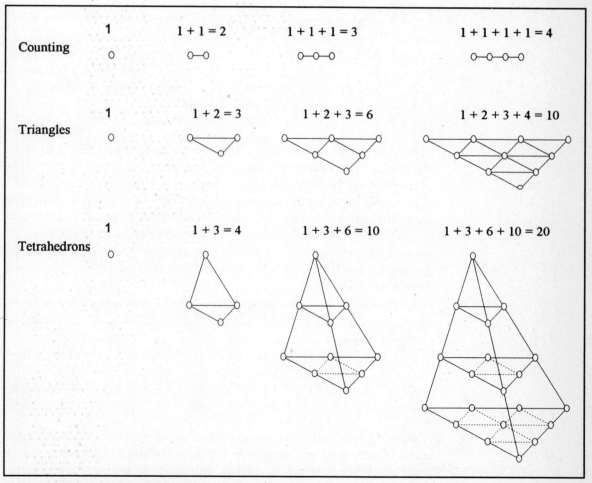

Figure 77. First order figurate numbers

Triangular numbers are one of a large class of numbers called figurates. This very physical way of thinking about quantities is generally the approach of ancient people, probably because of the nice patterns it can bring to numbers. We can see this pattern by taking a general approach to the idea of figurates. First, we have the one-dimensional or linear figurates, listed below. The first order of these is simply the counting numbers. The second order is every second number beginning with the first (what we call the odd numbers), and the third order is every third number beginning with the first.

LINEAR FIGURATE NUMBERS

Order	Series							
1	1,	2,	3,	4,	5,	6,	7, . . .	(Counting Numbers)
2	1,	3,	5,	7,	9,	11,	13, . . .	(Odd Numbers)
3	1,	4,	7,	10,	13,	16,	19, . . .	
4	1,	5,	9,	13,	17,	21,	23, . . .	

Next we have the two-dimensional or planar figurates. The first order of these are the triangular numbers, and they are properly defined as partial sums of the first order linear numbers, although that seems like a clumsy way of saying it. The second order are the squares, and they are the partial sums of the second order linear numbers, that is, partial sums of odd numbers. Notice that they are also what we normally call squares. Continuing this way, we get the pentagonal numbers by taking partial sums of the third order linear numbers. And then the hexagonal numbers, and so on.

PLANAR FIGURATE NUMBERS

Order	Series							
1	1,	3,	6,	10,	15,	21,	28,	. . .	(Triangular)
2	1,	4,	9,	16,	25,	36,	49,	. . .	(Square)
3	1,	5,	12,	22,	35,	49,	68,	. . .	(Pentagonal)
4	1,	6,	15,	28,	45,	66,	91,	. . .	(Hexagonal)

Moving up from these we get the three-dimensional or solid figurates. Needless to say, each order of these is formed by taking partial sums of the corresponding planar figurates. This gives us the tetrahedral, pentahedral, and other figurates.

SOLID FIGURATE NUMBERS

Order	Series								
1	1,	4,	10,	20,	35,	56,	84,	. . .	(Tetrahedral)
2	1,	5,	14,	30,	55,	91,	140,	. . .	(Pentahedral)
3	1,	6,	18,	40,	75,	126,	196,	. . .	(Hexahedral)
4	1,	7,	22,	50,	95,	161,	252,	. . .	(Heptahedral)

From here it is an easy matter to crack higher dimensions, although we would be at a loss to print pictures of such "figures." All of this comes together with a single formula that may seem daunting at first but is really quite simple. Let $N_{d,i,n}$ be the nth number of the ith order of dimension d. Then:

$$N_{d,i,n} = \frac{1}{d!} \frac{(n+d-2)!}{(n-1)!} \quad [ni-(i-d)]$$

The additive way in which each type of figurate is generated may remind you of Chu Shih-chieh's triangle, which is reproduced in Figure 78. If you rotate the triangle, you find the first order of the figurates at each dimension.

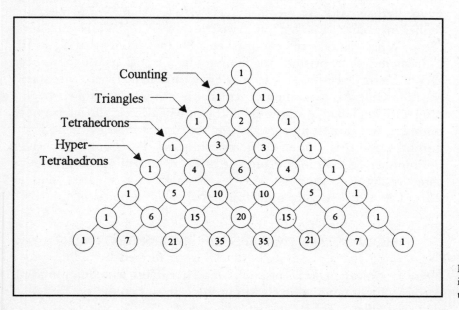

Figure 78. The figurates in Chu Shih-chieh's triangle

The first order figurates—the counting numbers, the triangular numbers, the tetrahedral numbers, and so on—are useful for their ability to count combinations of things. For counting numbers, this application is obvious. Among the triangular numbers, T_n is the number of ways that $(n+1)$ objects can be taken two at a time. In the third dimension, the nth tetrahedral number is the way to take $(n+2)$ objects three at a time. Moving up to the fourth dimension, the nth hyper-tetrahedron is the way to take $(n+3)$ objects four at a time. And so on.

To bring all this together, consider the five objects $\{a,b,c,d,e\}$. How many sets are there taking the objects two at a time? The answer is $T_4 = 10$:

1: $\{a,b\}$	4: $\{a,e\}$	7: $\{b,e\}$	10: $\{d,e\}$
2: $\{a,c\}$	5: $\{b,c\}$	8: $\{c,d\}$	
3: $\{a,d\}$	6: $\{b,d\}$	9: $\{c,e\}$	

How many sets are there taking objects three at a time? The answer is the third tetrahedral number, 10, which you can verify. How many sets are there taking objects four at a time? The answer is the second "hyper-tetrahedron," 5. The ability of this series to count different combinations of things may explain a fairly cryptic ancient Greek passage in which Pythagoras asks a merchant, "How do you count?" The merchant replies, naturally enough, "One, two, three, four . . ." Pythagoras says, "Stop. What you take to be four is ten." He meant only that $T_4 = 10$.

In more serious matters, the figurates have a curious use in number theory. Pierre de Fermat, the famous French mathematician, once stated the following: All natural numbers (that is, the whole numbers beginning with one) may be expressed as the sum of at most three triangular numbers, and at most four square numbers, and at most five pentagonal numbers, and so on for all the planar figurates. For example, consider the number 26. We may express it as $15 + 10 + 1$ (that is, at most three triangulars), and as $25 + 1$ (at most four squares), and as $22 + 1 + 1 + 1 + 1$ (at most five pentagonals). And so on.

HOW MANY POINTS OF INTERSECTION?

Here is a pleasant little research area for readers who enjoy finding patterns. I will not give an answer in this case, although I can't pretend that triangular numbers are not involved.

We have p dots on a top row, and q dots on a bottom row. We draw line segments between every dot on the top to every dot on the bottom. Our only restriction is that the dots must be so arranged that three lines may not intersect at a single point, except of course at the extremes. Obviously, there must be $p \cdot q$ line segments in all, but how many points of intersection are there?

In Figure 79(a), we show that for two and three dots there will be three points of intersection, which we abbreviate by saying $P(2,3) = 3$. Similarly, in Figure 79(b), we show that $P(3,3) = 9$.

Is it possible to find $P(x,y)$ given only x and y? What, for example, is $P(26,54)$, without drawing a figure of 1404 lines? The first step in research of this sort is always to collect more data. But there is no need to do this blindly. Notice that $P(x,y) = P(y,x)$, since this is simply a

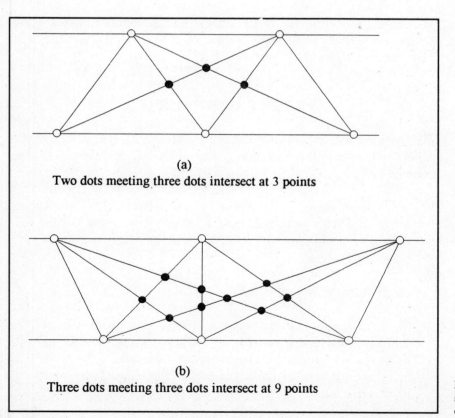

(a)
Two dots meeting three dots intersect at 3 points

(b)
Three dots meeting three dots intersect at 9 points

Figure 79. Counting the number of times lines can cross

matter of turning a figure upside down. So to begin with, find $P(2,y)$ for several values of y, then $P(3,y)$, and so on. I have started this table in Figure 80.

x	2					3				
y	2	3	4	5	...	3	4	5	6	...
$P(x,y)$	1	3	6	10		9	18	30	45	

One look at this table should lead you to guess that $P(2,y) = T_{y-1}$, or the $y-1$th triangular number. That's a good guess, although it by no means proves that the pattern continues indefinitely. What about $P(3,y)$? These are not the sequence of triangular numbers, but do you notice something peculiar about them? Divide each by 3. Think of it this way: Every pair of dots on the top row, when combined with every pair of dots on the bottom row, will produce a single point of intersection.

Continue the table for other values, and remember that a good pattern is one that can be stated elegantly.

By the way, $P(26,54) = 465,075$.

ANCIENT BARRELS . . .

The triangular numbers turn out to be useful in another puzzle of the *Propositiones*, although it may not appear immediately obvious. This is Problem 12:

> A father, when dying, gave to his sons 30 barrels, of which 10 were full of wine, 10 were half full, and the last 10 were empty. Divide the wine and flasks, so that each of the three sons receive equally of both barrels and wine.

Alcuin's solution is very simple:

> To each son will come ten flasks as his portion. But divide them as follows: give the first son the 10 half-full barrels; then to the second give 5 full and 5 empty barrels; and similarly to the third, and there will be equal division among the three sons of both wine and barrels.

That is a perfectly correct solution, but unfortunately it is not actually solved in general principles; it is only thought out by trial and error until one solution is found. That other solutions are possible is obvious, but Alcuin does not consider them. For example, the table below lists two other ways of partitioning the barrels, both of which satisfy the problem:

	FIRST SOLUTION			SECOND SOLUTION		
	Full	Half	Empty	Full	Half	Empty
First son	1	8	1	2	6	2
Second son	4	2	4	3	4	3
Third son	5	0	5	5	0	5
Total barrels	10	10	10	10	10	10

Notice that in each solution, a son receives exactly 10 barrels and exactly 5 barrels' worth of wine. Still other solutions are possible. In fact, the more interesting question is not to find any one way of partitioning the barrels, but to find the total *number* of ways of doing so.

And in doing this we will make the problem more general still. We ask the question not of 30 barrels, but of N full barrels, N half-full barrels, and N empty barrels. These, once again, are to be divided among three people, with all three receiving the same number of barrels and the same amount of wine. We will let f_i, h_i and e_i be the number of full, half-full, and empty barrels received by person i, where of course i may be 1, 2, or 3. The problem tells us that:

$$\text{the first son receives } f_1 + h_1 + e_1 = N \text{ barrels}$$
$$\text{the second son receives } f_2 + h_2 + e_2 = N \text{ barrels}$$
$$\text{the third son receives } f_3 + h_3 + e_3 = N \text{ barrels}$$

Furthermore, since the total contents before division must come to $(N + \frac{1}{2}N)$ barrels of wine, and the three people must receive exactly one-third of this, then each person must receive exactly $\frac{1}{2}N$ barrels of wine. The empty barrels cannot add to the contents, therefore:

$$f_i + \frac{1}{2}h_i = \frac{1}{2}N$$

These two equations can be combined to show that $f_i = e_i$, again for each person. This is a restraint on the problem that may not be immediately obvious, and it was certainly overlooked by Alcuin, yet it arises from the nature of the problem itself: In any valid solution, the number of full barrels received by any one person must be equal to the number of empty barrels. Notice that this is true of Alcuin's solution and of the other two given above.

All this enables us to get a firmer grip on the problem. A solution will take the form of a triplet of numbers (f_1, f_2, f_3), that is, the number of full barrels received by each person. We need not worry about the other barrels, since these will always be strictly determined by the number of full barrels. The number of empty barrels will be the same triplet, and the number of half-full barrels can be easily computed from these two, since $h_i = N - f_i - e_i$. For example, Alcuin's solution can be stated simply as (0, 5, 5). This means that the first son receives 0 full barrels (and therefore 0 empty and 10 half full), and the second son receives 5 full barrels (and 5 empty and 0 half full), and the third son receives the same.

A moment's thought will reveal something about the triplet (f_1, f_2, f_3) that may not seem obvious but is nevertheless of extreme importance: Each one of these numbers must be less than or equal to $\frac{1}{2}N$. In other words, the number of full barrels received by each person must be, at most, half the total number of full barrels. If this were not so, then a person would receive more than N barrels between the full and empty barrels alone, which is not allowed.

Thus, the problem reduces to this: In how may ways can I find triplets of numbers subject to two conditions—first, the triplets must sum to N (because they represent the total number of full barrels); and second, each number in the triplet must be less than or equal to $\frac{1}{2}N$. So stated, the problem is still not very simple. To keep things specific, let us assume $N = 10$, that is, we will work with Alcuin's original puzzle. We can begin by creating a list of all possible triplets of the numbers 0 through 10. Then we can go through this list and check off all those for which the three numbers sum to 10. And of these, we can check off all those for which all three numbers are 5 or less. This is the outline of the list, to show how it can be done systematically:

(0,0,0)	(0,0,1)	(0,0,2)	. . .	(0,0,10)
(0,1,0)	(0,1,1)	(0,1,2)	. . .	(0,1,10)
(0,2,0)	(0,2,1)	(0,2,2)	. . .	(0,2,10)
.	.	.		.
.	.	.		.
.	.	.		.
(10,10,0)	(10,10,1)	(10,10,2) . . .		(10,10,10)

The list, of course, will go on for $11^3 = 1331$ entries, and after this is done we must proceed with the tedious task of crossing off the invalid triplets. But we still would not have a general solution. Instead, if we want to find the number of ways to share, say, 12 of each type of barrel, we will need to draw a new list.

Fortunately, there is an easier way. We can create a triangular list like the one in Figure 81 below (ignore for the moment the heavy outline within the triangle):

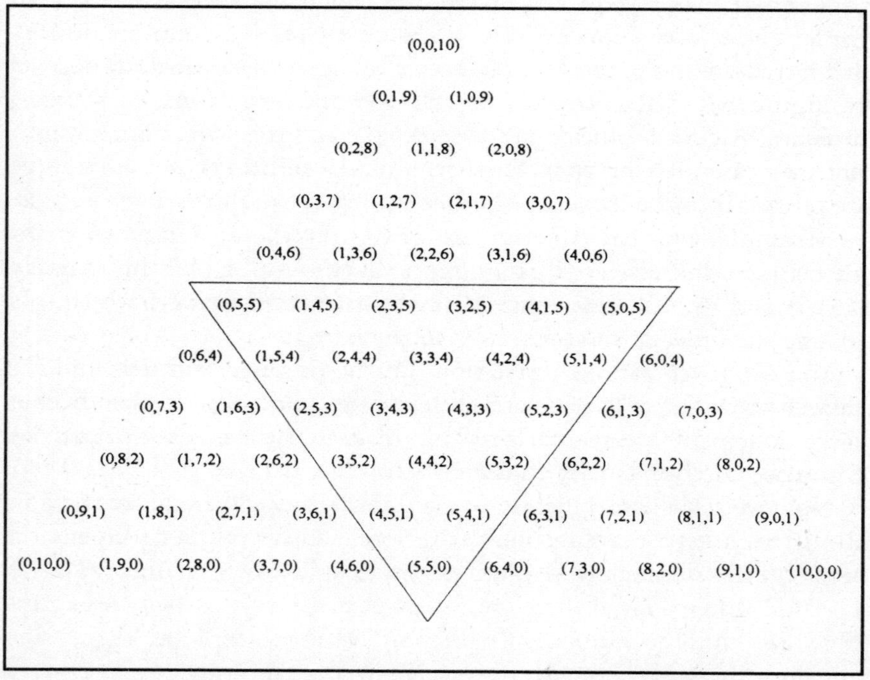

Figure 81. Sharing 10 barrels

The rules for creating this list are really quite simple. In the first row there is one triplet of numbers, in the second two, in the third three, and so on. There will always be $N + 1$ rows; in our case, since $N = 10$, there are eleven rows. Consider the first number in each triplet. Along each row, we start at the left with zero and ascend as far as we must to complete the row. Next, consider the second number in each triplet. Along each row, we start at the right with zero and ascend enough to complete the row. Finally, consider the third number in each triplet. The first row is always N, the second always $N - 1$, and so on.

If you look at the list, you can see why it is so important in solving Alcuin's barrel-sharing problem. Every triplet in it is a triplet that sums to 10, which is one of the two conditions we needed for solving the puzzle.

How many triplets are in this list? Obviously, it must be T_{11}, which as we saw previously, is equal to $\frac{1}{2}(11)(12) = 66$. This is much more amenable than the 1331 triplets we had previously.

We can begin now to go though the list and check off all those that satisfy Alcuin's second condition, namely that each of the three numbers be less than or equal to $\frac{1}{2}(10)$, but this is not necessary. All such triplets have very cooperatively gathered themselves into an upside-down triangle in the center. You can see them in the marked-off portion of Figure 81. These triplets are all the answers to Alcuin's barrel problem. Alcuin's solution is there (0,5,5), and the two alternate solutions we gave are next to it. Furthermore, the solutions that are unique are pushed into the corner. The other triplets are permutations of these. For example, consider Alcuin's answer (0,5,5); the upside-down triangle contains the answers that are immediately implied by this, namely (5,0,5) and (5,5,0). These are all really the same answer; we simply change the order of the sons we give the barrels to.

You can place various restrictions on the problem and still find the answer in this upside-down triangle. For example, let us specify that every son must receive at least one of each type of cask. Then we eliminate all triplets that contain a zero.

Now we ask the original question: How many solutions are there in all? If we accept permutations as different answers, then the answer must be the number of triplets in the upside-down triangle. This is $T_6 = 21$. In general, if there are N barrels of each type, then we express N as $2q$, and the number of different solutions will be T_{q+1}. The solutions themselves can be read in the triangular array.

This, at least, will work if N is an even number. If it is odd, then express N as $2q + 1$, and the number of different solutions will be T_q. In Figure 82, we work out a complete solution for the case in which $N = 9$, and once again the solutions can be found in an upside-down triangle, with the unique solutions pushed into the corner. Since $9 = 2(4) + 1$, the total number of solutions, counting permutations, is $T_4 = 10$.

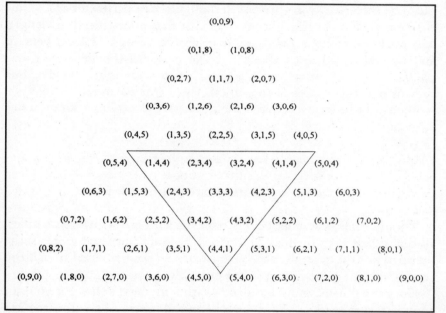

Figure 82. Sharing 9 barrels

... AND MODERN TRIANGLES

Alcuin's barrel-sharing problem has been disguised recently in the more modern garb of "combinatorial geometry." That title sounds like a mouthful, but it refers only to the study of the number of different types of geometric figures. This is a fairly modern type of problem, one that became popular only in the last half century or so, which makes it all the more surprising that Alcuin was able to publish the prototype of it. The correspondence between the two problems was first noted by David Singmaster.

The problem at hand first came to light in the 1970s: How many triangles are there with integral sides and perimeter N? If you try building a few triangles, you will find that certain combinations of sides are not permissible. For example, let N = 10, and assume that (a,b,c) is a triangle with sides equal to lengths of a, b, and c. Obviously, (3,3,4) is a proper triangle—that is, we can get three sticks of lengths 3, 3, and 4 respectively and bring them together into a triangle that must have a perimeter of length 3 + 3 + 4 = 10. But (6,3,1) is not a proper triangle. The three sticks in this case certainly have a perimeter of 10, but their ends cannot be brought together. The first side, which has a length of 6, is too long for the other sides to reach when they are brought end to end. We can be arbitrary about (2,3,5), the so-called degenerate triangle, or a triangle that has "collapsed" into a straight line. For our present purposes, let us choose to call them true triangles.

What all this means is that if the three sides of a triangle are x, y, and z, then:

> x must be less than or equal to y + z
> y must be less than or equal to x + z
> z must be less than or equal to x + y

That is, each side must be less than the sum of the other two sides. But if $x \leq y + z$, then $2x \leq x + y + z$. And since (x+y+z) is the perimeter of the triangle, then x must be less than or equal to half the perimeter. The same is true of the other two sides.

Does any of this sound familiar? With a moment's thought you can convince yourself that what the problem calls for is all possible triplets of numbers that sum to 10 and for which each number is less than or equal to half of 10. Already you can see that this problem is identical to Alcuin's barrel-sharing problem! A complete listing of the triangles in our case of N = 10 may be found in Figure 81, and once again the unique answers are those in the corner. Furthermore, there is an interesting correspondence between the triplets in the two cases. In Alcuin's barrel-sharing problem, some triplets represented permutations of the unique solutions, or different ways of giving the barrels to the three sons; in this case, they represent triangles that are formed by rotating and reflecting the unique solutions.

The outer rim of the triangular array of numbers are those for which the triangles are "degenerate." They can only arise when N is even, and if you wish to exclude them from the answer, then we are left with the two following rules:

If N is even, then let $N = 2q$. The number of triangles with perimeter N is T_{q-1}. For example, if $N = 10$, then there are $T_4 = 10$ such triangles.

If N is odd, then let $N = 2q + 1$. The number of triangles with perimeter N is T_q. For example, if $N = 7$, then there are $T_3 = 6$ such triangles.

In each case our rules will count all triangles, including rotations and reflections.

A MODERN COMBINATORIAL PROBLEM

When first looking at Alcuin's puzzle of sharing barrels, we came across a curious concept. "The more interesting question," we said, "is not to find any one way of partitioning the barrels, but to find the total *number* of ways of doing so." This is the first hint of a whole area of dizzying puzzles called combinatorial puzzles.

An example of a fairly difficult combinatorial puzzle is this: In how many ways can q objects be partitioned into at most three parts? Let $q = 6$; then we have the following partitions:

(1)	6				
(2)	1 + 5	(3)	2 + 4	(4)	3 + 3
(5)	1 + 1 + 4	(6)	1 + 2 + 3	(7)	2 + 2 + 2

In other words, there are 7 ways to partition six objects into at most three parts. Finding these partitions is itself a little bit of a trick, requiring a fairly clear head. Notice that we do not include such partitions as $2 + 3 + 1$, since this is the same as $1 + 2 + 3$, and that we *do* include $1 + 5$ as a partition, since we want *at most* three parts.

Here is a brief table for readers who wish to check their answers while partitioning other sets of q objects into at most three parts. The fun job of actually finding the partitionings I leave to you:

q	Number of Partitions
0	1
1	1
2	2
3	3
4	4
5	5
6	7
7	8
8	10
9	12
10	14
11	16
12	19
13	21

The series in the table on the left we will call N_q. For example, $N_0 = 1$, $N_1 = 1$, $N_2 = 2$, $N_3 = 3$, and so on. Deriving a general formula for this series is enormously difficult. The formula is recursive, meaning that each new number depends on a value of a previous number. More precisely, $N_{q+6} = N_q + q + 6$. You can verify a few examples. Looking at the end of the table, you can see that $N_{13} = 21$, so a set of 13 objects should be partitioned in 21 different ways.

It turns out that this series becomes important in answering yet another aspect of Al-cuin's barrel-sharing puzzle, and its cousin, the triangle puzzle. Remember that earlier we gave only the total number of solutions to the puzzle, including permutations and "degenerate" answers. Remember also that the unique, nondegenerate solutions all tucked themselves into a corner of the upside-down triangle. It is reasonable to ask for a count of these solutions. This we do in the table on the right, for each value of the number of barrels.

This series we will call A_q, in honor of Alcuin. For example, $A_5 = 1$, $A_6 = 2$, $A_7 = 1$, and so on.

Number of Barrels	Number of Unique non-Degenerate Solutions
5	1
6	2
7	1
8	3
9	2
10	4
11	3
12	5
13	7
14	7
15	5
16	8
17	7

The series on the right we will call A_q, in honor of Alcuin. That is, $A_5 = 1, A_6 = 2, A_7 = 1$, and so on. Is there any order to this series at all? Yes, and the order may be found in the previous series N_q. Look at the odd positions in the series, that is, $A_5, A_7, A_9. \ldots$ We have 1, 1, 2, 3, 4, 5, 7 . . . This is simply the series N_q starting at $q = 0$.

Now look at the even positions in the series, that is, $A_6, A_8, A_{10}. \ldots$ We have 2, 3, 4, 5, 7 . . . This again is the series N_q, this time starting at $q = 2$.

Thus, the series A_q is actually an interleaving of the series N_q. And Alcuin's barrel-sharing puzzle is an interleaving of a more serious combinatorial problem. It is almost mind-boggling to see how so many seemingly unrelated problems come together. Here again, credit for bringing everything together belongs to David Singmaster.

POURING WINE ON A RHOMBOID POOL TABLE

We have seen that Alcuin's problem of sharing barrels was related, at some level, to two other problems, although sometimes the relationship was well hidden. It is always a great pleasure to find this, since it hints that perhaps deep down, at some sublime level of abstraction, all puzzles are essentially the same. Here another classic puzzle comes to mind, although this time the kinship is not in the spirit of the puzzle, but in the method of solution. It was invented by a sixteenth-century Italian mathematician, Niccolò Fontana, known by his nickname, Tartaglia, "the Stutterer." (Tartaglia claimed that as a young boy, when Italy's wealth was being sacked by invaders, he developed his severe speech defect when a French soldier slashed his face. All writers take this story seriously, but of course it is nonsense to think a single incident, no matter how frightening, could effect a lifelong stammer.) Here is Tartaglia's problem:

> Three containers measure 3, 5, and 8 quarts respectively. The first two are empty, but the last is filled with wine. By pouring the wine from one container to another without ever losing any, and using no other measures, is it possible to end up with exactly two equal measures of wine?

(We will soon see a very simple graphic solution of this problem, so you may wish to struggle with it first.) The initial state of the problem may be represented as (0,0,8), where the three numbers represent the amount in each of the three containers, from smallest to largest. If we pour the 8-quart container into the 5-quart container until the latter is filled, the state of the problem becomes (0,5,3). If we next pour the 5-quart container into the 3-quart container, we have (3,2,3). Notice that in each case, the sum of the three numbers is always 8, since we neither increase nor decrease the total amount of wine.

When stated in terms of triplets, does it not sound like a strange variation of Alcuin's barrel-sharing problem? To see how similar the solution is, we will use a graph like Figure 81, but this time we will not bother to name all of the nodes. The number of nodes along any one side of the triangle will be 8, the total quantity of wine. Each node in this graph represents a possible state of the three containers, and the three numbers of the triplet associated with the node may be read off the sides of the triangle. The right side of the triangle represents the act of exchanging wine between the 3- and 8-quart containers; the left side, exchanging wine between the 5- and 8-quart containers; the bottom side, exchanging wine between the 3- and 5-quart containers. No other exchange is possible. Thus, as you pour wine from one container to another, you are actually moving along from node to node on this graph. The constraints of the problem are such that the proper nodes do not lie within an upside-down triangle this time, but rather a rhombus. Nodes outside this rhombus assume a container holds more wine than is physically possible. All of this is illustrated in Figure 83.

Since there is so much packed into this graph, it may be useful to look closely at Figure 84, where we demonstrate two steps in the puzzle. First, we begin with the 3-quart container empty, the 5-quart container full, and the 8-quart container holding the remaining 3 quarts. We pour the second container into the first until the first is full. Then we pour the first container into the third until the first is empty. The top of Figure 84 shows how this is done graphically.

Certain obvious constraints in the problem can be translated into its graphical representation. Since you can only alter two containers at a time, you will always move along one of the lines parallel to a side of the triangle. Furthermore, when pouring one container into another, it makes no sense to stop before the first container is empty or the second is full, otherwise you will lose track of how much wine is in either

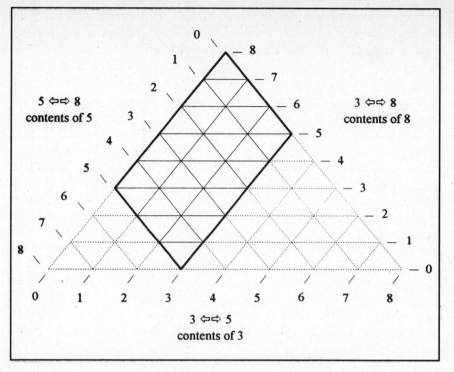

Figure 83. A graphic
representation of
Tartaglia's problem

container. Graphically, this means that if you move from one node to another, you must move all the way until you bump into an edge of the rhombus. Essentially, Tartaglia's problem amounts to starting at node (0,0,8), traveling along the lines according to the rules stated above, and ending at node (0,4,4).

How can we do this? The easiest way is to start at the end with node (0,4,4) and call this 0. Then take all possible routes (there are only two) and follow them to the end (remember in doing this that you cannot go outside the rhombus). The node you arrive at should be labeled 1, since it is one "step" away from the last node.

Now from the node labeled 1, take all the routes once again to the end, and label this 2, since this node is 2 steps away from the last step. If a node already has a label then it is not changed.

Continue in this way until you arrive at the beginning of the problem, namely (0,0,8). The label this node receives is the least number of steps needed in Tartaglia's pouring problem. The solution itself can be read off backward by starting at (0,0,8) and moving from node to node in order of descending labels. The solution to the problem is graphed in Figure 85. Reading backward, we get the following:

Step	0	1	2	3	4	5	6	7	8
3-quart	0	3	0	3	1	1	0	3	0
5-quart	0	0	3	3	5	0	1	1	4
8-quart	8	5	5	2	2	7	7	4	4

Figure 84. Pouring wine from one container to another

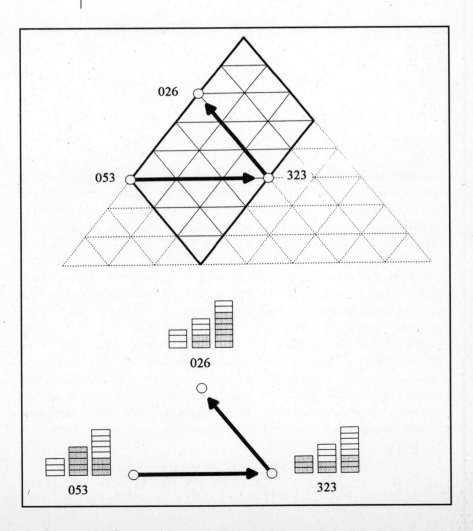

Figure 85. One solution to
Tartaglia's problem

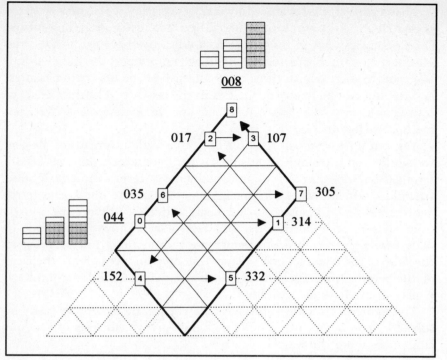

[Pool players may find something familiar in Figure 85. Stare at the figure until you see only the heavy lines of the rhombus and the path traced by the solution. It is the path a billiard ball would take if it were played on a rhomboid pool table.]

Another solution is possible, and this, too, may be found in Figure 85, but it will also require seven steps.

One of the irritating aspects of the problem is that no general solution can be found. If we change the sizes of the containers, we have to start over again for a solution. For example, assume now that we have 2-, 4-, and 6-quart containers, the first two of which are empty and the last of which is filled. How many moves are needed to get two equal measures of 3 quarts each? Or, assume we have 5-, 7-, and 9-quart containers, and again only the last is filled. How quickly can you juggle the contents so that we have 3 quarts in one container and 6 quarts in another? It is impossible to know beforehand. We do not even know, beforehand, if a solution is possible—which you should take as a warning.

The truly remarkable aspect of this type of graphic solution is that it points to an all-encompassing logic, and not just a specific solution. Consider a variation in the problem in which we have 4-, 5-, 10-, and 10-quart containers of wine, the first two empty and the last two full. We want to end up with three quarts in each of the first two measures, and the rest can be in any quantities in the last two. The difference, of course, is that now we have four and not three containers. Will our methods still work?

Yes, but now we must expand things to a higher dimension. Before, we worked on a triangle, one side for each container; now we need a tetrahedron, one *face* for each container. (A tetrahedron is a solid triangle—remember that in our scheme for figurate numbers a tetrahedron was one dimension higher than a triangle.) Before, we moved from node to node on the triangle's face; now we move from node to node *within* the tetrahedron. Before, we moved along lines parallel to the sides of the triangle; now we move along planes parallel to the faces of the tetrahedron. Each node has associated with it four numbers, which always have the same sum.

The figure is difficult to produce and the puzzle may more easily be solved by common sense. The table below gives each state of the four containers along the way:

Step	4-quart	5-quart	10-quart	10-quart
0	0	0	10	10
1	0	5	10	5
2	4	1	10	5
3	0	1	10	9
4	4	1	6	9
5	4	0	7	9
6	0	4	7	9
7	4	4	3	9
8	3	5	3	9
9	3	0	8	9
10	3	5	8	4
11	3	3	10	4

The pretty symmetry in the problems for three and four containers—changing a triangle into a tetrahedron—points to something higher in the solution. The graph is not really answering the specific problem; it is illustrating the logic behind it. The beauty of the design is that we can extend the logic and let it take us to ideas that would normally be inconceivable. What would happen, for example, if we had five containers? Obviously, we need a four-dimensional triangle of nodes, a hyper-tetrahedron. We cannot imagine such a contraption, but we know how it works. We know that it has five "sides," each a solid tetrahedron, and each of its nodes is associated with five numbers, which always sum to a constant. That is really all we need to know, for without too much more effort we can actually work with the hyper-tetrahedron, just as though we were holding it in our hands.

THE INNOCENT AND THE OBSCENE

During Alcuin's time, the Bishop of Exeter, a man named Leofric, gave to his cathedral a book of English verse. Toward the end of the book there are several riddles, a pastime much loved in Alcuin's England. One of them you might find interesting:

> I'm a wonderful thing, a joy to women, to neighbors useful. I injure no one who lives in a village save only my slayer. I stand up high and steep over the bed; underneath I'm shaggy. Sometimes ventures a young and handsome peasant's daughter, a maiden proud, to lay hold on me. She seizes me, red, plunders my head, fixes on me fast, feels staightway what meeting me means when she thus approaches, a curly-haired woman. Wet is that eye.

I'm sure the reader already knows the obscene answer, but like all riddles there is also an innocent "correct" answer, which I am mean enough not to give. I am always reminded of this riddle when I think of Alcuin and Alcuin's age—a curious mixture of the innocent and the obscene, where every act is layered with several meanings, some of which we still do not understand. It's a fitting end to Alcuin's world—a riddle that we misunderstand, just as he misunderstood his puzzles.

I Was Regarded with Astonishment

WHAT I MYSELF HAVE LEARNED FROM THE ARABIC MASTERS THROUGH REASON IS QUITE OTHER THAN WHAT YOU, SEDUCED BY A MASK OF AUTHORITY, HAVE ALLOWED TO ENSNARE YOU AS IN A HALTER. FOR WHAT NAME FITS AUTHORITY BETTER THAN THAT OF HALTER? YOU ALLOW YOURSELF TO BE LED BY AUTHORITY LIKE A BEAST THAT KNOWS NOT WHITHER OR WHY IT IS BEING DRIVEN.

—*QUESTIONES NATURALES*, ADELARD OF BATH

ONE INTERESTING FEATURE OF ALCUIN'S BARREL-SHARING problem that we saw in the last chapter is that it had many possible solutions. Alcuin gave only one of these, and seemed to be satisfied with that. It is possible that this overly simple approach to what is, at bottom, an enormously interesting problem is due to one basic limitation: Alcuin and his readers did not possess a positional number system. That is, they did not have the tools to get to the meat of the problem.

The same situation occurs in Problem 32 of the *Propositiones*:

> A gentleman has a household of 20 persons and orders that they be given 20 measures of grain. He directs that each man should receive three measures, each woman two measures, and each child half a measure. How many men, women, and children must there be?

Alcuin gives only 1 answer: 1 man, 5 women, and 14 children. This time there are no other solutions, unless we allow for the case of no women at all, in which case we have 4 men, 0 women, and 16 children.

Problem 34 is nearly identical, except this time there are 100 measures of grain to be divided among 100 people, again such that a man should receive three measures, a woman two, and children one-half. Alcuin again gives only one solution: 11 men, 15 women, and 74 children. This time, however, there are clearly 6 distinct and valid solutions given by the equations $(2+3n)$ men, $(30-5n)$ women, and $(68+2n)$ children, for all n from 0 through 5. (If you allow 0, then another solution is given by setting $n = 6$.)

The point of the two problems, of course, lies not in their solutions but in the fact that there is a different *number* of solutions for each. This was probably the intention of whoever designed them. But it was a point that Alcuin missed.

PRECIOUS THINGS

But the Arabs of Alcuin's time most definitely did not miss the point. They are probably the source of many of Alcuin's problems. It is interesting to look at an Arab version of a different kind of barrel-sharing problem. The following is of uncertain origin; it appears in several collections of Arab puzzles, but it probably existed in oral tradition long before the collections were written:

> A man leaves 45 casks of wine of which 9 are full, 9 are three-quarters full, 9 are half full, 9 are one-quarter full, and 9 are empty. His five sons want to divide the casks in such a way that each son receives the same amount of wine and the same number of casks. Furthermore, each son wants to receive at least one of each kind of cask, and no two sons want to receive the same number of every kind of cask.

Understand the problem correctly. Each son must receive a total of 9 casks, and among these 9 casks, there must be at least one of each kind—that is, at least 1 must be full, 1 three-quarters full, and so on. The total quantity of wine contained in each son's 9 casks must be exactly one-fifth the total quantity. And no son wants the same assortment of casks that a brother also gets.

This is certainly much more difficult than the barrel-sharing problem in Alcuin's *Propositiones*. The great jumble of restraints placed on the solution makes it qualitatively different from the former, and we will not be able to solve it in the usual way.

The respective numbers of each kind of cask that any one son receives will be called *a, b, c, d,* and *e,* from full to empty respectively. Each type of cask contains a certain volume of wine, which is best measured in quarter-casks. For example, a full cask (there are *a* of these) contains 4 quarter-casks of wine; a half-full cask (there are *c* of these) contains 2 quarter-casks of wine; and so on. Thus we know that

$$a + b + c + d + e \quad\ = \ 9 \text{ casks}$$
$$4a + 3b + 2c + 1d + 0e = 18 \text{ quarter casks of wine}$$

These two equations must be true for each son. There are many numbers that will solve these equations, but if we ignore ones that contain a 0 (since each son must receive at least one of each kind of cask) and if we restrict ourselves to only whole integers (since a single barrel cannot be divided), then after a little trial and error we end up with only the following eight:

Solution	a	b	c	d	e
1	3	1	1	1	3
2	2	1	2	3	1
3	2	1	3	1	2
4	2	2	1	2	2
5	1	1	5	1	1
6	1	2	3	2	1
7	1	3	1	3	1
8	1	3	2	1	2

In every solution above, there are a total of 9 casks, and the total amount of wine amounts to 18 quarter-casks. For example, in the first solution there are $(3+1+1+1+3) = 9$ casks, and $3(4)+1(3)+1(2)+1(1)+3(0) = 18$ quarter-casks.

Every one solution is correct, but only for one son. We need the subset of five solutions from the table above that will work for all five sons simultaneously. Furthermore, we must choose the five solutions in accordance with the other restraints in the problem: All the barrels must go to someone, and no two sons can have the same number of each kind of barrel. This means that we cannot use solutions 1 through 5 for the five sons, since this would require ten full (type *a*) barrels (we only have nine) and only 6 three-quarter full barrels (type *b*), and so on. In fact, solution 5 can be eliminated immediately; it cannot appear in any subset of solutions since it gives five half-full (type *c*) barrels to one son, forcing us to give 1 half-full barrel to the other four sons, and four equations in which $c = 1$ cannot be found.

After we eliminate the fifth solution, the columns in the above table sum to 12, 13, 13, 13, 12. We want each column to sum to 9, so we must cross off two solutions that sum to 3, 4, 4, 4, 3. One possibility is to cross off solutions 4 and 6. Thus the five sons would receive the following barrels:

Solution	*a*	*b*	*c*	*d*	*e*
1 (son 1)	3	1	1	1	3
2 (son 2)	2	1	2	3	1
3 (son 3)	2	1	3	1	2
7 (son 4)	1	3	1	3	1
8 (son 5)	1	3	2	1	2

Now each row sums to 9, each column sums to 9, no two sons receive exactly the same assortment of barrels, and each son receives 18 quarter-casks of wine. Two other combinations are possible, but I leave these for you.

Problems of this sort share several characteristics. First, several different solutions are possible. Second, certain restraints are made, or implied, that allow us to cancel some solutions that are only mathematically possible. This last characteristic is what makes the problems so entertaining. There is always a little head-scratching to do even after we have solved them mathematically.

If we emphasize the first characteristic, such puzzles are called indeterminate. They were very popular throughout the world, although China and India and the countries of the Middle East were among the first to create them. (The latter countries probably learned of them from China.) In the middle of the tenth century, the scholar Abu Kamil brought a few of the most instructive ones together in a twenty-page manuscript called *The Book of Precious Things in the Art of Reckoning*. His often-quoted introduction very nicely sums up their uncanny ability to gnaw at the brain, even after they have been solved:

In the name of God, the compassionate and merciful. The writer is Shodja ibn Aslam, known by the name Abu Kamil. I am familiar with a special kind of problem which circulates among high and low, among learned and simple people, which they enjoy and which they find new and beautiful. But when one asks about the solution, one receives inaccurate and conjectural replies and they see in them neither principle nor rule. Many men, some distinguished and some humble, have asked me about problems in arithmetic and I replied to them for each separate problem with the single answer when there were no others. But often a problem had two, three, four and more answers and often there was no solution. Indeed it happened to me in one problem which I solved that I found very many solutions. I considered the matter more penetratingly and came upon 2676 correct solutions. At this my surprise was great and I had the experience that when I told of the discovery, I was met with astonishment or was considered incompetent or those who did not know me had a false suspicion of me. Then I decided to write a book on the subject of such computations to facilitate the study and bring understanding nearer. This I have now begun and I shall declare the solutions for those problems which have several solutions and for those which have only one and for those which have none, all by means of an infallible method.

The idea of finding "principle and rule," or for that matter, an "infallible method," is something that would not have occurred to Alcuin or to other Europeans of his time. It was, in the tenth century, a wholly Arab trait. One reason for the trait is the set of curious symbols in Figure 86.

This, of course, is the Arab version of the numbers 1 through 9 and their Indian ancestors. It is easy to see that our own symbols originated here. The symbols themselves are of little importance, but behind them is the decimal number system, which contains the kernel of all mathematics. The symbols, and the system behind them, would not reach Europe until the beginning of the thirteenth century, when another book, the *Liber Abaci* by Leonardo (Fibonacci) of Pisa, would gather the collected wisdom of the Chinese and the Arabs and bring it all to a Europe that was beginning to expand. In the spread of the symbols from the Far East to Europe, Abu Kamil's *Precious Things* played an important role.

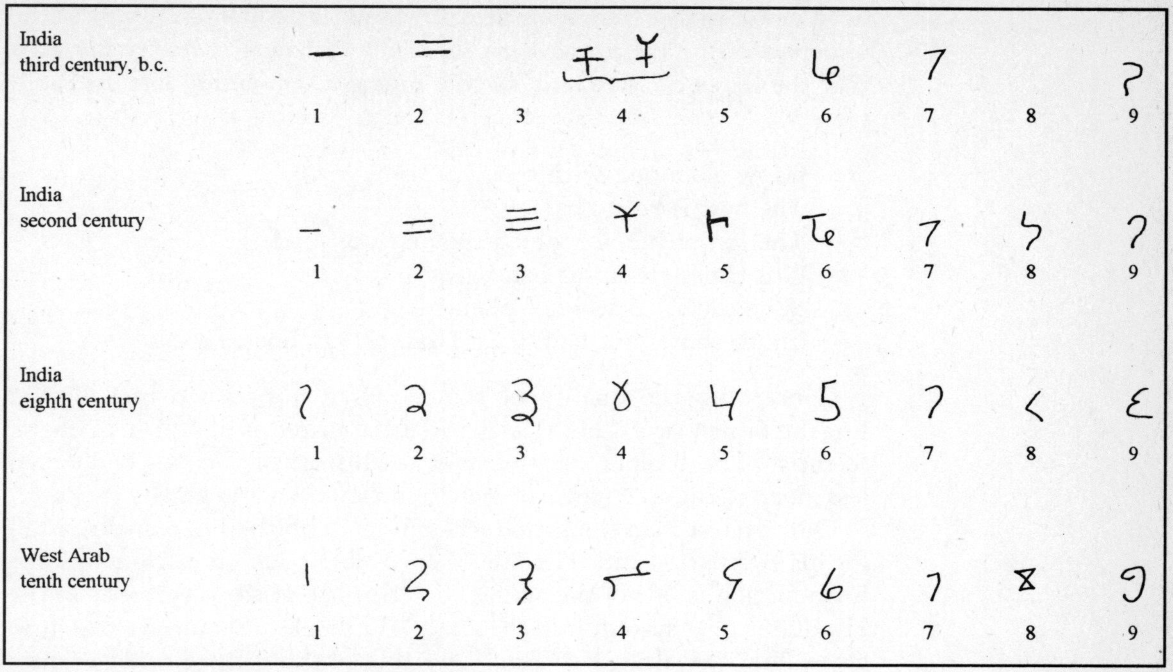

Figure 86. The development of Arabic numbers

TALKING JACKALS AND THE
MEANING OF HISTORY

As Figure 86 shows, it is likely that the Arab world acquired its numbers from contact with India. A fascinating story is told by Rabbi Ben Ezra, the Spanish-born Jew who became famous in the twelfth century as a historian, philosopher, and biblical commentator. Early in life, he seems to have been something of a failure in business. "I strive to grow rich," he once wrote, "but the stars are against me. If I sold shrouds, none would die. If candles were my ware, the sun would not set till the day of my death." After anti-Semitic pogroms forced him to leave Spain, he devoted himself entirely to scholarship and built a reputation that is second only to his contemporary, Maimonides. His philosophy was still sufficiently well known in the nineteenth century that the poet Robert Browning used him as a voice of uncommon wisdom for one of his monologues in *Dramatis Personae*.

In his biblical commentaries, Ben Ezra asserts that life must be understood in its entirety; what separates humans from mere brutes is that the latter can live only for the moment. Browning has the rabbi say:

> Grow old along with me!
> The best is yet to be,
> The last of life, for which the first was made:
> Our times are in his hand
> Who saith, "A whole I planned,
> Youth shows but half; trust God: see all, nor be afraid!"

Concerning the quality of the rabbi's historical writings, David Eugene Smith says, "He was as careful a writer as any of his time, a scientist of high repute, a student of the history of sciences, and a man less given to the acceptance of mere tradition than was usually the case."

Our interest is in the introduction that Rabbi Ben Ezra had written for his translation into Hebrew of an Arabic book on astronomy. The introduction is one of the earliest descriptions of the acceptance of the Hindu number system into the Arab Middle East. Should we take it at face value? Certainly, Ben Ezra is writing of things he did not witness firsthand, but considering his respect for the truth it is likely that his account, although it seems a little too colorful, comes from definitive Arab sources that are now lost. The introduction begins:

> In the name of the Most Holy and Revered, in whose help I trust, spake Abraham ibn Ezra the Spaniard. In ancient times there was no wisdom and no [true] religion among the sons of Ishmael, the tent dwellers, until the [author of the] Koran came and gave to them from his heart a new religion.
>
> After him there appeared many sages among them, who wrote many books on their laws; but at last there appeared a great king in Ishmael, called e's Saffah, who heard that there were many sciences in India. And he gave orders to search for a scholar who should know the language of India and that of Arabia, so as to translate for him one of their books of wisdom, although he feared that a calamity might befall him [that is, the translator], since profane sciences [were then permitted] in Ishmael in the book of the Koran alone, and whatever of the sciences they received [by tradition] was [believed to be] therein.

"Ishmael" means the Arab territories, and the "sons of Ishmael" means the Arabs themselves. The reference is to the biblical story of Abraham and his illegitimate son, from whom all Semites other than Jews were believed to be descended. Rabbi Ben Ezra tells us that this Arab king was curious about Hindu mathematics, but could not learn more about it for religious reasons; for this curiosity betrayed a belief that there were some truths not to be found in the Koran, which could be interpreted as blasphemy.

> [He had heard that] in India there was a book, very important in the councils of the kingdom, that was arranged in the form of stories put in the mouths of dumb creatures, the large number of pictures rendering the book very valuable in the eyes of the reader. And the name of the book was *Kalilah we-Dimnah*, which means the Lion and the Bull, because the first [chapter] of the book refers to them. And the above named king fasted forty days, hoping to see the angel of dreams who should allow him to translate the book into Arabic. Then he had a dream in harmony with his thoughts. He thereupon sent for a Jew who lived in his time and who knew the two languages, and he gave him command to translate the book, since he feared that if an Arab should translate it he might die.

Some of this might seem fanciful, but actually it has the strong ring of truth. First, the book *Kalilah we-Dimnah*. There really *is* such a Hindu book in which mathematical ideas are placed in the mouths of dumb creatures. In fact, many Hindu books on mathematics have a look of phantasmagoria. But the title is taken from two talking jackals who play an important role in the stories. The lion and the bull appear only in the first chapter. Second, the king is said to have fasted until an angel appeared in his dreams. This, too, is probably correct. It is in fact a little startling to learn how much of the Arab Golden Age depended on angels and dreams. For example, the Arab philosophers had long wanted to translate Greek writings, but would not do so until one of them claimed to have seen an angel speaking to Aristotle in his dreams. It's rather amusing to find that a Jew was made to do the actual translation: the idea apparently is that as a nonbeliever, the Jew would escape any calamity that might befall an Arab.

And when he saw how wonderful the book was, and so it really is, he was overcome by a desire to know more. Then he gave great wealth to the Jew so that he might journey to the city of Arin on the equator, under the signs of the Ram and the Scales, where the day throughout the year is equal to the night, thinking ["]Perhaps he will succeed to bring one of their wise men to the king.["] And the Jew went [there] and indulged in many subterfuges, after which, for a large sum, one of the wise men of Arin agreed to go to the king, and the Jew swore to him that he would not detain him beyond a year and then he would return him to his home. Then this scholar, whose name was KNKH, [was taken to the king] and taught the Arabs the bases of number, that is, the nine numerals.

Rabbi Ben Ezra's written Hebrew is composed entirely of consonants, but around these he places various marks to indicate the interpolated vowels. This is common among languages that do not think of vowels as separate sounds, but only tones that shape the preceding consonants. For some reason, the name KNKH was not given these markings. Quite possibly this scholar was Kanka, the Hindu mathematician who is thought to be the first to study amicable numbers. Two numbers are said to be amicable if the proper divisors of each can be summed to produce the other. For example, 220 and 284 are the smallest amicable numbers. The proper divisors of 220 are 1, 2, 4, 5, 10, 11, 20, 22, 44, 55, and 110, which sum to 284. And the proper divisors of 284 are 1, 2, 4, 71, and 142, which sum to 220. The study of amicable numbers harks back to a time when everything about numbers was thought to be significant. Today, they are nothing more than a curiosity. Notice that even Ben Ezra refers to the "nine numerals," showing again the inability to recognize zero as a distinct number.

[After the book was translated] there arose a great scholar in Ishmael who knew the secrets of the wisdom of counting. . . . This scholar was [Abu Jafar] Mohammed ibn Mūsâ al-Khowârezmi and all later Arabic scholars do their multiplications, divisions, and extraction of roots as is written in the book of the [Hindu] scholar which they possess in translation.

This scholar al-Khowârezmi is one of the most frequently cited authors in the history of mathematics, but for a very strange reason. His name means Mohammed, the father of Jafar and the son of Mũsâ, the Khwarizmian. His book *Algebr w'al-Mugabala* made its way to the Europeans, who then corrupted the first word, *Algebr*, meaning "reduction" in Arabic, into the word algebra, and used it as it is still used today. The name al-Khowârezmi itself was corrupted into the English word algorism, which at one time meant any method of calculation. It was used that way in *The Song of the Algorismus*, a French poem of the early thirteenth century:

> Here begins the algorismus.
> This new art is called the algorismus, in
> which out of these twice fine figures 0987654321
> of the Indians we derive such benefit.

When this poem was translated into English, the corruption of history was so bad that even poor al-Khowârezmi would not recognize himself:

> This book is called the book of Algorism, and this book treats the
> Craft of Numbering, which Craft is called also Algorism. There
> was a King of India, the name of whom was Algor, and he made
> this his craft, and, after his name, he called it Algorism.

It's all a sad, strange story, but try to unravel the meaning of history and this is all you get: A Moslem paid a Jew to take from the Hindus a book about talking jackals, and the Christian world has never been quite the same.

BY MEANS OF AN INFALLIBLE METHOD . . .

The indeterminate problems found in Abu Kamil's *Book of Precious Things* have enjoyed popularity throughout nearly all cultures and all times. Many of them were gathered together from diverse sources by Oysten Ore, a distinguished professor of mathematics at Yale University, who believes this general class of problem may have originated in either India or China. He was able to find the earliest example of it in a

Hindu work of A.D. 500. It is reasonable to assume it spread from India to the Arab countries. Here are three that he mentions. You may wish to solve them first before reading too much further:

> From sixteenth-century Germany, the first puzzle has it that a party of 20 persons pays a bill for 20 groschen. The party consists of men, women, and maidens, each man paying 3, each woman 2, and each maiden $1/2$ groschen. How many men, women, and maidens were at the party?

The problem can be reduced to two equations that must be solved simultaneously. Using m for the number of men, w for women, and c for children, we have:

$$m + w + c = 20$$
$$3m + 2w + \tfrac{1}{2}c = 20$$

> From seventeenth-century France, the second puzzle has 41 persons, men, women, and children, take part in a meal at an inn. The bill is for 40 sous and each man pays 4 sous, each woman 3, and every child $1/3$ sou. How many men, women, and children were there?

The two equations this time are:

$$m + w + c = 41$$
$$4m + 3w + \tfrac{1}{3}c = 40$$

> Finally, from twentieth-century America, here is a puzzle that was common among GIs at Guadalcanal: A man has a theater with seating capacity of 100. He wishes to admit 100 people in such a proportion that will enable him to take in $1.00 with prices as follows: men 5¢, women 2¢, and children 10 for 1¢. How many of each must be admitted?

The two equations are:

$$m + w + c = 100$$
$$5m + 2w + \tfrac{1}{10}c = 100$$

Obviously, these problems are nearly identical; after all, each presents us with two equations in three unknowns. It should be possible to find a general solution for all of them. Abu Kamil did in fact find such a method, as he stated, and it is nearly identical to the modern method. What follows may seem thick with equations at times, but it is important to look behind the equations and remember that they are only meant to mirror common sense.

We will use the second problem as an example, since it has a few twists that the others do not. The equations are:

$$m + w + c = 41$$
$$4m + 3w + \tfrac{1}{3}c = 40$$

Typically, the number of unknowns is always one greater than the number of equations, as it is in our problem. This assures that there will always be an infinite number of solutions, or none at all. Typically, if there are an infinite number of solutions, some physical consideration in the problem places a restraint on the algebra. For example, in this problem we cannot allow a fractional or negative number of men, women, or children. For such reasons we know that the number of children must be some multiple of three, in order to change the term $\tfrac{1}{3}c$ in the second equation into a whole number. Let $c = 3x$. We can think of x as a child-triplet, and we can specify that children must always come in threes. Now we get:

$$m + w + 3x = 41$$
$$4m + 3w + x = 40$$

If we multiply the last equation by 3 and subtract the first from it we get only one equation in two unknowns:

$$11m + 8w = 79$$

This last equation is something like a combination of the other two. Any value of m and w that satisfies this last equation must also satisfy the first two equations simultaneously. Now solve for w to get:

$$w = 10 - m - \tfrac{1}{8}(3m+1)$$

Remember now that our major constraint is that all variables must be positive integers. Any integer for m will force w to be an integer as long as the last term, $\frac{1}{8}(3m+1)$, is an integer also, which will be the case any time $(3m+1)$ is a multiple of 8. This happens when $m = 5$, or 13, or 21. But for any value of m greater than 5, we will be left with a negative number of women. Therefore, there is only one answer: 5 men, 3 women, and 33 children. This satisfies the terms of the problem, because there are $(5+3+33) = 41$ people in all, and they have spent $(4\cdot5) + (3\cdot3) + (\frac{1}{3}\cdot33) = 40$ sous.

The other puzzles mentioned above can all be solved in a similar way. They require the same mix of arithmetic and good common sense.

It is interesting to look at puzzles of this sort more graphically in order to see how they work. To do so, we will ignore what the numbers stand for and just look at the equations themselves. And we will use simpler equations—not ones in three unknowns, but only in two unknowns:

$$y = 6x + 1$$
$$y = 3x + 1$$

These two equations can be easily graphed, as in Figure 87 below. Notice no term in the equation is raised to a power, which is why these indeterminate problems are properly called linear indeterminate.

x	$6x + 1$	$3x + 4$
-5	-29	-11
-4	-23	-8
-3	-17	-5
-2	-11	-2
-1	-5	1
0	1	4
1	7	7
2	13	10
3	19	13
4	25	16
5	31	19

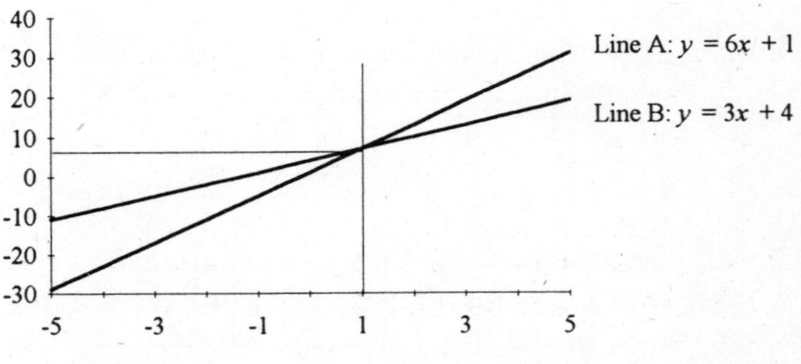

Line A: $y = 6x + 1$

Line B: $y = 3x + 4$

Figure 87. Two equations, two unknowns

Line A contains all points that will satisfy the first equation, and line B contains all points that satisfy the second equation. But only the single point of intersection—that is, the point that lies on both lines—will satisfy both equations simultaneously. This point will answer the problem we are working on, but only if it meets the physical restraints of the problem. The typical restraint is that the point must have integer coordinates. Had the two lines been the same, then there would be an infinite number of solutions. Had the lines been different but parallel, then there would be no intersection, and the puzzle would have no answer.

Now, all of the puzzles we have seen have equations in three unknowns. Such equations will produce planes instead of lines. There will be two such planes, and these may be parallel—in which case the puzzle has no solution—or they may intersect. But if planes intersect, they will not do so in a single point, but in a straight line. This is the straight line we found when we manipulated the two equations above

$$m + w + 3x = 41$$
$$4m + 3w + x = 40$$

and produced from them the single equation

$$11m + 8w = 79$$

The infinite points on this line must be restricted from some element of the puzzle; in our case we were forbidden to consider negative or fractional answers.

FROM GANITA-SARA-SANGRATA TO THE *SATURDAY EVENING POST*

Three sailors and their pet monkey are shipwrecked on an island. They spend all day gathering a pile of coconuts and decide to divide them in the morning. But in the night, one sailor awakes and decides to take his third. He divides the pile into three equal parts, but there is one coconut extra, which he gives to the monkey. He then takes and hides his third and puts the rest back in a pile. Then another wakes up and does exactly the same, and then the third. In the morning, they divide the pile that remains into three equal parts, again finding one extra coconut, which they give to the monkey. How many coconuts were there at the start?

This indeterminate problem first appeared in 850 in the Ganita-sara-sangrata by Mahavira. It reappeared in 1926 in a short story published in *The Saturday Evening Post*, although the three sailors were changed to five and there was no final coconut to toss to the monkey at the end. The first change only made the problem more unwieldy because the numbers get so large, while the second change added some awkward considerations. An analysis of the *Post* problem, and the amusing story of the minor storm that it created, is told by Martin Gardner.

When stripped of sailors, coconuts, and monkeys, the puzzle is about numbers, pure and simple, one of the earliest such examples. It was obviously invented by a people who have discovered something quite new and extraordinary, the number system itself. You can see here the beginnings of a playful kind of number theory. One can almost restate the problem in which numbers themselves are the only character:

> *The number theory version*: A number, when reduced by 1, is a multiple of 3. Take $2/3$ of the remainder, and you again arrive at a number that is 1 more than a multiple of 3. Repeat this operation 2 more times, and you always arrive at a number that is 1 more than a multiple of 3. What is the number?

The trappings of the sailors and monkeys is only meant to make this problem a little less abstract, as though those who invented it did not know they were actually asking a question about numbers. But in the solution that follows, notice how often we are forced to rely on properties of numbers alone, for example, that two numbers have no factors in common, or that another number is necessarily an integer.

The difficulty of the problem will be seen by anyone who attempts it. We are inclined to argue backward. Thus, at the end, there is some number that is evenly divisible by 3. Very well, there are exactly 3 coconuts. This was obtained by throwing 1 away, so there must have been 4 immediately before. This number in turn was obtained when the last sailor took $1/3$ of the pile left to him, so it represents $2/3$ of the pile. Therefore, the last sailor was left with exactly 6 coconuts, and 7 before he tossed 1 to the monkey. This in turn must have been $2/3$ of the pile left to the previous sailor, but now there is no integer x such that $^2/_3 x = 7$. So things break down. So we start over, and assume that at the end there was some different number evenly divisible by 3, such as 6, and we build up from there, until hopefully we can completely reconstruct the transactions. This procedure will take a long time, however, and it will not leave us with the "principle and rule" that Abu Kamil spoke about.

Let A be the number of coconuts at the start. When the first sailor discards 1 coconut and takes his share, there are B left. That is, $^2/_3 (A-1) = B$, or $2(A-1) = 3B$. Similarly, C, D, and E are the number of coconuts left after the subsequent divisions. We can construct the following equations.

$$2(A-1) = 3B$$
$$2(B-1) = 3C$$
$$2(C-1) = 3D$$
$$2(D-1) = 3E$$

Through methods we have already seen, we can eliminate three unknowns and arrive at a single equation:

$$16A = 81E + 130$$

This is easy to solve just by trial and error, but that will not give us the general solution.

At this point we should remember the story of the man with 17 camels. Not knowing his arithmetic, he wanted to give one-ninth to his first son, one-half to his second, and the rest to his third. How to divide them? The lawyer added one of his own camels, making 18. Then he gave 2 to the first son, 9 to the second, removed his camel and gave the rest, 6, to the third.

Similarly, in this problem we will add 2 coconuts to help with the arithmetic. (We will soon see why 2 was chosen.) Now we can write the equation above as

$$16(A+2) = 81(E+2)$$

Unlike the story of the man and his camels, however, adding these two coconuts is actually good arithmetic. It is easy to verify that the two equations above are exactly the same.

The term on the right must be an integer divisible by 81. Therefore the term on the left, $16(A+2)$, must also be divisible by 81. But 16 has no factors in common with 81, so the term $(A+2)$ itself must be divisible by 81. Now we have

$$\frac{(A+2)}{81} = K$$

where K is an integer. Thus $A = 81K - 2$, or 79 (when $K = 1$), or 160 (when $K = 2$), or 241 (when $K = 3$), and so on, where each term is 81 more than the previous term. The simplest answer is 79 and we can reconstruct the whole operation from here.

> The first sailor found 79 coconuts, threw 1 to the monkey, divided the rest into three piles of 26, kept 1 pile, and replaced the remaining 52.
>
> The second sailor threw one to the monkey, divided the remaining 51 into three piles of 17, kept one pile, and replaced the remaining 34.
>
> The third sailor threw one to the monkey, divided the rest into three piles of 11, kept one pile, and replaced the remaining 22.
>
> The next day, the sailors together threw one to the monkey, and divided the rest into three piles of 7. Each kept one pile and thought everything was fair.

The reader can see that other answers, such as 160 or 241, will also work. The secret is that each number is 81, or 3^4, more than the previous number. Thus, this extra 81 will always be able to figure in the four divisions.

Now then, why did we add 2 coconuts to serve as a catalyst here? The secret is in the behavior of the first sailor. He had to throw 1 coconut to the monkey in order to make the remaining number divisible by 3. He could have done the same by *taking* 2 coconuts from the monkey instead.

We can now state a simple solution to the general problem of the monkey and the coconuts. Assume there are s sailors and m monkeys. To keep things perfectly general, assume also that there are o operations.

The value for o is usually $s + 1$, since all sailors are suspicious of the others and at the end they divide the coconuts one last time. (The value of o may differ if we assume, for example, that some sailors are *not* suspicious.) Then the number of coconuts at the start will be equal to

$$s^o - (s-1)m$$

This solution will always work, but if the value of m is greater than or equal to $(s-1)^{o-1}$, then the solution will produce a negative number of coconuts for the last division. In terms of the pure Number Theory statement of the puzzle this poses no problem at all. But if the idea of negative coconuts seems silly, one can always add s^o repeatedly until the negative number disappears. Divide m by $(s-1)^{o-1}$, and find the largest integer that does not exceed this value. That is the number of times you must add s^o.

Since all of this may seem needlessly confusing, let us bring everything together with a fairly complicated example. Five sailors find a pile of coconuts, and 2 of them are suspicious of the others. One arises to take his share but finds that 17 coconuts must be discarded to monkeys. The second arises and does the same. At the end all sailors take one-fifth of what remains, and again find that 17 remaining coconuts must be discarded. How many coconuts were found initially?

None of the sailors are very bright, since it should never have been necessary to discard 17 coconuts. But we are only interested in the numbers. Here, $s = 5$, $o = 3$ (two divisions from the suspicious sailors, and once more at the end), and $m = 17$. According to our solution, the number of coconuts must be

$$s^o - (s-1)m, \text{ or}$$
$$5^3 - (5-1)17 = 57$$

The first suspicious sailor finds 57 coconuts, discards 17, and divides the remaining 40 into five piles of 8, takes one pile, and leaves 32.

The second suspicious sailor finds these 32 coconuts, discards 17, and divides the remaining 15 into five piles of 3, takes one pile, and leaves 12.

In the morning, all the sailors find these 12 coconuts, discard 17, and of the remaining -5, divide them evenly among themselves.

In numbers alone this makes perfect sense, but if you do not like the negative coconuts at the end, then add 5^6 to the answer, getting $57 + 125 = 182$. You can verify that this, too, will work.

ARCHIMEDES' REVENGE

There is an even more difficult and more ancient problem that has acquired a classic status. This is the famous Cattle Problem that, at one time or another, attracted the attention of nearly every great mathematician. Legend has it that Archimedes, the legendary mathematician of ancient Greece, created the problem as a way of taking revenge on his enemies. It is, in fact, well known that Archimedes worked on the problem, and possibly altered it to make it devilishly difficult, but it is very unlikely that he first created the puzzle. Archimedes is today ranked as one of the three greatest mathematicians that have ever lived, the other two being Isaac Newton and Carl Friedrich Gauss. During his own lifetime, he was equally venerated. Long after his death, civilizations that only knew of his fame used his name as a synonym for anything obtusely intellectual, much as we today use the name Einstein. Cicero, for example, often said, "That is a book for Archimedes," meaning, "That is a very difficult book indeed."

Whatever its origins, however, the Cattle Problem is the last word on indeterminate puzzles. Reading it today in its original form gives an almost awe-inspiring sense of the type of diversion that attracted the people of Archimedes' time:

> If thou art diligent and wise, O stranger, compute the number of cattle of the Sun, who once upon a time grazed on the fields of the Thrinacian isle of Sicily, divided into four herds of different colors, one milk white, another a glossy black, the third yellow, and the last dappled. In each herd were bulls, mighty in number according to these proportions: Understand, stranger, that the white bulls were equal to a half and a third of the black together with the whole of the yellow, while the black were equal to the fourth part of the dappled and a fifth, together with, once more, the whole of the yellow. Observe further that the remaining bulls, the dappled, were equal to a sixth part of the white and a seventh, together with all the yellow.

This is simple enough. Let

W be the number of white bulls;
B be the number of black bulls;
Y be the number of yellow bulls;
D be the number of dappled bulls.

Then all we are told is:

$$W = (\tfrac{1}{2}+\tfrac{1}{3})\, B \ + Y \ \dots\dots\dots\dots \quad (1)$$
$$B \ = (\tfrac{1}{4}+\tfrac{1}{5})\, D \ + Y \ \dots\dots\dots\dots \quad (2)$$
$$D \ = (\tfrac{1}{6}+\tfrac{1}{7})\, B \ + Y \ \dots\dots\dots\dots \quad (3)$$

So far we know only about the bulls. The story continues to describe the cows:

These were the proportions of the cows: The white were precisely equal to the third part and a fourth of the whole herd of the black; while the black were equal to the fourth part once more of the dappled and with it a fifth part, when all, including the bulls, went to pasture together. Now the dappled were equal in number to a fifth part and a sixth of the yellow herd. Finally, the yellow were in number equal to a sixth part and a seventh of the white herd.

This, too, is really very simple. Let

w be the number of white cows;
b be the number of black cows;
y be the number of yellow cows;
d be the number of dappled cows.

Then we are told:

$$w = (\tfrac{1}{3}+\tfrac{1}{4}) \ (B+b) \ \dots\dots\dots\dots \quad (4)$$
$$b \ = (\tfrac{1}{4}+\tfrac{1}{5}) \ (D+d) \ \dots\dots\dots\dots \quad (5)$$
$$d \ = (\tfrac{1}{5}+\tfrac{1}{6}) \ (Y+y) \ \dots\dots\dots\dots \quad (6)$$
$$y \ = (\tfrac{1}{6}+\tfrac{1}{7}) \ (W+w) \ \dots\dots\dots\dots \quad (7)$$

The problem requires no special skills at this point, although the numbers will get forbiddingly large. Archimedes says as much:

> If thou canst accurately tell, O stranger, the number of cattle of the Sun, giving separately the number of well-fed bulls and again the number of females according to each color, thou wouldst not be called unskilled or ignorant of numbers, but not yet shalt thou be numbered among the wise. But come, understand all these conditions regarding the cows of the Sun.

Now we are given certain complications that some authorities credit to Archimedes. Certainly, it is this part of the puzzle that makes its solution rather arduous:

> When the white bulls mingled their number with the black, they stood firm, equal in depth and breadth, and the plains of Thrinicia, stretching far in all ways, were filled with their multitude.

That they stood "equal in depth and breadth" possibly means that the number of white and black bulls together must be a perfect square number. This makes the problem almost impossible to solve. But one of the strangest accomplishments of number theory is that, while it could not state the answer exactly, it could discover, in the late 1800s, that the answer must have 206,545 digits, and the first three of these were 776. To understand exactly how big this number is, number theorists often use a graphic image: Imagine a sphere with a radius equal to the distance between the earth and the Milky Way, and imagine the cows are the size of electrons—the sphere could not hold this many cows. Three Canadians found the exact number using God knows how many hours of computer time; it was printed (in very small type) in *The Journal of Recreational Mathematics*.

The usual custom at this point is to cheat. Cows are longer than they are wide. If they are "equal in breadth and depth," therefore, the number of white and black bulls must be a rectangular number, and not a square. This, aside from being a hilarious cop-out, will make the problem solvable. But there is more:

> Again, when the yellow and the dappled bulls were gathered into one herd they stood in such a manner that their number, beginning from one, grew slowly greater till it completed a triangular figure, there being no bulls of other colors in their midst nor none of them lacking.

This simply means that $(Y+D)$ must be a triangular number, or a number of the form $\frac{1}{2}n(n+1)$, as we saw in a previous chapter.

> If thou art able, O stranger, to find out all these things and gather them together in your mind, giving all the relations, thou shalt depart crowned with glory and knowing that thou hast been adjudged perfect in this species of wisdom.

Fair enough. The problem contains nothing special in principle, but there are so many unknowns and the solutions grow so large, that it is nearly impossible to solve without the aid of a computer. Fortunately, the results are now known. In the following, give n any value at all and you will arrive at one possible solution to equations 1 through 7 above.

$$W = 10366482n \qquad w = 7206360n$$
$$B = 7460514n \qquad b = 4893246n$$
$$Y = 4149387n \qquad y = 5439213n$$
$$D = 7358060n \qquad d = 3515820n$$

Now, of all these possible answers, we must find those for which $(Y+D)$ is a triangular number. That $(W+B)$ should be a rectangular number will follow automatically. There is only one possible answer here:

$$W = 1,217,263,415,886 \qquad w = 846,192,410,280$$
$$B = 876,035,935,422 \qquad b = 574,579,625,058$$
$$Y = 487,233,469,701 \qquad y = 638,688,708,099$$
$$D = 864,005,479,380 \qquad d = 412,838,131,860$$

And the total number of cows is 5,916,837,175,686. And Archimedes has his revenge.

I FOUND VERY MANY SOLUTIONS . . .

The method we have previously looked at can be used to solve any type of linear indeterminate problem, although the part of the solution that requires common logic will always present fresh considerations. Sometimes these can overpower the problem. An extreme example is the last problem mentioned by Abu Kamil, alluded to in his introduction, having 2676 solutions. This number, 2676, is given by Abu Kamil himself as the number of solutions he actually found. For countless decades this was considered correct until the English mathematician Thomas H. O'Beirne decided to open the matter once more and it was found that a puzzle first mentioned in A.D. 900 was not to be solved correctly until the twentieth century. The problem itself is simple to state:

> You have 100 drachmas and you are told to buy 100 birds. Of the birds, Ducks are sold at 2 drachmas each, Hens at 1 drachma, Doves at 2 for 1 drachma, Ringdoves at 3 for 1 drachma, and Larks at 4 for 1 drachma. How many of each type of bird was purchased?

We assume that at least one of each species must be purchased. This problem can be solved like the previous one, but this time the number of solutions is so great that it quickly becomes unmanageable. We will present here the alternate method originated by O'Beirne. The method is remarkable in the way it gathers together all the competing considerations posed in the problem and boils it all down to something quite simple. What should be kept in mind, however, is that this method looks very much like the more mathematical method used previously. If the problem were solved mathematically, the solution would look esoteric; O'Beirne's method is straightforward. Yet they are both the same. As you follow the solution and begin to juggle around the Ducks, Hens, and so on, you will behave very much like a mathematician juggling the unknowns of an equation.

First, we will capitalize on the fact that the number of birds to be purchased is equal to the amount of money to be spent. This will allow us to group certain species of birds together, creating packages in which the number of birds equals the cost of the package. We will use the symbol P_x for these packages, where x is the number of birds, or the cost of the package in drachmas. We have the following:

$$P_3 = 1 \text{ Duck and 2 Doves} \qquad (3 \text{ birds for 3 drachmas})$$
$$P_5 = 2 \text{ Ducks and 3 Ringdoves} \ (5 \text{ birds for 5 drachmas})$$
$$P_7 = 3 \text{ Ducks and 4 Larks} \qquad (7 \text{ birds for 7 drachmas})$$
$$P_{5'} = 2 \text{ Ducks, 1 Dove, 2 Larks} \ (5 \text{ birds for 5 drachmas})$$

Hens do not need to be packaged, or if you prefer, each Hen is its own package, since a Hen sells at 1 for 1 drachma.

So the puzzle that once had five different species now has only four, the packages above. All solutions can be stated in terms of these packages; the number of Hens need not be mentioned since we just load up on these in order to complete the number of birds (and the cost of the transaction) to 100. A simple purchase is the following:

P_3 : 1 Duck, 2 Doves	costing	3	drachmas
P_5 : 2 Ducks, 3 Ringdoves	costing	5	drachmas
P_7 : 3 Ducks, 4 Larks	costing	7	drachmas
15 Birds	costing	15	drachmas
+ 85 Hens	costing	85	drachmas
100 Birds	costing	100	drachmas

Notice how the method of packaging insures that the two columns sum to the same amount. Previously, the simultaneous equations had the same effect. Notice how our commonsense approach imitated the thinking of a mathematician—or is it the other way around?

If we ignore the Hens, which merely serve as filling, then any proper solution to this problem must take one of the forms:

1) one or more of each of the packages P_3, P_5, and P_7; or
2) exactly one package $P_{5'}$, one or more of the package P_5, and perhaps, but not necessarily, one or more of the packages P_3 and P_7.

It is never necessary to have more than one package $P_{5'}$, since you will find that, after looking at the makeup of the packages, $P_{5'} + P_{5'} = P_3 + P_7$. These combinations will insure that one of each species is present. The number of birds in all, whatever the form, must be at most 99, since we have to save room for the Hens.

We can simplify things further. After the Hens are dismissed, the number of birds remaining in a proper solution will be equal to some multiple of 3 plus some multiple of 7 plus, possibly, 5 more birds. A number theorist would go to some lengths to prove this, but look how easy it is for us. P_3 and P_7 are obviously seen as multiples of 3 and 7 respectively. If there are packages of 5, either as P_5 or $P_{5'}$, then these can be paired together in twos to create a package of 10 birds, or as 3 + 7 birds. The only other possibility is that there remains an odd package of 5. This accounts for our qualification above that there are possibly 5 more birds. Thus, every solution (ignoring the Hens) can be written in the form $(3a+7b) < 100$, or $(3a+7b+5) < 100$.

Look at Figures 88(a) and 88(b). Each figure contains several bins arranged horizontally by increasing multiples of 3 and vertically by increasing multiples of 7. (Some aspects of the figures may seem confusing now, but they will be explained shortly.) Into each bin we will place one or more solution. We can imagine that there is a computer churning out all combinations of the five species. After it has one combination it checks to see if it matches the constraints of the problem. If so—that is, if it is a proper solution—it dispenses with the Hens and arranges the remaining birds into packages and finds the relevant multiples of 3 and 7. If there is no odd package of 5 left over, then it places the solution into the appropriate bin of Figure 88(a). If there is, it places the solution into the appropriate bin of Figure 88(b).

Notice that the value of the bins of Figure 88(a) can never exceed 99, so we can always add the Hens. And the bins of Figure 88(b) can never exceed 94, so we can always add the package of 5 as well as the Hens.

All solutions can be placed in one or another bin. For example, the computer will at some point find the solution "11 Ducks, 3 Ring-doves, 3 Doves, 10 Larks, and 73 Hens." It sees that this is correct, so it throws out the Hens, and divides the rest into the packages: $P_5 + P_{5'} + P_3 + P_7 + P_7$. The solution goes into Figure 88(a), since there is no odd package of 5 left over. Furthermore, it goes into the bin that has two multiples of 3 and three multiples of 7. This bin is shaded in the figure.

Each bin has at least one solution; Abu Kamil's problem is to find the total number of solutions. It is surprisingly simple to find how many solutions are contained in a bin. The trick is to look at the number of different ways we can interpret the combinations of the bin. Look again at the shaded bin in the position of two multiples of 3 and three multiples of 7 in Figure 88(a). We take this to mean that there are 2 multiples of 3 and 7, and a group of 7 left over. We know that the solutions here have $(2 \cdot 3) + (3 \cdot 7) = 27$ birds (and therefore 73 Hens). There are three solutions in this bin, the first of which we have already seen:

	First Solution		Second Solution		Third Solution
$3-7$	$\rightarrow$	$P_5 + P_{5'}$	$\rightarrow \quad P_5 + P_5$	$\rightarrow$	$P_5 + P_5$
$3-7$	$\rightarrow$	$P_3 + P_7$	$\rightarrow \quad P_3 + P_7$	$\rightarrow$	$P_5 + P_{5'}$
7	$\rightarrow$	P_7	$\rightarrow \quad P_7$	$\rightarrow$	P_7
(73 Hens)	$\rightarrow$	(73 Hens)	$\rightarrow \quad$ (73 Hens)	$\rightarrow$	(73 Hens)

The reader can verify that in each solution all species are present, the number of birds is always 100, and the cost is always 100 drachmas.

As a general rule, if there are n 3–7 combinations in a bin of Figure 88(a), there are $2n - 1$ solutions in the bin. And if there are n 3–7 combinations in a bin of Figure 88b, there are $2n$ solutions in that bin.

This is why we have combined the bins into L-shaped regions, where each bin in the region has the same number of 3–7 combinations. The precise number is written at the foot of the L. At the top of each L we write the number of bins in the region, the number of solutions in each bin, and having multiplied the two numbers we have the number of solutions in the region.

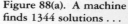

Figure 88(a). A machine finds 1344 solutions . . .

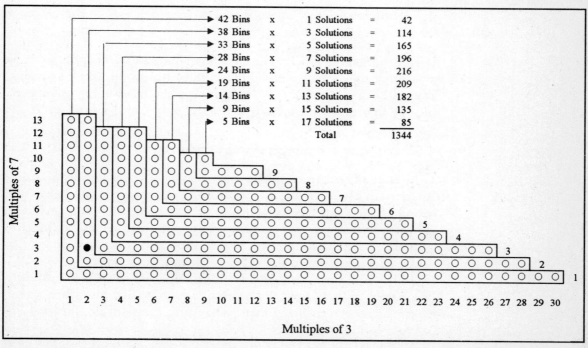

42 Bins	x	1 Solutions	=	42
38 Bins	x	3 Solutions	=	114
33 Bins	x	5 Solutions	=	165
28 Bins	x	7 Solutions	=	196
24 Bins	x	9 Solutions	=	216
19 Bins	x	11 Solutions	=	209
14 Bins	x	13 Solutions	=	182
9 Bins	x	15 Solutions	=	135
5 Bins	x	17 Solutions	=	85
		Total		1344

Multiples of 7

Multiples of 3

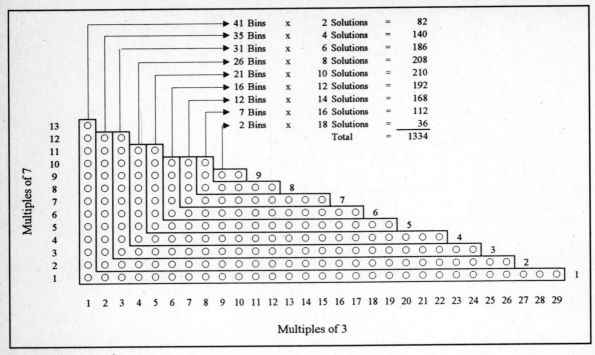

41 Bins x	2 Solutions =	82
35 Bins x	4 Solutions =	140
31 Bins x	6 Solutions =	186
26 Bins x	8 Solutions =	208
21 Bins x	10 Solutions =	210
16 Bins x	12 Solutions =	192
12 Bins x	14 Solutions =	168
7 Bins x	16 Solutions =	112
2 Bins x	18 Solutions =	36
	Total =	1334

Figure 88(b). . . . and
another 1334 solutions

Figure 88(a) has in all 1344 solutions. These are of the form $3a + 7b$ plus some number of Hens. Figure 88(b) has in all 1334 solutions. These are of the form $3a + 7b + 5$ plus some number of Hens. Between the two figures there are 2678 solutions. Abu Kamil was off by 2.

WATER AND WIND

The time of the Arab Golden Age, of which Abu Kamil was a part, lasted from the seventh to the fifteenth century, roughly the same period as the Dark Ages in Europe, of which Alcuin was a part. The gold faded in subsequent centuries, but it is worth remembering that without this golden age, the world, especially the Western world, would have very little today of what it considers its own.

Quite some time after Abu Kamil died, there lived in the Middle East a man named Omar. By profession he was, like his father, a tent maker, and so he took the name Khayyám. Early in life, however, he showed great talent as a mathematician, once referring to himself whimsically as "Khayyám, who stitched the tents of science." Today he is best known for the poetry he wrote to relax between bouts of mathematical research, especially a collection of quatrains known as *The Ruba'iyat*. Its popular English translation was by Edward FitzGerald, and in a fitting metaphor of what has befallen Middle Eastern history, the Westerner played fast and loose with the text, changing much of it into a drunken revelry told in rhymes and meters that just don't work. The loud references to drunkeness were misinterpreted. It is true that drinking appears often in *The Ruba'iyat*, but sometimes it is just a play on the Arab word *maisara*, which means "prosperity," but which sounded to the Persian ear like "wine is good," giving a comical double meaning to certain prayers. (As a Persian, Omar would have resented his forced conversion to Islamic fundamentalism.) Other times it is merely a gesture toward one of life's simple, harmless pleasures, as it is in the *Psalms*: "Wine maketh glad the heart of man." Many years later, Robert Graves did a second, more faithful translation, causing much of the drunkenness to disappear. One passage in particular seems appropriate (in what follows "Saki" is a wine-bearer):

> Some ponder long on doctrine and belief,
> Some teeter between certitude and doubt.
> Suddenly out of hiding leaps the Guide
> With: "Fools, the Way is neither that nor this."
>
> Most of them, gone before we go, my Saki,
> Drowse in their dusty bed of pride, my Saki.
> Drink yet again and hear the truth at last:
> "Whatever words they spoke were wind, my Saki."

....

> In childhood once we crouched before our teacher,
> Growing content, in time, with what he taught;
> How does the story end? What happened to us?
> We came like water and like wind we went.

Whatever that last line originally meant, and whatever it is taken to mean today, it simply is not true of the Arab Golden Age itself. For virtually all of the great Europeans who were to come later owed a substantial debt to the "water and wind" of the Arabs.

The Merchants of Pisa and the Digits of the Hindus

THERE IS A PART OF THE WORLD THAT LAGGED EMBARrassingly behind both Africa and China. The people of this region were backward and primitive and even its most prominent citizens would not have been able to communicate with the Arabs on an equal level. This region is Europe, or the West, a term that is now synonymous (even in present-day China and Africa) with science and technology. No one who lived in the West even as late as the thirteenth century could have predicted this development.

The great change can be credited to a number of circumstances, but among them certainly was the writings of a young Italian who traveled throughout much of the world toward the end of the twelfth century and hungrily digested all that he found. The "nine digits of the Hindus" fascinated him. This is the system that developed first in China, then traveled to India, and from there to the Arabs. To convey its meaning he decided to publish, in 1202, *Liber Abaci*. The book marked the end of Europe's doldrums. The title is often translated literally as *The Book of the Abacus*, but in Italy the word "abacus" referred not only to the well-known calculating aid but to the operations performed on it as well. A better translation is *The Book of Computation*. Copies of the book were almost lost, but in the 1860s a well-to-do prince, Baldassare Boncompagni, scoured the libraries of Europe, found what he could, set up a printing press in his own palace, and preserved much of it.

Considering the status of the author, it is a little distressing to report that not much is known about him. His name was Leonardo, and in thirteenth-century Italy surnames were not widely used. As his fame grew, and honors were bestowed on him, he took the name of the city of his birth, so he is sometimes called Leonardo Pisano, or Leonardo of Pisa. Because of the reputation of his father, Bonacci, as a state official, he sometimes took the name Leonardo Fibonacci, meaning *filius*, or son of, Bonacci. The last is the one that stuck, and today he is called simply Fibonacci.

What was the man's background? It is likely that he was schooled on Alcuin's *Problems to Quicken a Young Mind*, but aside from that we know little else. The opening paragraph of the *Liber Abaci* is the closest we have to an autobiography:

> After my father's appointment by his homeland as state official in the customs house of Bugia [in western Africa] for the Pisan merchants who thronged to it, he took charge; and, in view of its future usefulness and convenience, had me in my boyhood come to him and there wanted me to devote myself to and be instructed in the study of calculation for some days. There, following my introduction, as a consequence of marvelous instruction in the art, to the nine digits of the Hindus, the knowledge of the art very much appealed to me before all others, and for it I realized that all its aspects were studied in Egypt, Syria, Greece, Sicily, and Provence, with their varying methods; and at these places thereafter, while on business, I pursued my study in depth and learned the give-and-take of disputation. But all this even, and the algorism, as well as the art of Pythagoras I considered as almost a mistake in respect to the method of the Hindus. Therefore, embracing more stringently that method of the Hindus, and taking stricter pains in its study, while adding certain things from my own understanding and inserting also certain things from the niceties of Euclid's geometric

art, I have striven to compose this book in its entirety as understandably as I could . . . Almost everything which I have introduced I have displayed with exact proof in order that those further seeking this knowledge, with its pre-eminent method, might be instructed, and further, in order that the Latin [that is, Italian] people might not be discovered to be without it, as they have been up to now. If I have perchance omitted anything more or less proper or necessary, I beg indulgence, since there is no one who is blameless and utterly provident in all things.

This set the tone for Europe. First, Fibonacci borrowed what he could from the rest of the world. Even a casual glance through the *Liber Abaci* will show several familiar puzzles, some even from the Ahmes Papyrus, although, of course, Fibonacci came by them from other sources. Second, the new numbers were linked from the beginning with commerce. This had never happened before, and in a curious way this link would actually free the number system so that it could reach heights never expected by those from whom Fibonacci borrowed. Third, and most important, is not something found above, but something that is missing: A salute to the Deity. The *Liber Abaci* was never tinged with religious overtones. Fibonacci assured that the "entrance into all obscure secrets" would be, at long last, a simple matter of logic.

THE FIGURES OF THE HINDUS . . .

If a single sentence can be called the most important sentence ever written, it is this one from the *Liber Abaci*:

These are the nine figures of the Hindus: 9, 8, 7, 6, 5, 4, 3, 2, 1. With these nine figures, and with this sign "0," any number may be written as will be demonstrated.

The puzzles of the *Liber Abaci* are a celebration of these figures and the number system behind them. Fibonacci's parlor game, which we mentioned in an earlier chapter, is actually a direct play on this number system:

A group of people are seated in a row, and one of them is wearing a ring on a certain joint of a certain finger. One person, who knows the whereabouts of the ring, computes a number as follows: He finds the wearer's position in the row, multiplies it by 2, adds 5, multiplies that by 5, and adds 10. Then he adds a number indicating the finger, and multiplies this by ten. Then he adds a number indicating the joint. When this number is announced, it is easy to pinpoint the ring.

For example, assume the person is the fifth in the row, and he is wearing a ring on the second joint of his third finger. We find the number:

$$((((((5 \cdot 2)+5) \cdot 5)+10+3) \cdot 10)+2) = 882$$

All we need do is subtract 350 from the number to get 532. The number in the hundreds column is the row position of the ring wearer, the number in the tens position is the finger, and the number in the units position is the joint. If we let

$$r = \text{the row position}$$
$$f = \text{the finger}$$
$$j = \text{the joint}$$

then the calculation will give us:

$$((((((r \cdot 2)+5) \cdot 5+10+f) \cdot 10)+j = 350 + 100r + 10f + j$$

After we subtract 350, we are left with the number rfj, written in the "Hindu figures" that had so impressed Fibonacci.

But the new number system came kicking and screaming into Europe. In 1299, nearly a century after Fibonacci published his book, Florence strictly forbade its use in commercial and legal transactions. One reason was that so many of the figures could be changed fraudulently with unpredictable results. A "1" is easily changed to "9," increasing a figure by 8, or 80, or 800, and so on. Another reason was probably the presence of the mysterious figure "0," a symbol of nothing. Even Fibonacci insisted that there were "nine figures of the Hindus," and separated "0" from these, though there are ten figures in all.

As late as 1508, a popular woodcut showed the debate between the "abacists" (those who kept to the old method) and the "algorists" (those who followed Fibonacci), although to judge by their expressions it is obvious who was winning (see Figure 89). A knightly romance, written not long after Fibonacci's book, pokes fun at the rivalry of the "Algorismus" and the "Abakuc":

> And here too comes out
> Lot, Prince of Norway,
> With I know not how many hundreds;
> If the Algorismus were still alive,
> and Abakuc, learned in geometry,
> They would have much to do
> To find the number of them all.

Figure 89. The Spirit of Arithmetic stands between the algorist (Boetius) and the abacist (Pytagorus)

Romantic poetry aside, there is very little difference between Abakuc and Algorismus. The first does on a wire-and-bead contraption what the second does on paper. In fact, Abakuc laid the groundwork for Fibonacci. The important figure here is Gerbert {Zhare-bare'}, a French scholar who tutored the children of the King of France toward the end of the 900s. He is responsible for introducing a new kind of abacus into Europe. The story is told by William of Malmesbury, a minor historian, that Gerbert, while studying under an Arab teacher in Spain, ingratiated himself with the teacher's daughter. During the course of the romance he managed to get the father drunk, and then stole an important manual on arithmetic. The manual very likely contained the Arabic figures that we saw previously, and perhaps also instructions on the use of a new kind of abacus. We know for certain that Gerbert used this abacus while teaching his students. Even long after his death, skilled calculators were said to be "gerberizing" in their functions.

Partly because of his computational skills, Gerbert, in his later years, was made Pope by Otto the Great, Holy Roman Emperor, and took the name Sylvester II. By this time, his gift in the art of calculating contributed to the belief, commonly held throughout Europe, that he had sold his soul to the devil, and his papacy fueled the fears of some who thought the world would end at the turn of the millennium. One particularly gruesome story will suffice to describe the sad disarray of Catholic Europe during this time. When Stephen VI was raised to the papacy in 897 he disinterred the body of his rival and predecessor, Pope Formosus. The corpse was mockingly dressed in papal gowns and paraded through the streets of Rome. *Then* Formosus was placed on trial and, needless to say, found guilty of any number of crimes. As punishment, the body was mutilated and thrown into the Tiber River. The entire sordid affair is known as the "Council of Cadavers." It was into this scene that Gerbert was made Pope, and to his credit he attempted several measures of reform. Alas, none survived.

Concerning the new abacus, descriptions of it say that it consisted of a board with twenty-seven compartments in a rectangular array. The columns of the array were marked off into threes, the prototype of our custom of marking off numbers into threes by commas. Into each compartment, Gerbert could drop various coins, each containing some variant of the Arabic number symbols. In later centuries the coins were manufactured with extravagant details, sometimes adorned with the heads of current monarchs, or with important proverbs such as, "Here Today, Gone Tomorrow."

The use of the abacus is shown in Figure 90, although we have used modern numerals written inside a smaller sample of the board's compartments. To get a feel of the abacus, simply imagine that the numbers represent the number of beads placed in each compartment. The figure shows a way of multiplying 25 by 4700.

One number, 25, is placed at the bottom. The other number, 4700, is placed at the top. The blank compartments represent zeros, which of course Gerbert could not symbolize. Between the two are the partial products. The 35 in the second row is 5 times 7, and so on for the other rows. The multiplication, $5 \cdot 7$, had to be memorized and could not be worked out independently on the board. Notice that rows are properly indented.

Finally, the partial sums are added together to arrive at the final answer, 117,500. The whole machinery was so close to present-day calculations that Gerbert could have tossed the board away and simply written his calculations on paper.

Figure 90. Gerbert's abacus

	Thousands			Units		
	Hundreds	Tens	Units	Hundreds	Tens	Units
Multiplicand			4	7		
			3	5		
		2				
		1	4			
		8				
Result	1	1	7	5		
Multiplier					2	5

A CHYLDE CAN DO IT

It is interesting to pause for a moment to see how slow Europe was in picking up the new method of multiplication. We take our cue from Robert Recorde, a mathematician and personal physician to Mary Tudor. In 1542 he published *The Grounde of Artes. Teachyng the Worke and Practice of Arithmetike*, a text that attempts to set out certain rules for arithmetic. Here, for example, is how Recorde multiplied 8 and 7.

> First set your digits one over the other. Then from the uppermost downwards, and from the nethermost upwards, draw straight lines, so that they make a St. Andrew's cross. Then look how many each of them lacketh of 10, and write that against each of them at the end of the line, and that is called the difference. I multiply the two differences, saying, "two times three make six," that must I ever set down under the differences.

> Take from the other digit, (not from his own), as the lines of the cross warn me, and that that is left, must I write under the digits.

If I take 2 from 7, or 3 from 8, (which I will, for all is lyke), and there remaineth 5, and then there appeareth the multiplication of 8 times 7 to be 56. A chylde can do it.

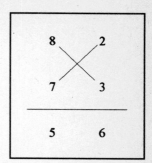

Figure 91 is Recorde's work sheet. The X in the figure, which Recorde calls "St. Andrew's Cross" may very well be the origin of the well-known symbol for multiplication.

Do you think this method is more or less sophisticated than the method of multiplication used by Gerbert? For that matter, is it more or less sophisticated than the one used by Ahmes?

Figure 91. Robert Recorde's worksheet

THE TERNARY SCALE

The effect that the number system had on Fibonacci can be seen in another problem in which the solution requires us to change the base, or radix, of the system. This is the problem of weights, made popular in 1624 by Claude Gaspar Bachet and now incorrectly credited to him:

> If you have a balance scale, what is the smallest number of weights needed to determine the weight of any unknown object that has an integral weight between one and forty?

The answer to this, like the answer to Fibonacci's parlor game, is contained in the number system itself, but this time we must shift our thinking away from the decimal base to the ternary base. The balance scale is a ternary instrument in the sense that a pan can occupy one of three states: up, down, or even. To determine the weight of any object with an integral weight between 1 and 40, we need only four weights, successive powers of three: 1, 3, 9, and 27. In Figure 92, we show how to weigh a 22-pound object.

In the ternary system, we use only three figures of the Hindus— namely 0, 1, 2—and all numbers are expressed as sums of multiples of powers of three. For example, the number 22 in ternary is 211 since

$$22 = 2 \cdot 3^2 + 1 \cdot 3^1 + 1 \cdot 3^0$$

Figure 92. The unknown
weight must equal 22

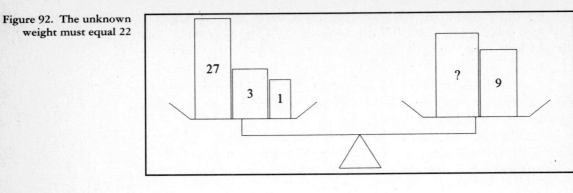

But if we allow ourselves to either add or subtract different powers of three, then we never need to multiply any of the powers. In this way

$$22 = 3^3 - 3^2 + 3^1 + 3^0$$

We use this method to solve Fibonacci's problem. The unknown object and all the negative weights are placed in one pan of the scale; the positive powers are placed in the opposite pan. The two pans, obviously, will balance.

Let's say your unknown object weighs instead 25 pounds. How to weigh it? Fiddle with the powers of three a little and you'll find that

$$25 = 3^3 - 3^1 + 3^0 \text{ or}$$
$$25 = 27 - 3 + 1$$

You can balance the object by placing 27 and 1 on one pan, and the 3 on the other pan along with the unknown object.

MORE SCALES

A simpler balance scale puzzle may show more clearly how to use the ternary number system.

Assume you have 27 coins, 1 of which is known to be heavy. How many weighings are needed in a balance scale, using no weights whatsoever, to find the coin?

It is easy to show that since $27 = 3^3$, exactly three weighings are necessary. The simplest solution is a contingency solution in which the coins that go into a weighing depend on the results of the previous weighing. Thus, begin by dividing the coins into three groups of 9 coins. Weigh one group against the other. The bad coin must be in the down pan or, if the pans balance, in the unweighed group. In either case, we have limited the suspects to only 9 coins. Divide these into three groups of 3 coins and again weigh one group against the other. As before, the results of the weighing will limit the suspects, this time to only 3 coins. Again, we divide these into three groups of 1 coin, and we repeat the procedure to get, finally, the bad coin.

The opposite of a contingency solution is a predetermined solution, in which the coins that go into a weighing are stated at the outset. (In this solution, try to think of Fibonacci's parlor game. The two are actually quite similar.) The easiest way to do this is to number the coins from 0 to 26, but using the ternary number system, as is done in Figure 93.

Now we play a game of twenty questions (actually, only three) and

Decimal	Ternary	Decimal	Ternary
0	000	14	112
1	001	15	120
2	002	16	121
3	010	17	122
4	011	18	200
5	012	19	201
6	020	20	202
7	021	21	210
8	022	22	211
9	100	23	212
10	101	24	220
11	102	25	221
12	110	26	222
13	111		

Figure 93. The first 27 ternary numbers

ask the scale to give us each of the three digits of the bad coin. Since the scale is a ternary instrument, it does not answer in the binary "yes/no" fashion, but in the ternary "up/down/even" fashion instead.

We start with the right-most digit. Place all the coins that have a 1 on the right pan, and all the coins that have a 2 on the left pan. If the right pan goes down, the scale tells us that the bad coin has a 1 in this digit; if it goes up it must be a 2; if the two pans are even, it must be a 0.

Move to the middle digit. Place all the coins that have a 1 on the right pan, and all the coins that have a 2 on the left pan. Once again, the scale will give us the middle digit of the heavy coin. Repeat everything on the left-most digit and you get the answer. Figure 94 shows the process when the bad coin is number 102.

Another scale puzzle, much more modern and sophisticated, is the odd-coin problem.

> Twelve coins have an equal weight, except one, which is either too light or too heavy. (We do not know which beforehand.) How many weighings do we need in a balance scale, using no weights whatsoever, to find the odd coin?

This is a perfect example of a puzzle arising because of a need to explain a phenomenon that does not normally arise in the real world. The problem attracted the attention of both physicists and computer scientists. The first saw in its solution an illustration of the concept of entropy; the second saw an example of information theory. It turned out that the two theories have much in common, although there is no reason to stretch the similarities too far.

There is a great deal to keep in mind here, since we must always remember that we do not know if the odd coin is light or heavy. If a pan in the scale goes down, that means the pan may have a heavy coin, or the opposite pan may have a light coin. We can show, however, that here again only three weighings are necessary.

The contingency method is diagrammed below in the "odd-coin slide rule" of Figure 95, which tells us how to perform the weighings with coins lettered from A to L. The first weighing is on the bottom row of the rule, the second is on the middle row, and the last is on the top. We move up depending on the outcome of each weighing, always going to the light side. The bottom row tells us how to begin. Weigh coins

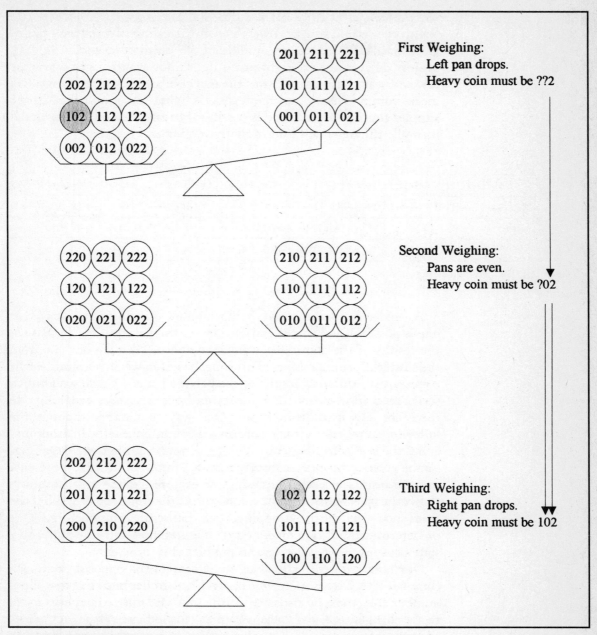

First Weighing:
    Left pan drops.
    Heavy coin must be ??2

Second Weighing:
    Pans are even.
    Heavy coin must be ?02

Third Weighing:
    Right pan drops.
    Heavy coin must be 102

Figure 94. Finding the heavy coin

(A,B,C,D) against (E,F,G,H); assume the left pan is light. Move to the left in the second row, and weigh (A,B,E) against (C,F,L); assume the pans balance. Move to the middle of the third row, and weigh (G) against (H); assume the right pan is light. Move to the right of the top row and read the answer: G was the odd coin and it was too heavy. (X^+ means coin X is heavy, and X^- means it is light). You might think that a simpler contingency method is possible, but any method that is fundamentally different will lead to more weighings.

A-	F+	B-	H+	D-	G+		C-	E+	I-	K+	J-	L-		L+	J+	K-	I+	E-	C+		G-	D+	H-	B+	F-	A+
A ←→ B		G ←→ H		E ←→ J			I ←→ J			L ←→ A				I ←→ J			E ←→ J				G ←→ H			A ←→ B		
(A,B,E) ←→ (C,F,L)							(A,I,J) ←→ (C,D,K)							(A,B,E) ←→ (C,F,L)												
(A,B,C,D) ←→ (E,F,G,H)																										

Figure 95. The odd-coin slide rule

A predetermined method is much more difficult. We know that one is possible, and that it can be done in three weighings, because of the results of the contingency solution above. We take our cue from the simple 27-coin problem. This time, however, we do not number the coins but the different results of the balance scale. At each weighing a scale can occupy one of three states, and there are three weighings, so there are 27 possibilities in all. One way to number them is the following: 1 represents the right pan dropping, 2 the left pan dropping, and 0 the two pans balancing. Thus, the results of the three weighings can be given a three-digit ternary number, from 000 to 222, representing the results of each weighing. For example, if the first weighing shows the pans balancing, the second shows the right pan dropping, the third shows the left pan dropping, then that result is number 012. Our predetermined solution must be so configured that only one coin, and a state of being light or heavy, can produce this number.

Our notation easily allows us to determine the opposite state of a coin. For if 012 is associated with, say A^+, then the mirror image of the number, 021, must be associated with the A^-. By mirror image we mean that 1 changes to 2, and 2 changes to 1. This indicates that if A^+ causes the right pan to drop on a weighing, then A^- must cause the left pan to drop on the same weighing.

From ternary 000 to 222 there are twenty-seven numbers in all. The number 000, which has no mirror image, is reserved for the case in which no coin is odd. Aside from this, we have thirteen pairs of numbers, but since there are only twelve coins we dispense with 111 and its mirror image, 222. The remaining numbers can be arranged in pairs, each with its mirror image, but we will do so in a way that maximizes the information—entropy?—in the system. How this is done will be explained shortly. First look at the table below:

Ternary number		Mirror image	
000			
001	(A^+)	002	(A^-)
010	(B^+)	020	(B^-)
022	(C^+)	011	(C^-)
021	(D^+)	012	(D^-)
100	(E^+)	200	(E^-)
202	(F^+)	101	(F^-)
102	(G^+)	201	(G^-)
220	(H^+)	110	(H^-)
112	(I^+)	221	(I^-)
210	(J^+)	120	(J^-)
121	(K^+)	212	(K^-)
211	(L^+)	122	(L^-)

Why did we place 001 on the left side and not its image 002? Why did we not reverse the order for this pair, or any of the other pairs? Because this arrangement will give us the most information. Look at just the left-hand column. Notice that among the first digits, four are 0's, four are 1's, and four are 2's. This is true also of the middle and last digits. Needless to say, this is the case for the right-hand column also, since these are only mirror images. Associated with each number is a coin and a state of being light or heavy. The association itself is wholly unimportant; I have simply gone down the list alphabetically. What *is* important is that all of one state is associated with a single column, and the opposite state is paired correspondingly.

From this table we can configure our predetermined solution. Consider, for example, A^+. We know that in its three weighings it must give us 001. Therefore, in the first weighing it may not appear in either pan, or in the second, and in the third it must appear in the right pan. And so on for the other coins. Our system of pairing the ternary numbers assures that in each weighing four coins will be present in either pan. Here is the configuration:

	Left Pan	Right Pan
First weighing:	FHJL	EGIK
Second weighing:	CDHK	BIJL
Third weighing:	CFGI	ADKL

Notice that if A is the odd coin and heavy, then the weighings are so designed that we will indeed get 001 as expected. Conversely, if we find the weighings give us 012, then we know that D is a light coin.

Look closely at the solution above. A computer scientist would say these weighings maximize information; that is, the weighings do not provide any redundancy. A physicist would say it maximizes entropy; that is, the coins are as "disorganized" as possible (notice that a coin never appears all three times with another coin). In this instance, information and entropy mean much the same. In this way, both the computer scientist and the physicist assure that the result of the weighings will point unequivocally to a single coin.

Soon after the puzzle appeared, a clever trick was produced to solve it and a poem written around it:

F. set the coins out in a row
And chalked on each a letter so
To form the words

F. AM NOT LICKED

An idea in his brain clicked.
And now his mother he'll enjoin

MA! DO   LIKE
ME TO   FIND
FAKE   COIN

(In other words, instead of using the letters A through L for the coins, use the letters FAMNOTLICKED. Then your three weighings are

MADO against LIKE, METO against FIND, and FAKE against COIN.)

> No two agree in their effect,
> As is by pen and patience checked.
> For instance, should the dud be "L"
> And heavy, here's the way to tell:
> First weighing, down the right must come;
> the others—equilibrium!

How many trials are necessary for a given number of coins? In general if there are $(3^n-3)/2$ coins, then n weighings are necessary.

THE TWENTY-SEVEN-CARD TRICK

The following is a simple but beguiling magic trick that Fibonacci might have appreciated. Like his parlor game about the hidden ring, its magic rests almost entirely on the properties of the number system; and like his puzzle about weights, it uses the ternary number system in order to hide its magic.

Let us assume that I have taken twenty-seven cards from a standard playing deck; for simplicity, I will use the 13 spades, 13 clubs, and the ace of diamonds to complete the set. A participant is asked to pick a card, which he does not reveal, and to choose a number from 1 to twenty-seven, which he does reveal—let us say he picks 12. I perform a simple computation, the nature of which you should try to guess—for the moment I will say only that it involves the ternary number system. Even though I do not know what card he has chosen, I will ask only three questions and ultimately arrange the deck so that this secret card, *which I do not know*, appears exactly in the twelfth position, as requested. (Notice that I need three questions to find one card among 27. How many weighings did I need to find a heavy coin among 27?)

To explain the game further, we will assume the secret card is the four of clubs, but remember that I do not know this. I array the twenty-seven cards faceup before the participant, as is done in Figure 96. Notice that I have dealt them in rows, not columns; the ordinal position of the deal is to the left of each card. The cards can be given a random shuffle, but for simplicity I have illustrated them in order.

Figure 96. The 27-card
                trick, part 1

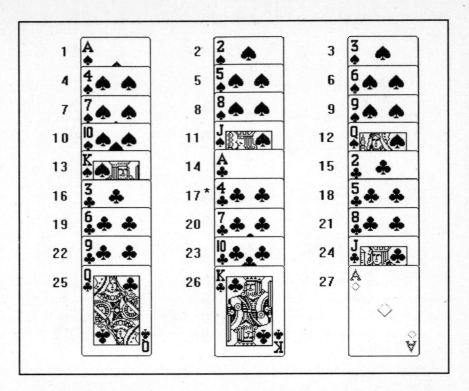

I ask the participant my first question, "What column does your card appear in?" and he tells me, "Column two." I pick up the first column and place it faceup in my hand, then the third column on top of this, then finally the second column on top of that. (Hint: the order in which I pick up the columns is due to my calculation above.) I turn the cards over, and array them again in three columns, as in Figure 97. Notice again that the dealing is done in rows.

I ask the participant my second question, "What column does your card appear in?" and he tells me, "Column three." This time my calculation tells me to pick up the columns in the following order: First the third column, then the second, then the first. As before, I turn the cards over and array them in three columns, as in Figure 98.

I ask the participant my third and final question, "What column does your card appear in?" and he tells me, "Column two." I pick up the cards in column one, then column two, then column three, turn them over and count them out. As the reader can see, the twelfth card will be the four of clubs, as predicted.

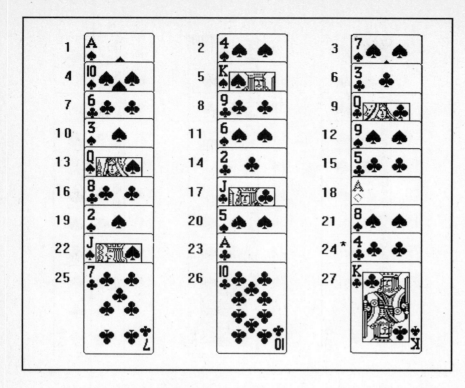

Figure 97. The 27-card trick, part 2

I will not explain the magic here, but leave it as a puzzle for you. Here are some clues. Is it really surprising that I was able to accomplish so much with three questions, since I was using only twenty-seven cards? Each card can be given a three-digit ternary number, just like the coins. My three questions amounted to asking for the three digits of the secret card.

Let us say that we did not want to put the card in a certain position, but just to locate it. How can we do this in three questions? I would array the cards as above and ask for the appropriate column. When I get the answer I know that the secret card is one of nine, so I can throw the others away, array the nine cards into three groups of three and again ask for the appropriate column. Now I know that the secret card is one of three. One more question, and I have all-too-obviously pinpointed the card. Is this not like the twenty-seven-coin puzzle?

Try the same trick in a different number system. The easiest, of course, would be the decimal system. If I had one hundred cards arrayed in ten columns of ten cards each, how many questions do I need to find.

Figure 98. The 27-card
        trick, part 3

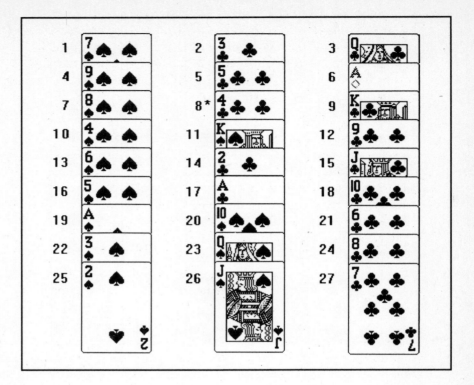

the secret card? How would I pick up the cards to make it appear in a certain position?

The trick works because of the way I pick up the columns after each of the three questions. The only important column is the one the participant tells me contains the secret card; the other columns can be picked up in any order. When the participant said he wanted the card in position 12, I found $12 - 1 = 11$, which in ternary is 102. Can you see how this tells me to pick up the column of cards?

AN ANCIENT CHINESE GAME

The *Liber Abaci* contains another guess-a-number game that turns out to be far more sophisticated than the parlor game above:

Let a contrived number be divided by 3, also by 5, also by 7; and ask each time what remains from each division. For each unity that remains from the division by 3, retain 70; for each unity that remains from the division by 5, retain 21; and for each unity that remains from the division by 7, retain 15. And as much as the number surpasses 105, subtract from it 105; and what remains to you is the contrived number.

Example: Suppose from the division by 3 the remainder is 2; for this you retain twice 70, or 140. [Fibonacci subtracts 105 from this immediately to get 35.] From the division by 5, the remainder is 3; from which you retain three times 21, or 63, which you add to the above 35; you get 98; and from the division by 7, the remainder is 4, from which you retain four times 15, or 60; which you add to the above 98, and you get 158; from which you subtract 105, and the remainder is 53. That is the contrived number.

This puzzle was also fashioned by Fibonacci into a parlor game:

From this rule comes a pleasant game, namely if someone has learned this rule with you; if somebody else should say some number privately to him, then your companion, not interrogated, should silently divide the number for himself by 3, by 5, and by 7 according to the above-mentioned rule; the remainders from each of these divisions, he says to you in order; and in this way you can know the number said to him in private.

The problem is actually a wonderful demonstration of what is now generally called the Chinese Remainder Theorem because its earliest appearance may be found in the *Sun Tzu Suan-ching* or the *Mathematical Classic of Sun Tzu*. (See Figure 99.) As with all classic Chinese works, we do not know its exact date, but very likely it was written about A.D. 200. By this time, of course, the Chinese were already quite masterful with their use of the positional number system.

As this quote from the *Mathematical Classic* shows, the original Sun Tzu problem is the source of Fibonacci's work:

We have things of which we do not know the number; if we count them by threes, the remainder is 2; if we count them by fives, the remainder is 3; if we count them by sevens, the remainder is 2. How many things are there? Answer: 23.

Method: If you count by threes and have the remainder 2, put 140. If you count by fives and have the remainder 3, put 63. If you count by sevens and have the remainder 2, put 30. Add these and you get 233. From this subtract 210 and you have the result.

For each unity as remainder when counting by threes, put 70.

For each unity as remainder when counting by fives, put 21.

For each unity as remainder when counting by sevens, put 15.

If the sum is 106 or more, subtract 105 from this and you get the result.

Neither Sun Tzu nor Fibonacci gives an explanation, and neither cares to make the solution very general. It is unlikely that Fibonacci was only quoting blindly, considering his skills as a mathematician, but all the same it seems unusual that he did so little to explain his method.

Let us see what is going on. First, the three numbers that are chosen to divide the original "contrived number" are, for both Fibonacci and Sun Tzu, 3, 5, and 7. There is nothing special about these numbers. We could use any set of numbers that are co-prime, that is, numbers that do not have divisors in common. We could have used, for example, the set of numbers 2, 3, and 5, or 8, 15, and 59649589127497217, although obviously this last set would be difficult to work with. We could not have used 4, 6, and 5, since 4 and 6 share a divisor. Furthermore, we do not need to limit ourselves to only three numbers; four or more would also work, but again the parlor game becomes more difficult.

Second, both authors seem to think that the contrived number can be any number at all. This is not true. The number must be a positive number less than the product of the three numbers we just spoke about. For example, both Sun Tzu and Fibonacci needed the contrived number to be less than $3 \cdot 5 \cdot 7 = 105$. Had they used instead 2, 3, and 5 as the divisors, then the contrived number had to be less than 30. In fact,

Figure 99. The Sun Tzu problem (Reprinted from Davis and Hersch, 1981)

今有物不知其數三三數之賸二五五數之賸
三七七數之賸二問物幾何
荅曰二十三
術曰三三數之賸一置一百四十五五數
之賸一置六十三七七數之賸二置三十
并之得二百三十三以二百一十減之即
得凡三三數之賸一則置七十五五數之
賸一則置二十一七七數之賸一則置十
五一百六以上以一百五減之即得

both authors probably settled on 3, 5, and 7 in order to get a fairly wide range of numbers while keeping the required divisions simple.

Third, after the remainders are found, they are multiplied by another set of numbers that both authors seem to pick out of the blue. But actually, these numbers are determined by the set of dividers. As an example, let us work with the original set of dividers: 3, 5, 7. We divided our number first by 3, then multiplied the remainder by 70. Where did 70 come from? It is a multiple of 5 • 7 that exceeds a multiple of 3 by exactly 1. Next we divided our number by 5, and multiplied the remainder by 21. Twenty-one is a multiple of 3 • 7 that exceeds a multiple of 5 by exactly 1. Lastly, we divided our number by 7, and multiplied the remainder by 15, which is a multiple of 3 • 5 that exceeds a multiple of 7 by exactly 1. Do you see the pattern? In each case, we take the two numbers that are not being used as a divider at the moment, and find the multiple of their product that exceeds a multiple of the divider by exactly 1.

You should be able to use different dividers, such as 2, 3, and 5, and devise a parlor game of your own.

This seems like a difficult way to guess a number, but the Chinese Remainder Theorem is one of the great tools of modern number theory. The Chinese used this theorem to predict the common period of different astronomical cycles, just as Fibonacci used it to predict a contrived number. Today it is an indispensable tool of computer science. To explain why it works we will keep the discussion fairly specific and use only the dividers mentioned by both Sun Tzu and Fibonacci, namely 3, 5, and 7. It is relatively easy to show that if you get a set of remainders from these numbers, then you have pinpointed a single number. Figure 100 is a table of the numbers 0 through 20 along with the remainders left behind by dividing them by 3, 5, and 7 respectively.

Remove the mystery from the table. The first column, listing the remainders on dividing by 3, is simply the series 0, 1, 2, 0, 1, 2 . . . The second column is the series 0, 1, 2, 3, 4, 0, 1, 2 . . . And the third column is 0, 1, 2, 3, 4, 5, 6 . . . These series always miss each other in the sense that no two series will restart at the same time. One upshot is that, given these three series, no two numbers can have the same set of remainders. For example, look at the set of remainders for 18: 0, 3, and 4. No other number has this set. This will be true as long as we limit ourselves to the first 105 numbers, because after this the entire table repeats itself.

Figure 100. 3, 5, and 7 are
relatively prime

N	Remainder when N is divided by 3	Remainder when N is divided by 5	Remainder when N is divided by 7
0	0	0	0
1	1	1	1
2	2	2	2
3	0	3	3
4	1	4	4
5	2	0	5
6	0	1	6
7	1	2	0
8	2	3	1
9	0	4	2
10	1	0	3
11	2	1	4
12	0	2	5
13	1	3	6
14	2	4	0
15	0	0	1
16	1	1	2
17	2	2	3
18	0	3	4
19	1	4	5
20	2	0	6

This property of uniqueness only works if the columns represent the remainders of co-prime numbers. If you delete the third column, and list instead the remainders left on dividing by 6 (the sequence 0, 1, 2, 3, 4, 5 . . .), you will find that the sets no longer uniquely identify a number. The problem is that 6 and 3 share a divisor.

At the very least you can see that given the remainders, it is always possible to find the original number. We need only look it up in this table. In practice, however, we cannot expect anyone playing Fibonacci's parlor game to keep such a long table in mind. We need a more general approach that can be worked out in numbers.

Let us assume that the secret number is n and the co-prime numbers we have chosen are a_p, b_p, and c_p. (Keep in mind that you could have used more than just three.) Also, assume that when we divide the secret number by these they leave the remainders a_r, b_r, and c_r. Finally, assume that the three associated multipliers are A, B, and C, which are computed as we showed above. Fibonacci and Sun Tzu found the number

$$N = A \cdot a_r + B \cdot b_r + C \cdot c_r$$

This number has a strange property. What do we get when we divide it by a_p? Obviously, a_p will divide the last two terms, since B and C were chosen specifically as multiples of a_p. So any remainder will be determined completely by the first term. Now A divided by a_p will leave a remainder of 1 (think of how we computed A), and therefore $A \cdot a_r$ will leave a remainder of a_r. Remember that the original secret number, n, also left a remainder of a_r when divided by a_p. Thus, we know that $(N-n)$ is evenly divisible by a_p. This may be a property of numbers that you have not heard of before, but you can find many examples: Both 18 and 8 leave a remainder of 3 when divided by 5, so the difference, $18 - 8$, is evenly divisible by 5.

What we have said about a_p may be said about the other divisors. Thus, we have:

$N - n$ is evenly divisible by a_p.
$N - n$ is evenly divisible by b_p.
$N - n$ is evenly divisible by c_p.

But a_p, b_p, and c_p are co-prime, so:

$N - n$ is evenly divisible by $(a_p \cdot b_p \cdot c_p)$

This, too, may be an unfamiliar property of numbers, but again, examples are easy to find. For example, 60 is evenly divisible by 2, 3, and 5, and since these numbers are co-prime, 60 is also divisible by $2 \cdot 3 \cdot 5 = 30$.

Now, obviously, when you divide N by $(a_p \cdot b_p \cdot c_p)$ you must get n as the remainder; and this was what Sun Tzu and Fibonacci both said.

MORE ON CO-PRIME NUMBERS

In Figure 101 is a 4 × 7 rectangle with the rows labeled from 0 to 3, and the columns labeled from 0 to 6. We have started putting the numbers 1 through 28 in the rectangle by starting in the upper left corner and proceeding by moving one square down and one square to the right. When this process takes us off the bottom of the rectangle (as happened with the number 5), we wrap around to the top; if it takes us off the right of the rectangle (as happens with the number 8) we wrap around to the left. Only part of the rectangle is filled. If you complete it, you can see that every number finds its way into a square.

4 and 7 are relatively prime, and all numbers between 1 and 28 will fit in a rectangle . . .

	0	1	2	3	4	5	6
0	1	9			5	13	
1		2	10			6	?
2			3	11			7
3	8			4	12		

. . . but 4 and 6 are not relatively prime. Where will 13 go?

	0	1	2	3	4	5
0	1		9		5	
1		2		10		6
2	7		3		11	
3		8		4		12

Figure 101.

Will this happen for rectangles of different sizes? Also in Figure 101 is a 4 × 6 rectangle, again with some numbers filled in. But this time when we get to the number 13, we should wrap our way around to the top and left and into the first cell—which is already taken. Why does the method work in one rectangle but not the other?

It is easy to see what is going on. By moving one down, one to the right we are recreating in a graphical way the remainders of each number when it is divided by the two dimensions of the rectangles. For example, in Figure 101 the number 15 will be placed in the cell at row 3, column 1. When divided by 4, its remainder is 3; when divided by 7, its remainder is 1. The method works only when the two dimensions of the rectangle are co-prime. The Chinese Remainder Theorem simply says that in this case a cell will hold one and only one number.

Fibonacci's guess-a-number game can be illustrated with a three-dimensional hexahedron, or six-sided solid. The dimensions of the solid are the three co-prime numbers chosen at the beginning. Start at a corner of the solid, and place the integers in it by moving one square down, one square to the right, one square back, and wrapping around a dimension when necessary. We are certain that all numbers will fit. When a secret number has been chosen, the three remainders left when the number is divided by the dimensions of the solid will pinpoint the number within the hexahedron.

(All of this is distantly related to magic squares. When numbers are placed in the *Lo Shu*, some numbers will collide. It is interesting to speculate that someone, while playing with magic squares, decided to try other dimensions in order to find a square in which collisions do not occur. Failing this, they moved on to rectangles. In time they developed a rule for the dimensions of collision-free rectangles. Thus, the Chinese Remainder Theorem. We do not know if this is the actual origin, but it is fascinating to think that the most important tool of number theory, like the Pythagorean theorem, may have started in a simple game.)

A more colorful example is illustrated in Figure 102. In the top portion, we give the four sides of a regular tetrahedron the numbers 1 through 4. Assume these numbers are inked, like a four-sided rubber stamp, then roll it about to stamp numbers on the plane. If we roll it back over the same area, the numbers will never mix. Of the regular solids, only the cube and octahedron will also cover the plane if rolled about. But the cube will definitely mix all its numbers. And the octahedron, if numbered in such a way that opposite sides sum to nine, will mix all even numbers, and all odd numbers, but never even and odd together. Why?

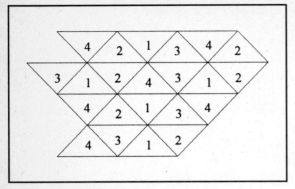

Figure 102. A tetrahedron never mixes numbers

Hint: Look at the number of faces that meet at a vertex on the solid and on the plane. For which solid are these two numbers co-prime?

VISIBLE POINTS ON A LATTICE

A lattice is an arrangement of dots sitting on the integer points of the x,y plane. This definition allows us to give the usual labels to the dots. In Figure 103, the two dark dots are $(1,2)$ and $(4,4)$. These dots are said to be mutually visible, since it is possible to join the two without passing through any other dot. Had we chosen $(2,2)$ and $(4,4)$ instead, the two dots would not be mutually visible.

In general, given the two dots (a,b) and (x,y), when are they visible, and when are they not? This problem is a little difficult to solve but very enjoyable. I will not give an answer, although a good start is to think in terms of co-prime numbers.

Figure 103. Mutually visible dots on a lattice

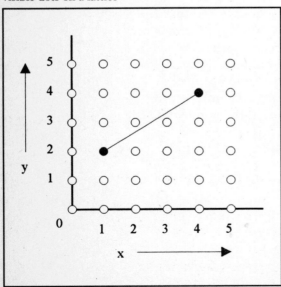

RABBITS AND BEES

Undoubtedly the most famous puzzle in the *Liber Abaci* is the Rabbit Problem. Over the years, it has been a source of some of the more fascinating pastimes in recreational mathematics, although it is doubtful that Fibonacci himself knew what he had stumbled upon. Here is the original problem along with Fibonacci's solution:

How many rabbits can be bred from one pair in one year?

A man has one pair of rabbits at a certain place entirely surrounded by a wall. We wish to know how many pairs can be bred from them in one year, if the nature of these rabbits is such that they breed every month one other pair and begin to breed in the second month after their birth.

Let the first pair breed a pair in the first month, then duplicate it and there will be 2 pairs in a month. From these pairs one, namely the first, breeds a pair in the second month. From these in one month two will become pregnant, so that in the third month 2 pairs of rabbits will be born. Thus there are 5 pairs in this month. From these in the same month 3 will be pregnant, so that in the fourth month there will be 8 pairs. From these pairs 5 will breed 5 other pairs, which added to the 8 pairs gives 13 pairs in the fifth month, from which 5 pairs (which were bred in that same month) will not conceive in that month, but the other 8 will be pregnant. Thus there will be 21 pairs in the sixth month. When we add to these the 13 pairs that are bred in the 7th month, then there will be in that month 34 pairs . . . [and so on 55, 89, 144, 233, 377 . . .] Finally there will be 377. And this number of pairs has been born from the first-mentioned pair at the given place in one year. You can see how we have done this, namely by combining the first number with the second, hence 1 and 2, and the second with the third, and the third with the fourth . . . At last we combine the 10th with the 11th, hence 144 with 233, and we have the sum of the above-mentioned rabbits, namely 377, and in this way you can do it for the case of infinite numbers of months.

This sequence of numbers is now universally called the Fibonacci sequence. The first two numbers in the sequence are equal to 1 and all subsequent numbers are equal to the sum of the previous two. According to one tradition, the numbers are labeled F_1, F_2, F_3, and so on, so that $F_n = F_{n-2} + F_{n-1}$. For reference the first several Fibonacci numbers are listed in Figure 104.

It is a simple matter to extend the sequence backward in order to find F_0, F_{-1}, F_{-2}, etc. What is F_0? According to our rule, we know that $F_1 + F_0$ must equal F_2; therefore, F_0 must be 0. Continuing this way, we get the full Fibonacci sequence:

$$. . . -8, 5, -3, 2, -1, 1, 0, 1, 1, 2, 3, 5, 8 . . .$$

The additive way that we generate the Fibonacci sequence indicates that it should be found somewhere in Chu Shih-chieh's triangle. And in

Figure 104. The first 50
Fibonacci numbers

N	The Nth Fibonacci Number	N	The Nth Fibonacci Number
1	1	26	121,393
2	1	27	196,418
3	2	28	317,811
4	3	29	514,229
5	5	30	832,040
6	8	31	1,346,269
7	13	32	2,178,309
8	21	33	3,524,578
9	34	34	5,702,887
10	55	35	9,227,465
11	89	36	14,930,352
12	144	37	24,157,817
13	233	38	39,088,169
14	377	39	63,245,986
15	610	40	102,334,155
16	987	41	165,580,141
17	1,597	42	267,914,296
18	2,584	43	433,494,437
19	4,181	44	701,408,733
20	6,765	45	1,134,903,170
21	10,946	46	1,836,311,903
22	17,711	47	2,971,215,073
23	28,657	48	4,807,526,976
24	46,368	49	7,778,742,049
25	75,025	50	12,586,269,025

fact it is easy to find there, although we must turn the triangle around slightly. In Figure 105, we give the triangle with its negative half. If you sum up the numbers in a diagonal, you get both parts of the Fibonacci sequence.

The sequence seems so strained and artificial that surely nothing useful can come from it. But surprisingly there are many phenomena in nature that are modeled by the sequence. In fact, Fibonacci himself just missed the boat in his story about rabbits breeding on schedule behind closed doors. He should have used bees instead. Ross Honsberger, a mathematician at the University of Waterloo, humorously describes the strange procreative behavior of the common honeybee:

One of [the honeybee's] distinguishing characteristics is a system of controlled reproduction. It seems that early in her career a queen

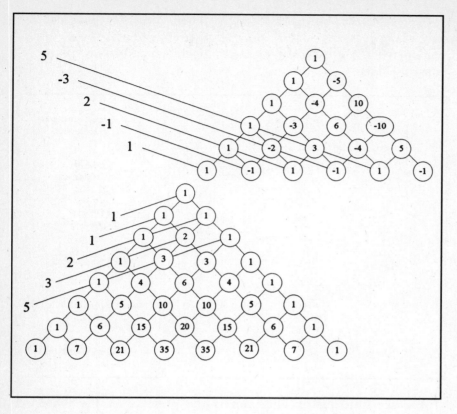

Figure 105. The Fibonacci numbers in Chu Shih-chieh's triangle

bee goes on a spree, collecting sperm from eager males who, I understand, immediately pass on to their reward (smiling, I trust). Now the queen bee produces many eggs, and it is the general rule that unfertilized eggs hatch into males and fertilized eggs into females. Thus male honeybees do not have fathers. The queen bee is able to store the collected sperm for months and even years and, upon information supplied by her attendants, she can regulate the gender of the offspring to meet the needs of the hive. Female bees are undoubtedly the superior sex; they do everything; in fact, the male's only function is in his role in the production of the prized female. There is no denying that we have here incontestable justification of the warning mothers have tried to pass on to their daughters since time immemorial—men are only good for at most one thing!

Figure 106 is a family tree for a hive of honeybees. The poor male has only one parent, 1 grandparent, 2 great-grandparents, 3 great-great-grandparents, 5 great-great-great-grandparents, and so on up the Fibonacci ladder.

Figure 106. The
generations of a honeybee

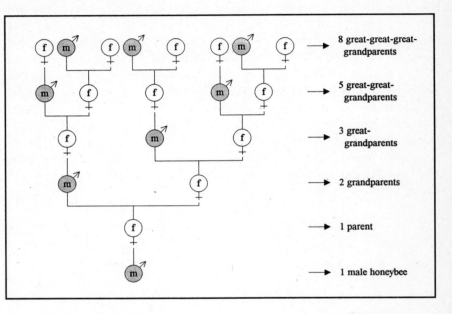

Another startling phenomenon is the presence of the Fibonacci sequence in phyllotaxis, or the arrangement of leaves on a stem. Figure 107 is a rather stylized drawing of a stem from the common cherry tree. Many stems like this can be found around your house. Notice that the leaves spiral around the stem as they move up. In the one pictured here, we must count five leaves and circle around the stem twice before we return to the same position on the stem. These two numbers form a fraction called the phyllotaxis:

Figure 107. Phyllotaxis on a cherry tree

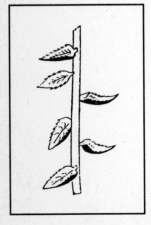

$$\frac{\text{Number of complete turns}}{\text{Number of leaves in a cycle}}$$

In Figure 107 the phyllotaxis is $2/5$. This will hold true for all stems on a cherry tree. In fact, every species holds strictly to a specific phyllotaxis. If you look at an elm tree you will find the phyllotaxis is $1/2$, meaning the leaves are found alternately on facing sides of the stem. On a pear tree it is $^3/_8$, and on the willow $^5/_{13}$. The numbers in every case throughout the plant kingdom are alternate numbers of the Fibonacci sequence. Is there evolutionary worth to this arrangement? We can only speculate, but probably the adherence to the Fibonacci sequence allows for the greatest amount of light to pass onto each leaf. If the phyllotaxis were some non-Fibonacci value, say $^5/_7$, then some leaves would be likely to block the sun from reaching other leaves.

The phyllotaxis ratio, and the Fibonacci sequence it is based on, has conditioned our sense of "natural beauty." If you were to draw a cherry tree stem similar to the one in Figure 107 but with a different, non-Fibonacci phyllotaxis, then it would look somewhat unnatural or lopsided. The same sense of naturalness can be found if we take the ratio of successive terms in the sequence. Such ratios are alternately greater than and less than the number phi, 1.61803398 . . . The following table shows this:

Less Than Phi	Greater Than Phi
$^1/_1 = 1.0000$	$^2/_1 = 2.0000$
$^3/_2 = 1.5000$	$^5/_3 = 1.6667$
$^8/_5 = 1.6000$	$^{13}/_8 = 1.6250$
$^{21}/_{13} = 1.6154$	$^{34}/_{21} = 1.6190$
$^{55}/_{34} = 1.6176$	$^{89}/_{55} = 1.6182$
$^{144}/_{89} = 1.6180$	$^{233}/_{144} = 1.6181$

As we proceed through the sequence the two sides of the table come to choke off at either side of the true value of phi, although we never quite get there. Like its cousin, pi, it is an irrational number. The easiest way to understand the number phi is to think of a stick marked off into two parts, the larger called x and the smaller called y, such that the ratio of the length of the whole stick to x is the same as the ratio of x to y. In numbers:

$$\frac{x + y}{x} = \frac{x}{y}$$

The ratio x/y is phi. What is the reciprocal of phi? It is simply phi − 1, or 0.61803398 . . . What is the square of phi? It is phi + 1, or 2.61803398 . . . Many people today—many mathematicians, in fact—believe that phi is the most pleasant ratio to behold, and they are all certain that this belief has an ancient pedigree behind it. Even careful writers repeat stories that great works of art, or certain ancient monuments, including the pyramids of Egypt, were constructed with phi in mind, but none of this is true.

NUMBER THEORY FOR AMATEURS

Some of the interesting characteristics of the Fibonacci sequence may not appear very obvious, and certainly they were not apparent to Fibonacci himself. For example, if a Fibonacci number is prime and greater than 4, then it must occupy a prime position. (Remember that a prime number is one that is evenly divisible only by itself and 1.) For example, 13 is a prime number, and it occupies F_7, and 7 is also prime. The converse is not necessarily true. That is, 31 is prime, but F_{31} is not; it equals $1,346,269 = 2417 \cdot 557$.

Another example: The sum of any 10 consecutive Fibonacci numbers will always be divisible by 11. For example,

$$3 + 5 + 8 + 13 + 21 + 34 + 55 + 89 + 144 + 233 = 605$$
$$\text{and } 605 = 11 \cdot 55.$$

Another example: Take any three consecutive terms in the sequence; then the product of the first and last of these three terms (that is, the terms of the phyllotaxis ratio) is equal to the square of the middle term plus or minus one. In symbols,

$$F_{n-1} \cdot F_{n+1} = F_n^2 \pm 1$$

This gives us:

$$3 \cdot 8 \ = 24 = 5^2 - 1$$
$$5 \cdot 13 = 65 = 8^2 + 1$$

Another example, this one somewhat more complicated but quite close to a serious problem in number theory: Let p be any prime number. Then, if p is of the form $(10k \pm 1)$, $F_p = ap + 1$. And if p is of the form $(10k \pm 3)$, $F_p = bp - 1$. In both cases, a and b are arbitrary integers. Once again, the converse is not true. Some examples will make this clear. Below we have some prime numbers of the form $(10k\pm1)$, then the associated Fibonacci number, and its expansion:

p = $(10k\pm1)$	F_p	=	Expansion
11	89	=	$11 \cdot 8 + 1$
19	4181	=	$19 \cdot 220 + 1$
29	514229	=	$29 \cdot 17732 + 1$
31	1346269	=	$31 \cdot 43428 + 1$

Next we do the same for some prime numbers of the form $(10k\pm3)$:

p = $(10k\pm3)$	F_p	=	Expansion
7	13	=	$7 \cdot 2 - 1$
13	233	=	$13 \cdot 18 - 1$
17	1597	=	$17 \cdot 94 - 1$
23	28657	=	$23 \cdot 1246 - 1$

Examples like this can be multiplied virtually endlessly. The sequence, in fact, is a kind of arithmetic system all to itself, in which anyone can prove interesting and sometimes quite useful theorems—somewhat like number theory for amateurs. For your benefit, I will begin a little system of theories below. Throughout, you can gain a sense of the thrill of discovery that professional number theorists achieve. Pay particular attention to the way one theorem builds on top of another.

Theorem 1: (Special Addition Theorem)

The sum of the first n Fibonacci numbers equals $F_{n+2} - 1$. That is, it equals the Fibonacci number just two past the end of the sequence in question, minus 1.

Proof: The defining characteristic of the Fibonacci series is that $F_n = F_{n-1} + F_{n-2}$. We can rewrite this as $F_{n-2} = F_n - F_{n-1}$. For example, $F_7 = F_9 - F_8$ or $13 = 34 - 21$. Now assume we want to add up the first 5 Fibonacci numbers, which we write below, along with their expansion. (For the moment, ignore the fact that some terms are canceled.)

$$1 \quad F_1 = F_3 - F_2$$
$$1 \quad F_2 = F_4 - F_3$$
$$2 \quad F_3 = F_5 - F_4$$
$$3 \quad F_4 = F_6 - F_5$$
$$5 \quad F_5 = F_7 - F_6$$

The sum of the first column is the same as the sum of the third column, but in this third column there are several terms that can be eliminated: The F_3's cancel out, and the F_4's, and so on. In fact, every number cancels out except two, which leaves us with $F_7 - F_2$, or since $F_2 = 1$, $F_7 - 1$. In our example, the sum of F_1 through F_5 is $F_7 - 1$, or simply $13 - 1 = 12$. Obviously, this can be generalized to prove our theorem.

Theorem 2: (General Addition Theorem)

The sum of any sequence of n Fibonacci numbers, F_r to F_{r+n-1}, will be equal to $F_{r+n+1} - F_{r+1}$.

This sounds complicated, so an example is in order. Take any set of consecutive Fibonacci numbers, not necessarily beginning with the first as we did with the first theorem, and the sum of these numbers can be found as follows: Find the Fibonacci number that is two further down in the sequence, then subtract from it the second number in the sequence. Consider the sequence between F_7 and F_{12}:

$$13 + 21 + 34 + 55 + 89 + 144 = 356$$

The Fibonacci number that is two terms further down the road is F_{14}, which is 377. Now subtract the second term in the original sequence, that is F_8, which is 21. This gives us 356, the correct sum. Notice this theorem holds true even if the sequence begins with the first term, so it makes a special case of our first theorem.

Proof: Consider two strings in the Fibonacci sequence, both starting with the first term. The first string goes up to F_{r-1}, the second goes up to F_{r+n-1}. Obviously the sequence in question is the difference between these two. In our example, we actually took the first twelve Fibonacci numbers and subtracted out the first six Fibonacci numbers. This left us with the string from F_7 to F_{12}. Thus we have in general:

$$(\text{Sum from } F_r \text{ to } F_{r+n-1}) =$$
$$(\text{Sum from } F_1 \text{ to } F_{r+n-1}) -$$
$$(\text{Sum from } F_1 \text{ to } F_{r-1})$$

By theorem 1, we have:

$$(\text{Sum from } F_r \text{ to } F_{r+n-1}) =$$
$$(F_{r+n+1} - 1) - (F_{r+1} - 1) =$$
$$(F_{r+n+1} - F_{r+1})$$

which proves our theorem.

Theorem 3: (The Distribution of Fibonacci Numbers)

Let n be any integer. Then between successive powers of n, there can be at most n Fibonacci numbers.

This, too, calls for an example. Let n be 4. Then between 4^2 and 4^3, or between 4^7 and 4^8, or in general between 4^k and 4^{k+1}, there can be at most only 4 Fibonacci numbers.

Proof: Assume the opposite, that is, between n^k and n^{k+1} there are $n + 1$ Fibonacci numbers, and let these be the numbers from F_{r+1} to F_{r+n+1} inclusive. (Notice there are $n+1$ numbers here). A mathematician would write:

$$n^k < F_{r+1}, F_{r+2} \cdots F_{r+n+1} < n^{k+1}$$

We wish to prove that this assumption will lead to a contradiction. Consider first the sum of the first $n - 1$ of these. We already know how to find this by Theorem 2:

$$F_{r+1} + F_{r+2} + \ldots + F_{r+n-1} = F_{r+n+1} - F_{r+2}$$

Now it is simple algebra to solve for F_{r+n+1} to get:

$$F_{r+n+1} = (F_{r+1} + F_{r+2} + \ldots + F_{r+n-1}) + F_{r+2}$$

Each of these terms is greater than n^k, by assumption, and there are n of these terms. Therefore:

$$F_{r+n+1} > n(n^k)$$
$$\text{or:}\quad F_{r+n+1} > n^{k+1}$$

which contradicts our initial assumption, and therefore proves our theorem.

This type of system can be built to any level of difficulty you wish to take it. Some of the theorems will be quite trivial, but others, such as our theorem 3, can border on fairly significant number theory. All of it points to the type of system building that professional mathematicians rejoice in.

The reader may have noticed that there was nothing in our proofs that assumed the first two numbers in our sequence were 1's. In fact this is not at all necessary! You can begin with any two numbers whatsoever to produce a General Fibonacci Sequence. You can see from this why our system of theorems was not all that trivial, since the theories refer to *any sequence of numbers that follows the Fibonacci pattern*. One can produce a trick of lightning calculation based on these theorems. For example, what is the sum of

$$5 + 32 + 37 + 69 + 106 + 175 +$$
$$281 + 456 + 737 + 1193 + 1930 + 3123$$

The terms above are the first terms of the General Fibonacci Sequence that begins 5, 32, and so on. So I used theorem 2 above, and continued the sequence for two more terms to get 8176, then subtracted the second term, 32, to get the answer: 8144.

PARTITIONING PENNIES

I have in my hand five pennies, and I partition them into piles of 1 and 2. In how many different ways can I do this? I can make piles of (2-2-1) or piles of (2-1-2), which I consider a *different* partitioning, and I can make piles of (1-1-1-2). I do not care that in some cases I have more piles than in others. I simply want to know the total number of distinct configurations. After a little head scratching I find I can make 8 different configurations in all, which I believe is exhaustive.

(1-2-2)	(1-1-2-1)
(2-1-2)	(1-2-1-1)
(1-1-1-2)	(2-1-1-1)
(2-2-1)	(1-1-1-1-1)

Given *n* pennies, in how many ways can I partition them into piles of 1 and 2?

MĀTRĀ-VṚTTAS AND GANITA KAUMUDI

Here is a very roundabout way of anwering that. *Mātrā-vṛttas* is a style of Sanskrit poetry that has no direct counterpart in European languages because of broad linguistic differences. Any example would miss the point, but it serves our purposes to say that the meters of *Mātrā-vṛttas* all have the same number of accents, while the number of syllables is allowed to vary. An accent may be light (*laghu*) or heavy (*guru*). The light accents we will symbolize as "1" and the heavy as "2." This translation into numbers is appropriate, since Indian poets sometimes play a combinatorial game in their verses. In *Mātrā-vṛttas*, if all meters are to have five accents, then some sample meters may run 2-2-1 or 2-1-2 or 1-1-1-2. All are acceptable because the total number of accents, found by summing the digits, is a constant 5, even though the first two meters have three syllables while the last has four. An early issue among Indian poets was: If a poem is restricted to meters of *n* accents, how many distinct meters are possible? The answer is F_{n+1}. For example, of meters with five accents there are exactly F_6, or 8.

This fact was known to Indian poets perhaps as early as 700 B.C. Furthermore, the poets had worked out a scheme for generating all the meters with a given number of accents. Let us say we want a list of all meters with six accents. We can poke about haphazardly, as I did with my pennies, but we will never be sure our list is complete. If instead we already have a list of all meters with four accents, we can append a *guru* (that is, a "2") onto each of these; and if we had a list of 5 accents, we can append a *laghu* (a "1") onto each of these. The combined list is our desired set, since it must be an exhaustive list of all meters of six accents exactly. If we do not have at our disposal the previous sets of four- and five-accented meters, then we build these the same way. The general approach of building on what comes before is nowadays called a "recursive algorithm."

An example will make everything clear. It is trivial to generate sets of meters with one and two accents. These are, respectively, {(1)} and {(2), (1−1)}. From these we generate meters with three accents by appending the appropriate *laghu* and *guru*:

(1)	➜	(1-*2*)
(2)	➜	(2-*1*)
(1-1)	➜	(1-1-*1*)

And now meters with four accents:

(2)	➜	(2-*2*)
(1-1)	➜	(1-1-*2*)
(1-2)	➜	(1-2-*1*)
(2-1)	➜	(2-1-*1*)
(1-1-1)	➜	(1-1-1-*1*)

In both cases, the italicized numbers are the *laghu* and *guru* that we have appended. If you count the number of meters in each set you will find you have 1, 2, 3, 5, 8, 13, 21 . . . and so on up the Fibonacci (or should we say Hindu) ladder. (F_1 is missing; perhaps the poets could say this is a meter with no accent.) The Indian scheme essentially creates a new set by combining two previous sets—a direct application of the Fibonacci principle.

I have symbolized the *laghu* and *guru* as "1" and "2" in order to show how Sanskrit poetry answers the question about pennies. If I have *n* pennies, then I can partition them into piles of 1 and 2 in exactly F_{n+1} ways. It is natural to generalize this question. If you have *n* pennies again, in how many ways can you partition them into piles of 3, 2, and 1? In how many ways can you partition them into piles of 4, 3, 2, and 1? I will not answer this for you, at least not directly, although hints follow shortly.

Figure 108 is a table of partitions for one, two, three, four, and five pennies. In each case, the partitioning is done into piles of 1 and 2. Of course, it is also a list of Sanskrit meters with the same number of accents.

1 Penny	2 Pennies	3 Pennies	4 Pennies	5 Pennies
(1)	(2)	(1-2)	(2-2)	(1-2-2)
	(1-1)	(2-1)	(1-1-2)	(2-1-2)
		(1-1-1)	(1-2-1)	(1-1-1-2)
			(2-1-1)	(2-2-1)
			(1-1-1-1)	(1-1-2-1)
				(1-2-1-1)
				(2-1-1-1)
				(1-1-1-1-1)

Figure 108. Table of partitions

Some time after Fibonacci—and independently of him—we find in India a complete generalization of this number sequence. The *Ganita Kaumudi* explains the construction of what it calls the "additive sequence":

> First keeping unity twice, write their sum ahead. Write ahead of that the sum of numbers from the reverse order [and in] places equal to the greatest digit. In the absence of [numbers in] places equal to the greatest digit, write ahead the sum of those [in available places].

That may seem a little cryptic, but it is really quite simple. It explains how to construct an infinity of "additive sequences" of which the Fibonacci sequence is a special case. Every sequence is defined by its "greatest digit," which we will call q. Let us say we want to construct the sequence for which $q = 3$. We begin, as always, by "keeping unity twice"—that is, with 1, 1. Now, to get the next digit, we sum the previous 3 digits (this is because $q = 3$). If 3 digits are not yet present, then sum as many as you have. The complete sequence for $q = 3$ is 1, 1, 2, 4, 7, 13 . . . (We now call this rather fancifully the Tribonacci sequence.) Or if we set $q = 4$, we get 1, 1, 2, 4, 8, 15, 28 . . . (the so-called Tetranacci sequence). The orginal Fibonacci sequence is just the case in which $q = 2$. Do the Tribonacci and Tetranacci sequences answer the paritioning problem mentioned earlier?

THE INDIAN MOUNTAIN AND THE CHINESE TRIANGLE

Let us look again at Figure 108. Under the column for five pennies, we find there is 1 partition of five piles, namely (1-1-1-1-1); 4 partitions of four piles, namely (1-1-1-2), (1-1-2-1), (1-2-1-1), and (2-1-1-1); and 3 partitions of three piles, namely (1-2-2), (2-1-2), (2-2-1). Is there any rule to this?

Yes, and it was well worked out in India in a mountain of numbers called the *mātrā-meru*. (In Hindu mythology, the *meru* is the mountain at the center of the earth.) It is made up of two rows of one cell, two rows of two cells, two rows of three, two rows of four, and so on. In Figure 109(a), we have built a mountain of ten rows altogether, but it is easily extended.

The last cell in each row is "1." The first cell in each odd-numbered row is "1." The first cell in even rows is, beginning at the top, "1," "2," "3," "4," and so on. The inside cells are more cumbersome to find. In the even-numbered rows an inside cell is equal to the cell above it plus the cell above that and to the right. In the odd-numbered rows, an inside cell is equal to the cell above and to the left plus the cell above that and to the right. Figure 109a shows the two types of twisting paths that an inside cell takes for rows 10 and 7.

This Indian mountain is actually the Chinese triangle rotated 45 degrees. To see the similarities, Figure 109(b) pushes the rows of the "*meru*" so that its cells are aligned on the right. Each column in this shifted mountain is identical to a side in the Chinese triangle.

The *meru*, however, is more convenient to use when dealing with Fibonacci numbers. The sum of the digits in each row produces the Fibonacci sequence. The digits themselves break down the corresponding Fibonacci number into a count of the different partitions. For example, the sixth row corresponds to $F_6 = 8$. This means that, for example, five pennies can be partitioned into 8 different piles of 1 and 2. But the *meru* breaks down this Fibonacci number into $1 + 4 + 3$, showing that there will be 1 partition of five piles; 4 partitions of four piles; and 3 partitions of three piles. Exactly what we saw above.

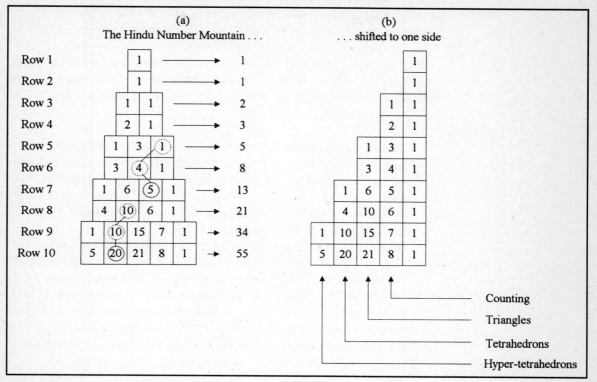

Figure 109.

THE ORIGINATORS AND THE BENEFICIARIES

IT IS USELESS, MY SON. I HAVE READ ARISTOTLE THROUGH

TWICE AND HAVE FOUND NOTHING ABOUT SPOTS ON THE SUN.

THERE ARE NO SPOTS ON THE SUN. THEY ARISE EITHER FROM

IMPERFECTIONS OF YOUR TELESCOPE OR FROM DEFECTS IN

YOUR EYES.

—AN UNNAMED SEVENTEENTH-CENTURY JESUIT PROFESSOR

It is probably safe to say that Western Europeans were dragged kicking and screaming into the modern world. Time and again we find a stubborn thick-headedness that cannot be found among other people. Can one imagine, for example, the Chinese saying sunspots do not exist simply because Confucius does not mention them? Yet such an attitude can be found frequently in the West. Even as late as 1612, when Galileo had actually observed the satellites of Jupiter, we find a Florentine astronomer writing:

> There are seven windows given to animals through which the air is admitted to the tabernacle of the body, to enlighten, to warm and to nourish it. What are these parts of the microcosms? Two nostrils, two eyes, two ears and a mouth. So in the heavens, as in a microcosm, there are two favorable stars, two unpropitious, two luminaries, and Mercury undecided and indifferent. From this and many other similarities in nature, such as the seven metals, et cetera, which it were tedious to enumerate, we gather that the number of planets is necessarily seven. Moreover, these satellites of Jupiter are invisible to the naked eye and therefore would be useless and therefore do not exist. Besides, the Jews and other ancient nations, as well as modern Europeans, have adopted the division of the week into seven days and have named them after the seven planets. Now if we increase the number of planets, this whole and beautiful system falls to the ground.

It is such a common phenomenon that one might call it a "law" of history: The originators are seldom the beneficiaries of their own work. On moral grounds alone, we may argue with that law, but it is a law all the same. The booty always goes to those who look on until all the hard work is done. When one considers how late the Europeans came into their own, that description seems quite fitting: people who looked on. You cannot escape the conclusion that all the real work was done by others, especially the Chinese and Egyptians, and even this had to be developed by the Arabs. What was presented to the Europeans was a finished product, a gift more valuable than anything owned by their predecessors. Yet when this gift was laid, unpaid for, on their doorstep, the Europeans largely ignored it. The irony, of course, is that today, and at least for the near future, this same Europe is seen by much of the world as the true originators.

In fairness, never before did any one people go as far as the western Europeans in their pursuit of science, nor in the openness with which they shared it. They developed their gifts to an extent unimagined previously, and turned it into a completely rational system, unencumbered by inept superstitions.

Graphs and Puzzles

IGURE 110 IS A VARIATION OF CHECKERS. ONE PLAYER PLACES a black marker in cell 2. The opponent places a red marker in cell 4. The two players then take turns moving their markers along the edges of the game board until one player takes the other's marker by moving into the same cell. What is the best strategy to follow? Can you see which player is assured of winning in seven moves or less, whether the player moves first or second?

The trick is to realize that the board is made up almost entirely of diamonds, although they have been stretched out of recognition. You can see one of the diamonds by starting at cell 4 and walking across four edges back to 4 again. All of the other cells, except 1 and 3, belong to similar diamond shapes.

Black is assured of winning if he always moves into a cell diametrically opposite the one occupied by Red. Red can then either move along the same diamond—in which case Black will take him on his next move—or go to a different diamond, in which case Black will follow again to the opposite cell. In this last case, Red faces the same two alternatives. Within seven moves, however, Red will be chased into a cell that has only two edges, in which case he is stuck.

What if Black moves first? In this case, Red has the opportunity of running away. Black's best strategy then is to "forfeit" his first move. Notice that to go from cell 2 to 3 requires only one move, but Black can do it in two by moving first to cell 1 and then taking the long edge around to 3. Essentially, by doing in two moves what he could have done in one, Black has positioned himself in second place. He can then follow the strategy above.

This strategy depends solely on the connections of edges and nodes on the board. It does not matter whether we stretch an edge so that it does not appear straight, or if we distort the entire board so that the diamond-shaped cells appear less like diamonds. As long as its "connectedness" remains intact, the strategy will work. Conversely, if we cut an edge so that two nodes, once connected, are now free of each other, or if we join two nodes that were once unconnected, the strategy will fail us.

When we are interested only in the connectedness of a figure, we call the figure a graph. Its geometric properties—such as its perimeter or its area—are of no interest whatsoever. In fact, we are free to change these at will by stretching and shrinking the figure. Although graph theory is a relatively new invention, there are many ancient puzzles built on a graph, perhaps the earliest being the etches that we saw on the temple at Kurna.

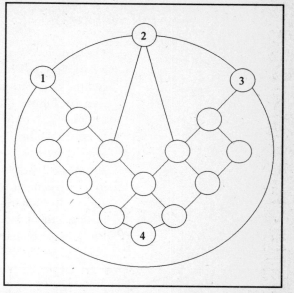

Figure 110. Can player 2 win in seven moves or less?

SEVEN BRIDGES

The great beauty of a graph is its ability to reduce cloudy, ill-formed puzzles into a wonderfully physical matter of lines and nodes. Here is such a puzzle. Consider all the people of the world. Some have shaken hands an odd number of times—call them type-O people—and others have shaken hands an even number of times—type-E people. Can you prove that at any given moment the number of type-O people must always be even? Surely not much can be said to answer this. Every nanosecond two people shake hands somewhere in the world and both will change their types. But really the problem is quite simple, and we will answer it shortly.

First, however, we can look at the problem that virtually started all of graph theory. This is the problem of the Seven Bridges of Königsberg. It was a game once played by the children of Königsberg while crossing the seven bridges, but it became famous when it attracted the attention of the prolific mathematician Leonhard Euler. Here is how Euler described it:

> The problem, supposedly quite well known, was as follows: At Königsberg in Prussia there is an island *A*, called "der Kneiphof," and the river surrounding it is divided into two branches as can be seen [in Figure 111]. Over the branches of this river lead seven bridges . . . Now the question is whether one can plan a walk so as to cross each bridge once and not more than once. I was told that some deny this possibility, others are doubtful, but that nobody affirms it. Wherefrom I formulated the following problem, framed in a very general way for myself. Whatever the shape of the river and its division into branches may be, and whatever the number of bridges, to find out whether it is possible or not to cross each bridge exactly once.

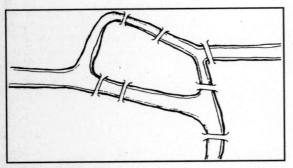

Figure 111. Euler's Seven Bridges of Königsberg

Obviously, the length of the bridges, or their distances from each other, does not change the nature of the problem. We are only concerned with the way they are connected to the islands—that is, we are only interested in the graph that they represent. In fact, it is easy to think of the problem as a simple paper-and-pencil game, dispensing with the bridges altogether. As a graph, the seven bridges of Königsberg are identical to the first drawing in Figure 112. Can this, or any of the others, be traced in a single stroke of the pencil without retracing any of the lines, in the way that the residents of Königsberg had to walk the bridges without retracing a step?

What you are trying to find is now universally called an Euler walk, and it is easy to show that none exists in the first graph above. Look at the nodes in any one of the graphs. Either they are even (they connect an even number of edges) or they are odd (they connect an odd number of edges). Assume a graph has an Euler walk; then every time you enter a node, you must be able to leave it—that is, every node must be even. The only exceptions to this are two nodes that *may* be odd, and in this case you must begin and end your walk at these nodes. Thus, in general, a graph will have an Euler walk only if the number of odd edges is either

0 or 2. More specifically, there will be a closed Euler walk (that is, you can return to the node of origin) if the number of odd edges is 0, and there will be an open Euler walk (that is, you cannot return to the node of origin) if the number of odd edges is 2.

The two other graphs in Figure 112 have respectively an open and a closed Euler walk, which the reader can easily find. The middle, of course, is a well-known figure played in many Western nations. More than likely it originated from the Königsberg problem. Quite typically, it is an open Euler walk, which is more difficult and therefore more entertaining than the closed variety.

The last is a rather intricate closed Euler graph similar to many found throughout Africa as a symbol of the seamless and eternal recurrence of life. The one shown here is perhaps the most interesting example; it is drawn by the storytellers of Angola while reciting the following gentle "fall-from-Eden" story (the story is repeated in Claudia Zaslavsky's book *Africa Counts*):

> At one time the Sun went to pay his respects to God. He walked and walked until he found the path which led to God. He presented himself to God, who gave him a cock and said to him: "See me in the morning before you leave." In the morning the cock crowed and woke up the Sun, who then went to see God. God said: "I heard the cock crow, the one I gave you for supper. You may keep him, but you must return every morning." This is why the Sun encircles the earth and appears every morning.
>
> The Moon also went to visit God, was

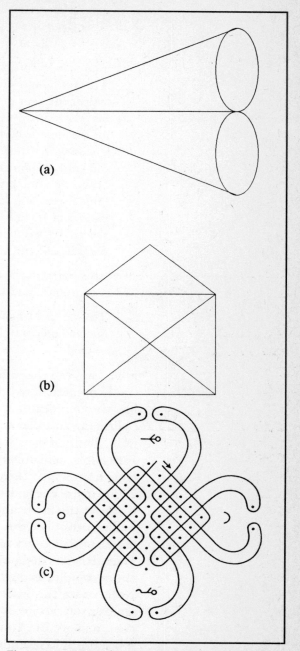

(a)

(b)

(c)

Figure 112. Which figure has an Euler walk? (Figure c reprinted from Zaslavsky, 1973)

given a cock, who also woke him up in the morning. So God said: "I see that you also did not eat the cock I gave you for supper. That is all right. But come back to see me every twenty-eight days."

And man in turn went to see God, and was given a cock. But he was very hungry after his long voyage and ate part of the cock for supper and kept the rest for his return trip. The next morning the Sun was already high in the sky when our man awoke. He quickly ate the remains of the cock and hurried to his divine host. God said to him with a smile: "What about the cock I gave you yesterday? I did not hear him crow in the morning." The man became fearful. "I was very hungry and ate him." "That is all right," said God, "But listen: You know that Sun and Moon have been here, but neither of them killed the cock I gave them. That is why they themselves will never die. But you killed yours, and so you must die as he did. But at your death you must return here." And so it is.

At this point in the story the lovely network at the bottom of Figure 112 is complete, and the storyteller explains its meaning:

The top of the figure is God, the bottom is man, on the left is the Sun and on the right is the Moon. The path is the path that leads to God.

Perhaps the closed Euler walk in the figure is meant to represent the single uninterrupted path of a human being, leading from God, into life, through death, and back to God again.

Proving an Euler walk exists is not the same as actually finding the walk. The best way to do the latter is to begin at a node and walk as far as possible, remembering to cross no edge twice. You will arrive at a node from which there is no valid exit. If you have not exhausted the graph, one of the nodes in your walk will be part of the uncrossed edges. Begin at this node and walk across the uncovered edges for a second walk. Then splice this path into the previous one. Repeat the process if there are still edges left uncovered. Eventually, the walk is complete. The method is demonstrated in the open Euler walk in Figure 113 in a figure complex enough to get lost in if not approached systematically. Notice that the walk begins at an odd node, as it must, and ends prematurely at the second odd node. The remaining nodes are now even, and we can conduct a closed walk across them, which is then spliced in to the original.

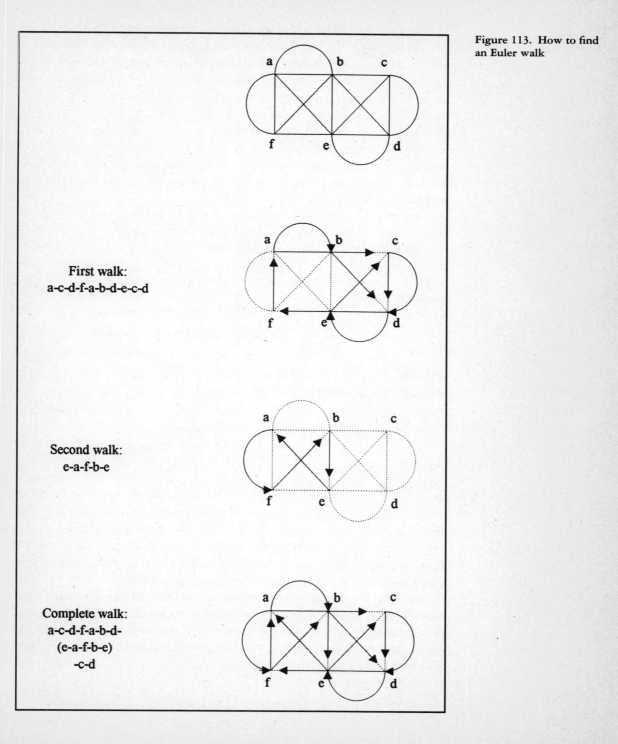

Figure 113. How to find
an Euler walk

First walk:
a-c-d-f-a-b-d-e-c-d

Second walk:
e-a-f-b-e

Complete walk:
a-c-d-f-a-b-d-
(e-a-f-b-e)
-c-d

The analysis can be made more complete. If a graph has more than two odd nodes it can not have an Euler walk of any kind, either open or closed. The graph, however, can be traced in two or more *distinct* lines. The exact number of lines needed is always half the number of odd nodes in the graph, and each line must begin and end at one of the odd nodes. This is a more general rule, which encompasses everything else that has been said. Thus, if a network has six odd nodes, three lines are needed to cover all the edges. If it has two odd vertices, one line is needed, as we have seen. And if there are zero odd vertices, no line is needed—which in some sense is true, since the path that is finally mapped out will circle back on itself.

This rule assumes that the number of odd vertices in a network is always even. Is this true? Yes, and the proof shows how it is possible to speak with a kind of mathematical rigor about figures that stretch and shrink at will. Let E_1 be the number of nodes that connect only one edge, E_2 the number that connect two edges, and so on. Then the number

$$(1 \cdot E_1) + (2 \cdot E_2) + (3 \cdot E_3) + (4 \cdot E_4) \ldots$$

must be even since it counts each edge twice, at its starting and ending node. Now consider the number

$$(2 \cdot E_1) + (2 \cdot E_2) + (4 \cdot E_3) + (4 \cdot E_4) \ldots$$

This must also be even, since every term in it has an even factor. Now subtract the first number from the second to get:

$$E_1 + E_3 + E_5 \ldots$$

This, of course, is the number of odd vertices in a network. It must be even, since it is the difference of two even numbers.

And this, if you missed it, is the answer to our hand-shaking problem above. Think of the people of the world as nodes on a page. When two people shake hands, draw an edge between the two nodes. The type-E people are the even nodes and the type-O people are the odd nodes. We have just shown that the number of type-O people in the world will always be even.

ONE-WAY ROAD SIGNS

The graphs in Figure 114 differ from others in that they are directed. This is why arrows have been placed on the edges: we should interpret these to mean that one may walk along the edge in only the indicated direction. Obeying these one-way signs, can you find an Euler walk in the first graph? How about the second? Can you find a general rule? We will use this rule in a later section on Memory Wheels.

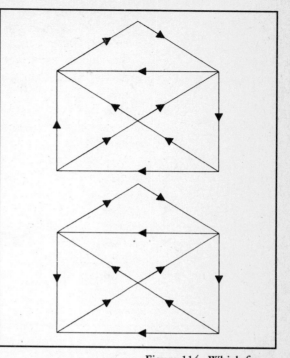

Figure 114. Which figure has a one-way Euler walk?

THE HIGHWAY INSPECTOR AND THE TRAVELING SALESMAN

In 1859 the mathematician William Hamilton invented a game that he called "Around the World," which, because of very close but very misleading similarities, is always mentioned immediately after Euler's problem of the seven bridges. He marketed the game originally as a regular dodecahedron (a twelve-sided solid) but played this way the game is very easy to solve (he never made much money on it). Instead we will use the two graphs in Figure 115.

Is it possible to travel along the edges of either graph in such a way that we pass each of the nodes exactly once? If so, and if you can return to the original node, then the path is called a closed Hamilton walk, and if you cannot return to the original node this way, it is called an open Hamilton walk.

This is very similar to the two types of Euler walks. Sherman K. Stein of the University of California called Euler's problem the "Problem of the Highway Inspector" who does not want to travel down the same road twice. And Hamilton's problem is the "Problem of the Traveling Salesman" who does not want to visit the same town twice. But the nature of the two puzzles should not be confused. In the Euler puzzle, we are to travel down every *edge* exactly once, and it is allowable to pass a node any number of times. In the Hamilton puzzle, we are to travel to every *node* exactly once, and it is allowable to skip an edge if necessary.

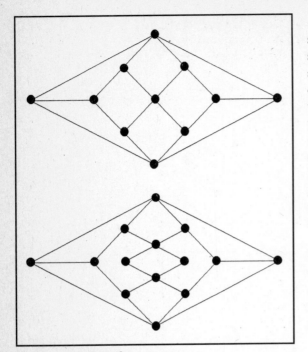

Figure 115. Which figure has a Hamilton walk?

But the most important distinction is a very sad one: The question of which graphs will have a Hamilton walk of either kind is still unanswered. Given a graph, I can tell you immediately whether or not it has an Euler walk, and whether that walk is open or closed. I can tell you this even before I have found the walk. I need do nothing more than count the number of nodes that have an odd number of edges leading from them. But consider again the two graphs above in Figure 115. They look very similar, yet one has an open Hamilton walk, the other has no Hamilton walk whatsoever.

If you found which is which, you have done so by tedious inspection. There is really no other way. We have only two theories to help us, both of which are clumsy and uninformative. Assume we have a graph before us and let the number of nodes be called n, and let the degree of a node be the number of edges meeting there. Then:

1) A graph has an open Hamilton walk if the sum of the degrees of every pair of nodes is at least $n - 1$.

2) A graph has a closed Hamilton walk if the sum of the degrees of every pair of nodes is at least n.

These two theories are almost laughably overstated. They are sufficient to guarantee a Hamilton walk, but they are by no means necessary. That is, if the theories are true for a graph, then the graph has a Hamilton walk, but even if they do not hold true there might still be such a walk. Also, do not be impressed by the precise terminology. They both really only say that if there are a good many edges evenly dispersed across the nodes, then there must be a Hamilton walk.

HAMILTON, EULER, AND YAMÁTÁRÁJABHÁNASALAGÁM

Although the Hamilton and Euler walks are wholly unrelated, the two come together as different views of an interesting problem called the Memory Wheel.

Consider the two digits 0 and 1. There are four distinct couplets we can get from these: 00, 01, 10, and 11. The most compact way to remember all four couplets is to write them within a "memory wheel," as is done in the top of Figure 116.

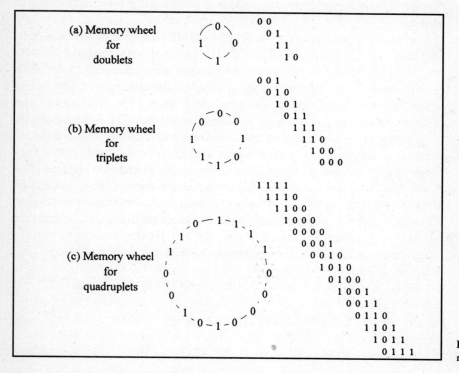

(a) Memory wheel
for
doublets

0 0
0 1
1 1
1 0

(b) Memory wheel
for
triplets

0 0 1
0 1 0
1 0 1
0 1 1
1 1 1
1 1 0
1 0 0
0 0 0

(c) Memory wheel
for
quadruplets

1 1 1 1
1 1 1 0
1 1 0 0
1 0 0 0
0 0 0 0
0 0 0 1
0 0 1 0
1 0 1 0
0 1 0 0
1 0 0 1
0 0 1 1
0 1 1 0
1 1 0 1
1 0 1 1
0 1 1 1

Figure 116. The first three memory wheels

Start at the twelve o'clock position and take the first two digits to find the first couplet, 00. Now move one digit, and take the next two to find the second couplet, 01. Moving on like this it is possible to find all four. Thus, the wheel is a very simple aid to memory.

There are two points to a memory wheel that must be kept in mind. First, there can be no wasted digits; that is, every possible couplet in a wheel must be distinct. Second, it must loop back on itself; that is, the digit that begins a wheel must be the first digit in the first couplet, as well as the last digit in the last couplet. Perhaps an easier way to understand the wheel is by stretching out the couplets, as is also done in Figure 116. Notice that the couplets have been so arranged that the last digit of one is the first digit of the next; this assures our first point, that we do not waste any. Notice also that the line can be made continuous, so the last digit of the last couplet is also the first digit of the first couplet; this assures our second point, that it loops back on itself. Thus, the problem of creating a memory wheel is essentially a matter of writing all couplets, and then rearranging them in a chained format.

Can we do the same for triplets instead? Yes. The memory wheel in this case is in the middle of Figure 116, and next to it we have written the chain of triplets. Notice now that the last *two* digits of a triplet must match the first two of the following triplet. Also in Figure 116 is the wheel and associated string of quadruplets. To see the difficulty in the problem, you may try to create a wheel for quintuplets and sextuplets.

In general, for any length n, there will be 2^n n-tuplets. These must be chained so that the last $n - 1$ digits of a tuplet match the first $n - 1$ digits of the following tuplet. The memory wheel that we get from the chain will have $n + 2^n - 1$ digits. You can see in this the great space-saving advantage of a memory wheel. Consider, for example, octuplets. There are 256 of these, producing a total of 2048 digits. A memory wheel compresses this into only 263 digits.

Of course, the interesting question is, Can we produce wheels like this for all possible n-tuplets? One approach to the problem, surprisingly, is the Hamilton walk. This is illustrated in Figure 117, for the wheel of triplets. In the figure, we list all possible triplets of digits on the nodes of a graph, and we draw lines between nodes that are possible successors. The lines in this case are directed, since we are not free to go backward. For example, from 001 we draw lines to 010 and 011, since both of these could come after 001 in our listing. We need only find a Hamilton walk on this graph and call out the nodes as we follow it in order to create our memory wheel.

This does not really answer our question. We have only translated it into a different question of Hamilton walks, which is not very useful, since the Hamilton walk has not been solved for general graphs. But fortunately we can also translate the problem into an Euler walk, which is much simpler to solve. The translation is surprisingly easy. In Figure 117, the nodes were the triplets, and the roads were the overlapping digits. In Figure 118 the roads are the triplets, and the nodes are the overlapping digits. Notice that between the nodes 10 and 00 there is a road marked 100, since this is the triplet that goes from one to the other.

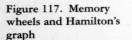

Figure 117. Memory wheels and Hamilton's graph

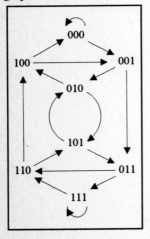

Once again, the lines are directed because we can only go in a certain direction. But if you solved the previous puzzle, you would know that a directed graph has an Euler walk if at each node the number of edges exiting is equal to the number of edges entering. This will give us a closed walk. If instead there are exactly two nodes that break this rule, one of which has one more edge exiting than entering, and the other has one more edge entering than exiting, then the walk is open. In the graph above, the walk is closed. This must always be the case, regardless of the length of the *n*-tuplets. Consider the node 00. There must be one line exiting—to 001—and one line entering—from 100. Since we are using only the numbers 1 and 0, there can be no other edges. Find the walk, and the roads will give you the listing for the memory wheel.

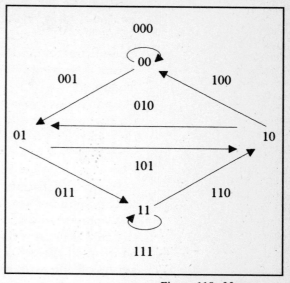

Figure 118. Memory wheels and Euler's graph

There are simple methods for finding a wheel of a given size. For example, begin with an *n*-tuplet made up of all zeros. Now place at the right the larger of the two digits, 0 or 1, which will not create a duplicate *n*-tuplet. Repeat this process until the wheel is complete. Try this method to obtain the simple quadruplet wheel above.

The idea of a memory wheel has a very interesting history. It was first used, believe it or not, by medieval Indian poets and musicians as a handy way of remembering all possible rhythms. The first "wheel" was the nonsense Indian word *yamátárájabhánasalagám*. Change the long syllables with accented vowels into 1 and the other syllables with unaccented vowels into 0 and you have the memory wheel for triplets. Since then, it has also been used in telegraphy, Teletype machines, probability theory, error detection and correction, and so on. In the early days of computer science, the memory wheel was an actual physical wheel that rotated until the appropriate *n*-tuplet had been found. For example, on the old-fashioned Teletype machines, when you struck a key you sent out a string of digits such as 01101110. The memory wheel was cranked around, electronically of course, until the specific string was found. The position of the wheel then indexed into the desired character for typing. The advantage of the wheel, of course, is that it took so much less space than a complete listing of octuplets.

A GAME WITH DOMINOES

1 have before me a set of dominoes in which each tile has a number from 0 to 4. I have thrown out the tiles that have doubles so that only ten remain, such as (0-1), (0-2), (0-3), and so on up to (4-4). The full set can be arranged as follows:

(0-1) (1-2) (2-3) (3-4) (4-0)
(0-2) (2-4) (4-1) (1-3) (3-0)

Notice the chaining order of the set: The last number of a domino is the first number of the next domino. This is even true of the last and first domino, so that we have something like a Domino Wheel.

Can this be done for all sets of dominoes? What if we used the set in which each tile has a number from 0 to 5? When is it possible, and when is it impossible? Can you use a graph to prove your solution?

GRACEFULNESS

Strictly speaking, any collection of nodes and edges can be called a graph, but we will restrict ourselves now to only those cases in which there are no edges connecting a node with itself, and no two nodes having more than one edge between them. This restriction will allow us to "number" a graph. This process of numbering simply means assigning a number to the nodes of a graph and then inducing from these a value for the edges. The induced value is simply the absolute difference between the two nodes that the edge connects. For example, let us say that we decide to assign the numbers 1 and 3 to two nodes; then the edge connecting them is given the value 2, since $2 = (3-1)$. Should we change the values of the nodes, then, of course, the values of the edges will change also. Some of the most fascinating problems in graph theory will arise when we try to number a graph in such a way that its nodes and edges possess a quality that is now called gracefulness.

To see what gracefulness means, consider the first numbered graph in Figure 119. The numbering of its nodes may seem arbitrary, but actually a good bit of thought went into it. It has six edges, and its nodes have been numbered in such a way that the edges were given *all* the values between 1 and 6. Furthermore, the values assigned to the nodes were kept between 0 and 6, and no two nodes have the same value, although, of course, not all values were used. When all these qualities are found, the graph is said to be gracefully numbered.

The second graph in Figure 119 is *not* gracefully numbered—we are forced to give two edges the number 2—but nevertheless it is still a graceful graph. This is because it is possible to change the numbering of

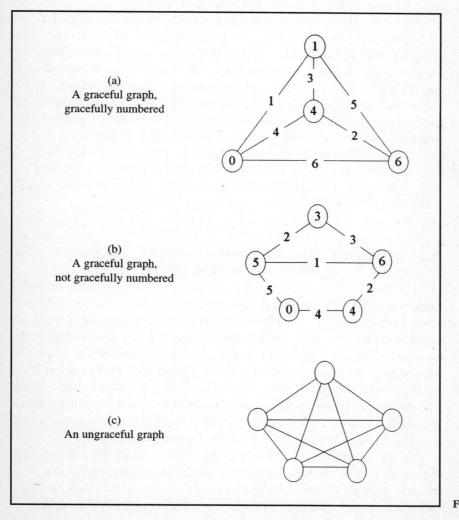

(a)
A graceful graph,
gracefully numbered

(b)
A graceful graph,
not gracefully numbered

(c)
An ungraceful graph

Figure 119.

the nodes in a way that the edges, as before, will have the values 1 through 5. It just happens that in this instance the numbering is not graceful. I will let you find the proper numbering. There are five edges in the graph, so remember that the nodes must be assigned values between 0 and 5 (no two the same) in such a way that the edges have all the values between 1 and 5.

The third graph in Figure 119 is also not gracefully numbered, but in this case the graph itself is not graceful. Try as you may, you will never be able to find a proper numbering scheme.

Obviously, the quality of gracefulness is a quality of the graph itself. The connectedness of the first two graphs is quite different from the connectedness of the third. What is this difference? We do not know, but it is important to keep in mind that the question is not only a lot of fun to think about, it is also a fundamental question about space itself. The entire concept of graceful graphs, and most of the important questions surrounding them, is the work of a single man—Solomon W. Golomb, professor of mathematics and electrical engineering at the University of Southern California. As originally conceived, Professor Golomb's graceful graph had important applications in such diverse fields as X-ray crystallography and radio astronomy, but there is enough in the sheer pleasure of it to occupy our attention.

GRACEFUL CHESSBOARDS, TREES, AND CATERPILLARS

There are whole classes of graphs that can be shown to be graceful. One example of this is any graph that can be shaped into the corner of a chessboard, like the graph in the top of Figure 120. That such graphs are always graceful can be demonstrated with a constructive proof in which we give a general method for numbering the graph. Because the method never refers to the specific size of the graph, only to its connectedness, we know that it can be used for any graph whatsoever of this general form. In short, we know that all of these graphs are graceful, because we can construct one to any size demanded.

First we assign a number to the edges. This is easily done: We begin at the top and assign the numbers sequentially moving from right to left. But now we also want to sign these numbers. This is only slightly more complicated. For the vertical edges, begin with the left-most one

A chessboard graph . . .

... with labeled
edges . . .

... the final,
graceful version

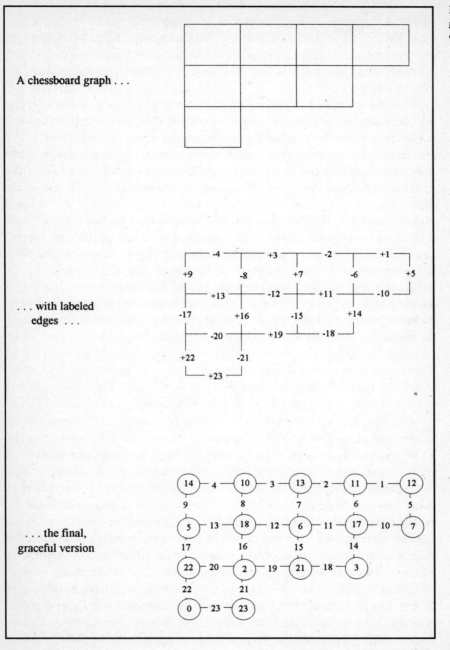

Figure 120. How to
gracefully number the
corner of a chessboard

at the bottom and make it positive; now sign all other vertical edges such that moving either rightward or upward the signs always alternate. Do the same for the horizontal edges; that is, begin with the leftmost one at the bottom and make it positive, then move rightward and upward alternating the signs. The result is shown in the middle of Figure 120.

Now we number the nodes. We begin with the node at the bottom left, and give it the value 0. Any node adjacent to it is given the sum of 0 plus the signed value of the edge connecting the two nodes. We spread out through the graph in this way, always moving up and to the right, giving a number to all the nodes. The bottom of Figure 120 is the final version. Find the values of the edges and you can see its gracefulness.

Another general class of graph is illustrated in Figure 121. It possesses two properties: First, it is possible to walk along the edges from any node to any other node; and second, it is impossible to walk along the edges from a node back to itself. Such graphs are said to be connected and acyclic, and they are called trees; the prototype is, of course, the family tree, in which the two restrictions amount to saying that every person on the tree is a descendant of all people higher up, and no person is his or her own ancestor. The tree in Figure 121 is obviously graceful, and if you play around with trees long enough, making them larger and more complicated as you go, you will be nagged by a very annoying question: Are all trees graceful?

Alas, I have no answer to give you. The question is already several decades old, and although the best minds from around the world have worked on it, no one knows for sure.

We do know, however, that certain types of trees are graceful. One type is illustrated in Figure 122, called a caterpillar. (One of the pleasures of graph theory is its playful terminology.) The caterpillar is made up of a single "backbone" of nodes, and a number of "feet" extending from the bone. *All caterpillars are graceful*. Once again we give a constructive proof, this one called the bipartite method. The unusual shapes given to the nodes of the caterpillar are meant to illustrate this method. First, we ignore its feet. Second, we alternately mark off the nodes of the backbone, using a square, then a circle, then a square, and so on. The feet extending from a specific node are all given a mark opposite that of the node from which they extend. Now proceed from left to right numbering all the squares sequentially beginning with zero. Then continue from right to left numbering all the circles sequentially. Be sure in this process to number both the nodes of the backbone and of the feet in the order in which they fall. When you are done you will find a graceful caterpillar. The edges are also numbered sequentially, which is characteristic of the bipartite method. The method will work regardless of the size or complexity of the caterpillar. Therefore, as we said, all caterpillars are graceful.

Caterpillars, as well as being a subclass of trees, are also examples of a special kind of graph called bipartite graphs. This means their nodes can be divided into two sets such that the nodes of one set are connected to the nodes of the other set, but nodes within a set are never connected to each other. You are finding the two sets when you mark off a node as being either a square or a circle. If all the nodes of one set are connected to all the nodes of the other set, then the graph is said to be a complete

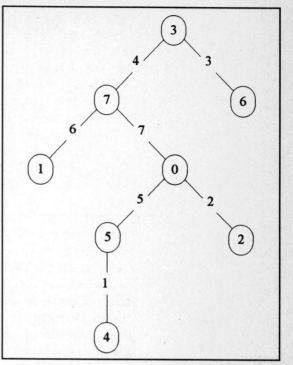

Figure 121. A graceful tree. Are all trees graceful?

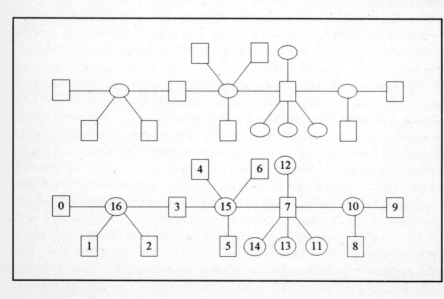

Figure 122. How to make a graceful caterpillar

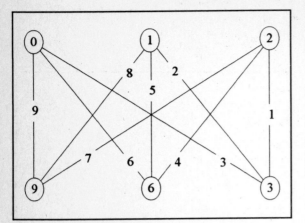

Figure 123. All complete
bipartite graphs are
graceful

bipartite graph, and these are known to be graceful. An example of a complete bipartite graph is in Figure 123. As we have seen, even if the bipartite graphs are not complete, but show the type of connectedness associated with caterpillars, then these, too, will be graceful.

Other types of trees have also been examined. For example, all trees with sixteen or fewer nodes are graceful. And so are all trees with fewer than five leaves, or nodes connected by only one edge. However, the question of whether or not trees in general, regardless of their quirks, are graceful remains one of the great unsolved questions of graph theory.

TREES THAT DECOMPOSE

The question is related to another problem, which is equally entertaining, namely the decomposition of complete graphs. A complete graph is one in which every node is connected to every other node, like the first graph in Figure 119. Such graphs are sometimes given the special name, K_n, where n is the number of nodes. The graph in Figure 119 is K_4.

Theory has it that if n is odd, then K_n can be decomposed into several copies of a single tree. We can be more specific. Let K_n be any complete graph in which n is odd. Then let $n = 2k + 1$. (This can always be done, because n is odd.) Then K_n can be decomposed into exactly n copies of a tree, the tree having exactly k edges. The decomposition of K_n, carried out in a hit-or-miss fashion, is never easy and should always be done in a cyclical manner. To do this, begin with a complete graph K_n in which the nodes have been numbered from 0 to $n - 1$. Now find on it an appropriate tree. Cycle around to the next copy of the tree by adding one to each node. If this should take you off the graph, then begin over again at zero. For example, let us say that you are working on the graph K_5, and your tree has the three nodes 1, 3, and 4. Then the next tree in the cycle will have nodes 2, 4, and 0. This tree in turn is cycled once more to produce the next tree, with nodes 3, 0, and 1, and we continue in this way until all n trees are produced.

In Figure 124 we try to decompose K_7 using two different trees.

Here, $n = 7$, so $k = 3$, and we try to decompose K_7 into 7 trees each with 3 edges. Had we used instead K_9, then $n = 9$, and $k = 4$, and we would decompose the graph into 9 trees each with 4 edges.

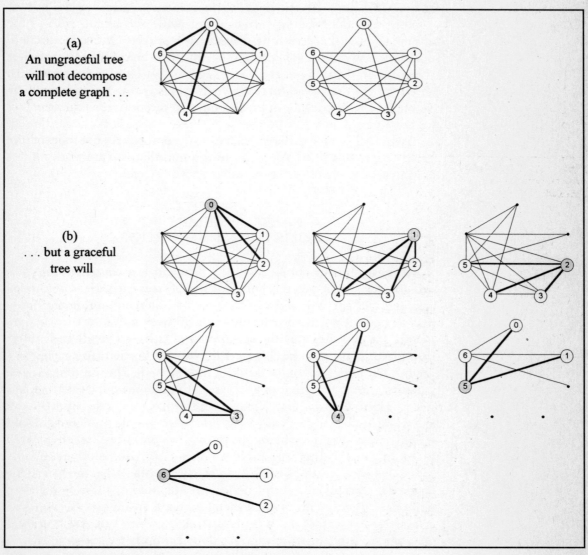

Figure 124. Decomposing a graph into copies of a graceful tree

Our first attempt fails rather quickly—one branch of the next tree is already used up, so there are parts of the graph left over. But in the second attempt we use a different tree, and the decomposition works fine. All of the edges have been used in one of the trees and at the end all of the edges have disappeared.

Now, why does the first attempt fail while the second works fine? Which trees will successfully decompose a graph? One sufficient, but not necessary, condition is that the tree must be gracefully numbered, as is the case in the second example in Figure 124. Thus, if you prove that all trees are indeed graceful, then you will also prove that all complete graphs K_n, with odd-n, can be decomposed into n trees. Two problems for the price of one.

Try to find trees of different shapes to decompose K_7 in order to fully grasp how it all works. You will quickly find that you are working in a new area somewhere between graphs and numbers.

A FIRST ATTEMPT AT A CONSTRUCTIVE PROOF

The most obvious approach to the problem is a constructionist approach. If we had a general "horticulture" of trees—that is, a method of producing larger trees from smaller ones while maintaining the original's gracefulness—then we could build all trees and show that they are indeed graceful. Begin with the simplest of trees—a single node numbered zero. This, of course, is graceful. Now the horticulturist can take a "twig"—a node and edge—and give its node the number 1 and "grapht" it to the original tree. The result is a somewhat larger tree, but just as graceful as the first. This larger tree has two nodes numbered 0 and 1. We take another twig, this time with a node numbered 2, and grapht it once again to the zero node, and we produce a larger, but still graceful, tree. To this we grapht another twig, and another, and . . .

Can we produce all possible trees this way? No. What we have done is taken a graceful tree with n nodes and graphted *to its zero node* a twig numbered $n + 1$. This is not general enough; an infinity of trees will escape our construction. To build all trees, we need to grapht a twig onto any node whatsoever, not just the one numbered zero.

We could save our horticultural method if we could prove that all graceful trees are "zero-rotatable"—that is, if we could show that any node could be given a zero and then all other nodes renumbered in some systematic way in order to preserve its gracefulness. Then we would indeed be able to grapht a twig onto an arbitrary node; we would need only to rotate the node to the zero position.

Unfortunately, trees are not zero-rotatable. The tree in Figure 125 is a counterexample. We have placed the zero in all of its nodes except the square one. In each case, the rest of the tree has been gracefully numbered, and it is an easy matter to grapht onto the zero node, wherever it may appear, a twig numbered 6 to build a larger graceful tree. But on the node marked with a square, a zero cannot appear. Notice that this does not mean a twig cannot appear on this node. If it did, then not all trees would be graceful. Instead, it only means that the numbering must be done all over again.

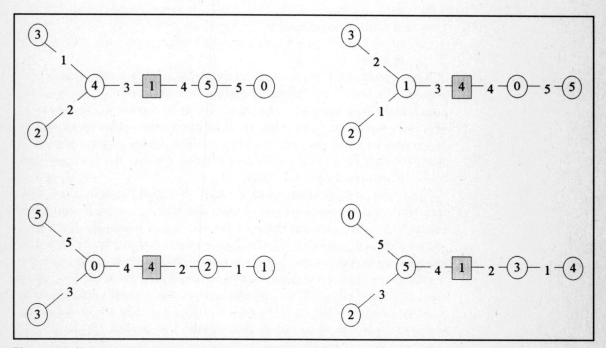

Figure 125. Zero can appear on any node except the square node

A SECOND ATTEMPT AT A
CONSTRUCTIVE PROOF

Other methods of horticulture are possible. The most powerful to date is one invented by R. G. Stanton and C. R. Zarnke. To show this method, look at Figure 126. In Figure 126(a) we begin with two trees already gracefully numbered. In Figure 126(b) we make one replica of the first and three replicas of the second, none of which are gracefully numbered anymore. Then in Figure 126(c) we graph everything together and produce a final monstrous tree in all its graceful glory. Imagine how difficult it would be to produce the final tree from scratch.

In explaining how all this is done, we will keep the discussion general so that it can be applied to larger trees at a later time. The first tree is called S, and it has s nodes (in our example $s=3$). The second tree is called T, and it has t nodes ($t=6$). We need to make a single replica of S (S_0) and s replicas of T (T_0, T_1 ... T_{s-1}), since a replica will later be graphted onto each node of S_0.

Begin with the single replica of S. This is easily done. We simply multiply each node by t.

The replicas of T are created by properly adding a multiple of t to some of the nodes. By "properly adding" we mean the following: Take an arbitrary node and call it the root. Then, on replica T_i, the root and all nodes separated from it by an even number of edges—the square nodes in part (b)—are increased by $i \cdot t$. The nodes that are separated from the root by an odd number of edges—the circular nodes in part (b)—are increased by $(s-1-i)t$.

That sounds complicated but actually it is quite simple. First consider the square nodes, separated from the root by an even number of edges. On T_0 we increase these by $0 \cdot t$ (0 in our example). On T_1 we increase these by $1 \cdot t$ (or 6). On T_2 we increase these by $2 \cdot t$ (or 12). And so on, so that on the last replica, T_{s-1}, we increase these nodes by $(s-1)t$. Now consider the circular nodes, separated from the root by an odd number of edges. These are changed in the opposite direction. On T_0, they are increased by $(s-1)t$ (or 12). On T_1, they are increased by $(s-2) \cdot t$ (or 6). And so on, so that on the last replica, T_{s-1}, they are increased by $0 \cdot t$ (or 0).

In part (c) we attach the replicas of T to the replica of S by joining identical nodes.

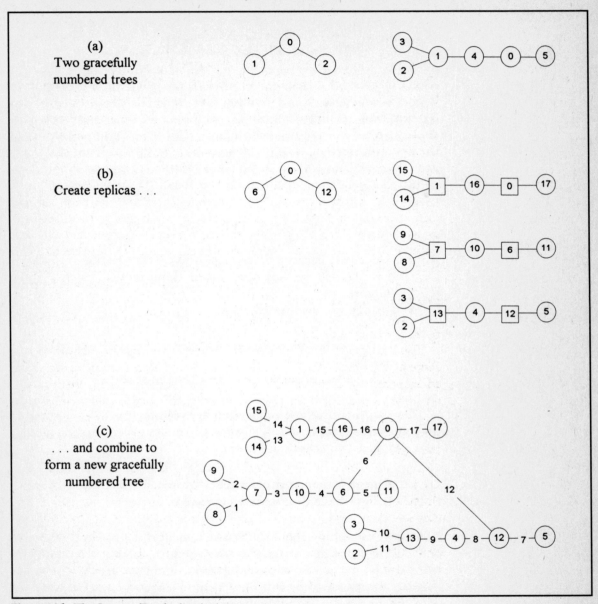

(a)
Two gracefully
numbered trees

(b)
Create replicas . . .

(c)
. . . and combine to
form a new gracefully
numbered tree

Figure 126. The Stanton-Zarnke horticulture

It is a simple matter to handle even larger trees this way. Furthermore, when you make your replica of S, you can add to the nodes an arbitrary constant between 1 and $t - 1$ inclusive. This will give your final tree either a different shape or a different numbering, but it will always be graceful. The method really is quite powerful. It is difficult to explain why it works, but I urge you to try it on fairly large trees, just to watch it work its magic. Of course, beginning with two trees each with two nodes, we can get a tree with four nodes, then eight nodes, and so on. But unfortunately we still fall far short of building all possible trees. Appropriately enough, we end the book with an unsolved puzzle: Are all trees graceful?

WE ARE THE ISHANGO

And so we are the Ishango all over again. We have never been anything else, and very likely we will never be anything more. That is a humbling thought.

The Ishango saw two statements:

1. Four etches can be carved on a bone, followed by four other etches.
2. Eight etches can be carved on a bone all at once.

They could not see any connection between the two, although to us the connection is so obvious that we would not even consider it a puzzle. We look at two other statements:

1. A graph is connected and acyclic—that is, it is a tree.
2. The graph can be gracefully numbered.

There is something about the first statement that implies the second, but like the Ishango we cannot see it. The first statement is about the space around us, while the second is about numbers. It is in this sense that our number system will once again change our world, just as it once changed the world of the Ishango. For the moment, the numbers are hidden from us; we have only etches on a bone. What did Ahmes say? "Accurate reckoning . . ." We are like the Bakairi counting one, two, tussling our hair, pointing at our toes, shouting *méra, méra.*

"... the entrance into the knowledge of all existing things and all obscure secrets." The Deity is one who has already played all possible games. Is space what it is because, in part, the Deity wanted all trees to be graceful? Otherwise, what would we do to puzzle ourselves?

Perhaps some future generation will write a new book of ancient puzzles that begins, instead of ends, with this tree, and treats it as though it is old business, fit only for a quaint and primitive mind. I, for one, can't wait to read it.

WE SHALL NOT CEASE FROM EXPLORATION

AND THE END OF ALL OUR EXPLORING

WILL BE TO ARRIVE WHERE WE STARTED

AND KNOW THE PLACE FOR THE FIRST TIME.

—T. S. ELIOT, *FOUR QUARTETS*

Postscript

SOMEONE VERY WISE ONCE SAID, "IF I QUOTE FROM ONE source, I am plagiarizing; if I quote from several sources, I am doing research." I have done research. Still, in order to keep the text flowing nicely, I may not have given credit when credit was due. I hope to correct that now.

The references that follow are balanced between puzzles and history, so readers may follow one or the other, but hopefully both. All references will lead readers to still more information. The bracketed numbers refer to the sources mentioned in the reference section.

INTRODUCTION

The general idea of a history of puzzles is being pursued by David Singmaster [64] in a work that has been under way for at least a decade now. It promises to be an exhaustive work on the subject, but it is still unpublished. Frank Swetz is another prolific author on the subject, and of his many books and articles, the reader may find [77] interesting. Puzzles in general, not necessarily their histories, are especially associated with one author, of course; he is Martin Gardner, with well over twenty-five books on the subject. It is impossible to write a single sentence about puzzles without finding it said better by him. Particular reference should be given to [24–27], but I have always believed there is a certain added pleasure in reading all his books in order.

There are many wonderful books on the history of mathematics, but I have chosen to give additional references to my two favorites. These are *The History of Mathematics: An Introduction* by David Burton [14], and *The Exact Sciences in Antiquity* by O. Neugebauer [53].

THE FIRST ETCHES

The Ishango bone was first written about by Jean de Heinzelin [37]. The belief that it may have been an ancient calendar is the idea of Alexander Marshack [48], whose book is an exhaustive account of many relics like the Ishango bone. Claudia Zaslavsky [87] also mentions the bone and a good deal more about ancient Africa in a book that is a true gem to read. The history of numbers is dealt with best by Graham Flegg [23], but John McLeish [49] also handles the subject nicely and places it in a mathematical context. Like many more recent books, this one, for better or worse, takes a decidely "ethnic look" at the subject. C. Stanley Ogilvy and John T. Anderson have written the first truly popular account of number theory [55], which also covers some of the early methods of calculation. The extension of the Russian Peasant algorithm to other moduli was first done by Beverly Gimmestad [31]. Philip J. Davis and Reuben Hersch [19] explain the difficult subject of the Riemann Hypothesis in a book that makes for great reading on many levels. What I have called the Conway sieve and the Ishango computer were first mentioned by John Horton Conway [17], who of course uses neither term. A fuller explanation of both subjects, again without using the terms, was done by Richard K. Guy [34].

I also want to mention Howard Eves's four (much too thin) volumes on quaint mathematical stories [22]—something like bedtime reading in mathematics.

THE ENTRANCE INTO ALL OBSCURE SECRETS

The Ahmes Papyrus, usually called the Rhind Papyrus, was translated by P. B. Chase and his colleagues [15]. You get an eerie sense of your ancestors rising up from the dust as you turn its pages. Concerning the mathematical content of the book, no one does as good a job as Richard J. Gillings [30]. A short but important footnote, and Gillings's reply to it, is found in Rising [61]. Gillings also wrote several articles that go into a bit more detail, especially [28–29]. Here, as elsewhere, Burton has the most readable history on ancient Egypt [14], but for other aspects of the times, see E. A. Wallis Budge [12–13] and Torgny Save-Soderberg [62]. A translation of the *Book of the Dead* was done by Budge [11]. The riddle of the vanishing camel, and its relation to Egyptian fractions, was explored by Ian Stewart [73].

Undoubtedly the finest account of the number pi, including a fascinating description of methods for computing it, is found in Petr Beckmann [5]. Like all of Beckmann's books, this one is cranky, iconoclastic, and meticulously researched. There is no one quite like him.

ON A TEMPLE ROOF

The etches that seem to be the beginning of Tic-Tac-Toe and other alignment games is covered by H.J.R. Murray [51]. The game of Morris is also covered by Murray, but the specific game I used was taken from Geoffrey Mott-Smith [50]. George Markowsky has the final say on the game of Numerical Tic-Tac-Toe [46–47], having created a computer program to find all possible moves, thereby ruining it for the rest of us. The book by Elwyn Berlekamp, John Conway, and Richard Guy [6] is a virtual encyclopedia of games, more than you can possibly play in a lifetime. The book is a joy to read even on a higher level, because of the many puns and inside jokes scattered throughout. (It is related to Conway's [16].) Its chapters on Tic-Tac-Toe leave you feeling like nothing more need be said, but some of the original details behind it may be found in Hales and Jewitt [35], Jerome L. Paul [58], and Oren Patashnik [57].

TO MEASURE THE HEAVENS

There is no single translation of the *Nine Chapters on the Mathematical Art*, although two of the chapters have been translated by Frank Swetz and T. I. Kao [78] and by Lam Lay Yong [86]. The preface to the book by Swetz and Kao has a sampling of the puzzles from other chapters as well. The interesting discovery that one of the problems in the *Nine Chapters* appeared later in *Mathematics Teacher* was noted by Swetz [77]. Julian Lowell Coolidge has a history of geometric methods in general [18], but some sections are out of date.

In fact, everything about China is out of date if it was written before the massive work on the subject by Joseph Needham [52]. The book, running to several very thick volumes, is too forbidding for most, but fortunately there is a shortened version of it by Robert Temple [79], apparently done under Needham's guidance. The latter is a plain good read that sacrifices none of the former's scholarship.

Finding the negative half of Pascal's triangle was first done by James Varnadore [82], who also found in it the negative half of Fibonacci's sequence.

Whether or not to include the section on tangrams was a difficult decision. Martin Gardner was one of the first to say that this game dated back to about 2000 B.C., but later changed his mind when Ronald C. Read [60] showed that it was all a hoax. The Read book will occupy anyone who likes to fiddle with tans. The whole story of the hoax, and much more material, is given by Gardner [26]. Swetz [77] leaves open the possibility that the game is indeed a very old one. The question concerning convex tangrams was asked and answered by Fu Traing Wang and Chuan-Chih Hsiung [84].

ON A TURTLE SHELL

Whole libraries can be filled with books about magic squares, and more are being written every day. The two most popular resources are W. S. Andrews [3] and William H. Benson and Oswald Jacoby [7]. The latter book has all the important information about the fascinating subject of magic cubes. The first magic cube, created by Robert Myers, was introduced to the world by Martin Gardner [26], although prior articles on the subject were later found. The Benson and Jacoby book goes into details. The story of Mohammed ibn Mohammed is told by Zaslavsky [87].

Magic graphs were first studied by R. M. Stewart [74–75], although the articles are rather difficult. Hartsfield and Ringel [36] give a nice summary.

SPEAK, WHO CAN

The first English translation of Alcuin's *Problems to Quicken a Young Mind*, along with very useful commentary, is scheduled to appear in the 1992 issue of *The Mathematical Gazette*, by David Singmaster and John Hadley [1], but after I went to press. I am indebted to Dr. Singmaster for sharing it with me. The history of Alcuin is told by the Right Rev. G. F. Browne [10], who takes the spiritual nonsense seriously, but includes most of Alcuin's letters. A more scholarly history is in Burton [14]. Alcuin's *Epitaph* and many other beautiful Latin verses may be found in Helen Waddell [83].

Many variations on the transportation problem are in Pierre Berloquin [8], a very entertaining collection of puzzles. Its updated Desert Fox variation was mentioned in A. K. Dewdney [21] and finally solved by D. R. Westbrook [85].

Figurate numbers are nicely described by Maurice Kraitchik [42], although this inexhaustible source of mathematical games may be found nearly anywhere. Gardner [26], as usual, has the best article. Martin D. Stern [71] tells the story of the use of triangular numbers in the Talmud. Stern's articles are always a reliable source of information about mathematics in the Middle East. I actually thought I invented the little puzzle on crossing lines until I found it in print barely a month later. I give credit to Richard Grassl and Robert Lochel [33], since I used their notation.

A cultural history of the jealous husbands problem was published by Marcia Ascher [4], who by now is very likely the foremost authority on the new study of "ethnic mathematics." Original variations of the problem were invented by Thomas H. O'Beirne [54]. And the last word on the problem as it appeared in Alcuin was written by Ian Pressman and David Singmaster [59], as part of the latter's work in translating the *Problems*.

The barrel-sharing puzzle was solved by many authors, but Singmaster [66] was the first to notice that it is identical to the problem of enumerating triangles with integer sides. The latter problem is also explained by Jordan, Walch, and Wisner [39].

Finally, Tartaglia's problem of wine measuring was first solved graphically by M.C.K. Tweedie [81], but O'Beirne [54] raises the problem to higher dimensions, literally.

I WAS REGARDED WITH ASTONISHMENT

There is no English translation of Abu Kamil's *Book of Precious Things*, which is surprising, since it is barely a pamphlet. For those of you whose German is at least as good as mine, Suter [40] has a translation. O'Beirne [54] gives most of the problems, as does Singmaster [65], although the latter gives many other similar problems along with their history. The story of the monkey and the coconuts is mentioned by Gardner [24], and the best and most general solution of the problem is due to Roger B. Kirchner [41]. The interesting story of Rabbi Ben Ezra is told by David Smith and Jekuthial Ginsburg [67].

THE MERCHANTS OF PISA AND THE DIGITS OF THE HINDUS

There is still no English translation of Fibonacci's *Liber Abaci*, although the classicist Richard E. Grimm tells me that he and Sherman K. Stein are embarking on one. More than I can say, I hope to see it. My Latin is fairly good, but I can translate only pieces of the original text, which Grimm tells me, in a personal letter, "is a mess." Problems from the *Liber Abaci* can be found in many sources.

Davis and Hersch [19] do a good job explaining the Chinese Remainder Theorem. O'Beirne [54], Gardner [25], and Calvin T. Long [44] each give different but related methods of solving the twelve-coin problem. (I called it the twelve-coin problem for my own reasons. The correct title is the Odd-Ball Puzzle.) The twenty-seven-card trick is explained in a recent article by Long [45], and Hugo Steinhaus [70] was the first to show how a tetrahedron can tesselate a plane without mixing colors. The Steinhaus book is a beautiful stream-of-consciousness puzzle book that even now, twenty years after its translation into English, is a marvel.

The Fibonacci sequence can be found in many sources, but the best elementary explanation is in Brother Alfred [2] and Ogilvy and Anderson [55]. More modern material is in Ross Honsberger [38]. The fact that the Fibonacci sequence was known in India was noted by Paramanand Singh [63].

GRAPHS AND PUZZLES

Since Euler and the Kurna Temple, graph theory is now too big a subject for one book. A very enjoyable elementary look is in Mitch Struble [76] and Oystein Ore [56], and something more advanced is in Richard J. Trudeau [80]. Zaslavsky [87] is the only one to have looked at the graph games of Africa. I found the fall-from-Eden story of Angola in her book.

Sherman K. Stein [69] has the best treatment of Euler and Hamilton, and this same book reprints his original article on memory wheels. Stewart [72] duplicates Stein, but then adds new information.

Graceful graphs is another subject that can occupy several books. The original work on the subject is due to Solomon Golomb [32] but he chose to announce the subject in one of Gardner's columns, reprinted in [27]. Dewdney [21], who took over Gardner's column, looked at the same subject from a different angle. R. G. Stanton and C. R. Zarnke [68] were responsible for the fascinating method of growing graceful trees. Sin-Min Lee and Kam-Chuen Ng [43] first discovered the method for creating a Graceful Young Tableau, which I have called the corner chessboard graph. Bloom, in a review article [9], summarizes the current information on graceful graphs, although by the time this book comes out, there will probably be more.

IF I HAVE PERCHANCE OMITTED ANYTHING MORE OR LESS PROPER OR NECESSARY, I BEG INDULGENCE, SINCE THERE IS NO ONE WHO IS BLAMELESS AND UTTERLY PROVIDENT IN ALL THINGS.

—LEONARDO FIBONACCI, *LIBER ABACI*

Glossary

THIS IS AN INFORMAL GLOSSARY, MEANT ONLY TO HELP readers who do not wish to hunt through the text for forgotten definitions. It differs from other glossaries in that it includes the names of important figures mentioned in the text, so that the pronunciation of their names and biographical information may be kept in one place. Modern names do not appear, but the reader may find them in the index and postscript instead. Items appearing in **bold** appear elsewhere in the glossary.

Abu Kamil Shuja ibn Aslam

A-bu′ Ka-meel′; Egyptian mathematician; lived c. 900. His short work *The Book of Precious Things in the Art of Reckoning* is an early example of a general method used to solve a class of problems, called **linear indeterminate equations**.

Ahmes

Ah′-mez; Egyptian scribe; lived c. 1650 B.C. As a scribe, Ahmes was responsible for copying the manuscript for *Directions for Attaining Knowledge into All Obscure Secrets*. It is not known how much of this is original to Ahmes.

Alcuin of York

Al′-kwin; English abbot and scholar; born in York, England, c. 732; died May 19, 804. Alcuin was the appointed head of Charlemagne's educational system, intended to be a model for much of western Europe. In a letter to the emperor, Alcuin refers to a collection of puzzles that he sent for the latter's enjoyment. This is believed to be the *Problems to Quicken a Young Mind*.

Binary Number System

The **positional number system** that uses a base of 2—that is, each digit is to be multiplied by the appropriate power of 2. For example, binary 101 is $(1 \cdot 2^2) + (0 \cdot 2^1) + (1 \cdot 2^0) = 5$. It is used in the **Russian Peasant algorithm**.

Binomial Coefficients

The coefficients in the expansion of $(x+y)^n$, where n is a positive integer. For example, if you expand $(x+y)^3$, you get $1x^3 + 3x^2y + 3xy^2 + 1y^3$. The numbers 1, 3, 3, 1 are the coefficients. The numbers make up a row in the **Chinese triangle**.

The Book of Precious Things in the Art of Reckoning

(c. 900). Written by **Abu Kamil**, the Precious Things are six problems of **linear indeterminate equations**. It is evidence of the sophistication of the Arab world during Kamil's time.

Chang Tshang

Kan Chan; Chinese mathematician; lived c. 200 B.C. Nothing is known of Chang Tshang's life except that he is believed to be the author of *Nine Chapters on the Mathematical Art,* a work that summarized a great deal of Chinese mathematics of the time. Doubts about the authorship remain because this work, and many others, were destroyed early on. Other mathematicians, notably Liu Hui, tried to reconstruct the work from memory.

Chinese Triangle

A ubiquitous pattern of numbers probably originating in China but found also in India and western Europe. It is sometimes called **Pascal's triangle**, after the mathematician who popularized it in the West. The triangle calls attention to the relationship between seemingly unrelated number sequences, including the **Fibonacci sequence, figurate numbers**, and **binomial coefficients**. If shifted 45 degrees, it becomes the **mātrā-meru** of India.

Composite Number

An integer that is not **prime**. That is, an integer other than 0 and ± 1 that has a proper divisor other than itself and 1. The first positive composite numbers are 4, 6, 8, 9, and 10.

Decimal Number System

The **positional number system** that uses a base of 10—that is, each digit is to be multiplied by the appropriate power of 10. For example, decimal 101 is $(1 \cdot 10^2) + (0 \cdot 10^1) + (1 \cdot 10^0) = 101$. This is the most common number system used throughout the world today. It was developed first by the Chinese sometime prior to the fourteenth century B.C., and probably traveled westward from there. The Egyptians independently discovered something similar, as evidenced in the *Directions for Attaining Knowledge into All Obscure Secrets.* It was brought from the Arabs to western Europe by **Fibonacci**.

Directions for Attaining Knowledge into All Obscure Secrets

(c. 1650 B.C.) A collection of problems copied by the scribe **Ahmes**. It displays the use of **unit fractions**, a **positional number system** that is functionally similar to the **decimal number system**, the **Russian Peasant algorithm**, and even **pi**.

Euler, Leonhard

Oi'-ler; Swiss mathematician; born in Basel, Switzerland, April 15, 1707; died in St. Petersburg, Russia, September 19, 1783. Commonly considered the Prince of Mathematicians, he is also credited as the father of **graph theory**.

Fibonacci

Fee-bo-nat'-chee; Italian businessman and mathematician; born in Pisa, Italy c. 1170; died c. 1240. Sometimes called Leonardo Pisano, he was one of the first, and certainly the most successful, of the Europeans to bring Arab mathematics to the West. His book *Liber Abaci* introduced the **decimal number system** to Europe and probably changed the course of history. The *Liber Abaci* also introduced the **Fibonacci sequence**, a rich source of highly entertaining puzzles in number theory. It should be noted that Fibonacci was a master mathematician in his own right.

Fibonacci Sequence

The sequence of numbers 1, 1, 2, 3, 5, 8, 13, 21 . . . in which each number is the sum of the previous two numbers. It can be generalized to the q-nacci system, in which each number is the sum of the previous q numbers. For example, the Tetranacci sequence is 1, 1, 2, 4, 8, 15 . . . The sequence was well known in India long before **Fibonacci**, but the latter invented it independently to solve the Rabbit Problem in his *Liber Abaci.*

Figurate Numbers

The number of discrete objects that can be arranged into various geometric shapes of different sizes. The number of billiard balls is a figurate number, specifically a **triangular number**, since they can be arranged in a triangle when racked up.

Graph Theory

The study of the position of objects placed on the plane, as opposed to the geometric properties (the area, perimeter, and so on) of such objects. There have always been games that could be called graph theoretical, but it was **Euler** who first made a systematic study of it.

Ishango

The name given to a Neanderthaloid people who settled around what is now called Lake Edward sometime during 8500 B.C. Among their remains is a bone with three notched columns. It is agreed that the notches represent a first use of a **unary number system**. Some think there is also evidence of doubling, and a very few believe they see an early inkling of **primes**.

Liber Abaci

(1202). Written by **Fibonacci**, the "Book of Computations" introduced the **decimal number system** of the Arabs into western Europe. The book contains the first mention of the **Fibonacci sequence** outside of India.

Linear Indeterminate Equations

A system of equations in which the number of unknowns is equal to or greater than the number of equations. The unknowns are not raised to a power, thus the word "linear." **Abu Kamil** made the first systematic study of such equations.

Magic Squares

A square array of numbers in which each row, column, and diagonal all sum to the same magic constant. Magic squares were first developed in China. Throughout history they have been invested with extraordinary mystical powers.

Mātrā-meru

The number mountain of India. The rules for its construction are needlessly complicated. It is simply the **Chinese triangle** shifted 45 degrees, but it calls attention to certain properties of what is now called the **Fibonacci sequence**.

Nine Chapters on the Mathematical Art

(c. 200 B.C.) A book that summarized much of Chinese mathematics known at the time. It is believed to have been written by **Chang Tshang**. Among its many firsts is the **decimal number system**, the use of zero and negative numbers, and the **right-triangle theorem**.

Pascal's Triangle

The **Chinese triangle**

Pi

The ratio of a circle's circumference to its diameter. It is likely that **Ahmes** knew something about it.

Positional Number System

A system in which the value of a digit depends on its position in the number. Each digit is to be multiplied by the appropriate power of the base. The power is determined by the position of the digit. If the base is 10, the positional number system is called **decimal**; if 2, **binary**; if 3, **ternary**; and so on. Positional number systems were developed independently in China and Egypt.

Prime Number

An integer other than 0 and ± 1 that has no divisors other than itself and 1. The first positive primes are 2, 3, 5, 7, and 11. Archaeologists generally believe the **Ishango** possessed a primitive understanding of prime numbers, but mathematicians dismiss the evidence. Primes are considered the atoms, or building blocks, of all other numbers. For example, the **composite number** 10 is made up of the primes 2 and 5, since $2 \cdot 5 = 10$.

Problems to Quicken a Young Mind

(c. 800) Believed to be the collection of puzzles that **Alcuin** sent to the Emperor Charlemagne for his amusement. Most of the problems likely came from the Arabs, Alcuin serving mainly as a conduit. He continually misunderstands how to solve most of them, and it is not known how Charlemagne fared.

Pythagorean Theorem

The **Right-triangle theorem**

Right-triangle Theorem

In a right triangle, the square of the hypotenuse is equal to the sum of the squares of the other two sides. The theorem probably originated in China, and it is wrongly credited to Pythagoras.

Roman Numerals

An example of a number system that is not a **positional number system**. It is not really a system at all, merely labels given to different quantities. Surprisingly, it was used throughout Europe as late as the eighteenth century. It was the system used by **Alcuin** in the ***Problems to Quicken a Young Mind.***

Russian Peasant Algorithm

A simple method of multiplication that uses the **binary number system**. Its origins can be found in the ***Directions for Attaining Knowledge into All Obscure Secrets.***

Ternary Number System

The **positional number system** that uses a base of 3—that is, each digit is to be multiplied by the appropriate power of 3. For example, ternary 101 is $(1\bullet3^2) + (0\bullet3^1) + (1\bullet3^0) = 10$.

Triangular Number

The most useful of the **figurate numbers**, the triangular numbers may be thought of as the partial sum of the integers. For example, $1 + 2 + 3 + 4 + 5$ is the fifth triangular number. It is easy to compute the nth triangular number as $1/2n\,(n + 1)$. The partial sums of triangular numbers are called tetrahedral numbers, and the partial sums of tetrahedral numbers are called hyper-tetrahedral numbers. And so on.

Unary Number System

The simplest and most primitive number system. Each stroke stands for 1, so that unary 111 is 3, and so on. Many primitive people developed the unary system, but there is some very slight evidence that the **Ishango** went further than others with it.

Unit Fractions

Any fraction of the form $1/n$. Except for the fraction $2/3$, unit fractions were the only fractions used by the early Egyptians, such as Ahmes. Like **Roman numerals**, unit fractions were used in Europe as late as the eighteenth century.

References

1. Alcuin of York, *Problems to Quicken a Young Mind*, trans. by John Hadley and David Singmaster, in *The Mathematical Gazette* (1992), pp. 102–26.

2. Alfred, Brother U., *An Introduction to Fibonacci Discovery*. San Jose: The Fibonacci Association, 1965.

3. Andrews, W. S. *Magic Squares and Cubes*. New York: Dover Publications, 1960.

4. Ascher, Marcia. "A River-Crossing Problem in Cross-Cultural Perspective." *Mathematics Magazine* 63 (1990), pp. 26–29.

5. Beckmann, Petr. *The History of Pi*. New York: St. Martins Press, 1971.

6. Berlekamp, Elwyn R., John H. Conway, and Richard K. Guy, *Winning Ways for Your Mathematical Play*. New York: Academic Press, 1982.

7. Benson, William H., and Oswald Jacoby. *Magic Cubes: New Recreations*. New York: Dover Publications, 1981.

8. Berloquin, Pierre. *The Garden of the Sphinx*. New York: Charles Scribner's Sons, 1985.

9. Bloom, Gary S. "A Chronology of the Ringel-Kotzig Conjecture and the Continuing Quest to Call All Trees Graceful," in *Topics in Graph Theory*, ed., Frank Harary, The New York Academy of Sciences (1979), pp. 32–51.

10. Browne, Right Rev. G.F. *Alcuin of York*. London: Society for Promoting Christian Knowledge, 1908.

11. Budge, E.A. Wallis, trans. *The Book of the Dead*. New York: Dover Publications, 1967.

12. _____. *Dwellers on the Nile*. New York: Dover Publications, 1985.

13. _____. *Egyptian Magic*. New York: Dover Publications, 1971.

14. Burton, David M. *The History of Mathematics: An Introduction*. Boston: Allyn and Bacon, 1985.

15. Chace, A.B., et al., eds. and trans. *The Rhind Mathematical Papyrus*. Oberlin: Mathematical Association of America, 1927.

16. Conway, John H. *On Numbers and Games*. New York: Academic Press, 1976.

17. _____. "Problem 2.4." *The Mathematical Intelligencer* 3 (1980), p. 45.

18. Coolidge, Julian Lowell. *A History of Geometrical Methods*. New York: Dover Publications, 1963.

19. Davis, Philip J., and Reuben Hersch. *The Mathematical Experience*. Boston: Houghton Mifflin Co., 1981.

20. Dewdney, A.K. *The Armchair Universe: An Exploration of Computer Worlds*. San Francisco: W.H. Freeman & Co., 1988.

21. _____. "Computer Recreations." *Scientific American* 131 (1987), pp. 128–31.

22. Eves, Howard. *In Mathematical Circles*. Boston: Prindle, Weber, and Schmidt, 1969.

23. Flegg, Graham. *Numbers Through the Ages*. London: Open University Press, 1989.

24. Gardner, Martin. *Second Scientific American Book*

of Mathematical Puzzles and Diversions. New York: Simon & Schuster, 1961.

25. _____. *Sixth Book of Mathematical Recreations.* San Francisco: W.H. Freeman & Co., 1971.

26. _____. *Time Travel and Other Mathematical Bewilderments.* San Francisco: W.H. Freeman & Co., 1988.

27. _____. *Wheels, Life and Other Mathematical Amusements.* San Francisco: W.H. Freeman & Co., 1983.

28. Gillings, Richard J. "Problems 1 to 6 of the Rhind Mathematical Papyrus." *The Mathematics Teacher* 55 (1962), pp. 61–65.

29. _____. "Think-of-a-Number Problems 28 and 29 of the Rhind Mathematical Papyrus." *The Mathematics Teacher* 54 (1961), pp. 97–102.

30. _____. *Mathematics in the Time of the Pharaohs.* Cambridge: MIT Press, 1972.

31. Gimmestad, Beverly J. "The Russian Peasant Algorithm." *The Mathematical Gazette* 75 (1991), pp. 169–71.

32. Golomb, Solomon W. "How to Number a Graph," in *Graph Theory and Computing*, Ronald C. Read, ed., New York: Academic Press, 1972.

33. Grassl, Richard, and Robert Lochel. "Where Have You Seen $n(n-1)/2$ Before?" *The Mathematical Gazette* 76 (1992), pp. 378–79.

34. Guy, Richard K. "Conway's Prime Producing Machine." *Mathematics Magazine* 56 (1983), pp. 26–33.

35. Hales, A.W., and R.I. Jewitt. "Regularity and Positional Games." *Transactions of the American Mathematical Society* (1963), pp. 222–29.

36. Hartsfield, Nora, and Gerhard Ringel. "Supermagic and Antimagic Graphs." *The Journal of Recreational Mathematics* 21(2) (1989), pp. 107–15.

37. de Heinzelin, Jean. "Ishango." *Scientific American* 131 (1962), pp. 128–31.

38. Honsberger, Ross. *Mathematical Gems III.* Washington: Mathematical Association of America, 1985.

39. Jordan, J.H.; Ray Walch, and R.J. Wisner. "Triangles with Integer Sides." *American Mathematical Monthly* (1979), pp. 686–89.

40. Kamil el Misri, Abu. *The Book of Precious Things in the Art of Reckoning,* trans. by Henrich Suter into German, *Bibliotheca Mathematica* (3) 11 (1910–11), pp. 100–20.

41. Kirchner, Roger B. "The Generalized Coconut Problem." *American Mathematical Monthly* (1960): 516–19.

42. Kraitchik, Maurice. *Mathematical Recreations.* New York: Dover Publications, 1953.

43. Lee, Sin-Min, and Kam-Chuen Ng. "Every Young Tableau Graph Is d-graceful." in *Combinatorial Mathematics: Proceedings of the Third International Conference*, Gary S. Bloom, Ronald Graham, and Joseph Malkevitch eds., pp. 296–302.

44. Long, Calvin T. "Magic in Base 3." *The Mathematical Gazette* 76 (1992), pp. 371–76.

45. _____. "The Twenty-Seven-Card Trick." *The Mathematical Gazette*, (1991), pp. 299–303.

46. Markowsky, George. "Numerical Tic-Tac-Toe—I." *The Journal of Mathematical Recreations*, 22(2) (1990), pp. 114–23.

47. _____. "Numerical Tic-Tac-Toe—II." *The Journal of Mathematical Recreations*, 22(3) (1990), pp. 192–200.

48. Marshack, Alexander. *The Roots of Civilization.* New York: McGraw-Hill, 1971.

49. McLeish, John. *Number: The History of Numbers and How They Shape Our Lives.* New York: Fawcett Columbine, 1991.

50. Mott-Smith, Geoffrey. *Mathematical Puzzles.* New York: Dover Publications, 1978.

51. Murray, H.J.R. *A History of Board Games Other Than Chess.* New York: Hacker Art Books, Inc., 1978.

52. Needham, Joseph. *Science and Civilization in China.* Cambridge University Press, 1954.

53. Neugebauer, O. *The Exact Sciences in Antiquity.* New York: Dover Publications, 1969.

54. O'Beirne, Thomas H. *Puzzles and Paradoxes.* New York: Oxford University Press, 1965.

55. Ogilvy, C. Stanley, and John T. Anderson. *Excursions in Number Theory.* New York: Oxford University Press, 1966.

56. Ore, Oystein. *Graphs and Their Uses.* New York: Random House, 1963.

57. Patashnik, Oren. "Qubic: 4 × 4 × 4 Tic-Tac-Toe." *Mathematics Magazine* 53 (1980), pp. 202–16.

58. Paul, Jerome L. Tic-Tac-Toe in n-Dimensions." *Mathematics Magazine* 51 (1978), pp. 45–49.

59. Pressman, Ian, and David Singmaster. "The Jealous Husbands and the Missionaries and Cannibals." *The Mathematical Gazette* 73 (1989), pp. 73–81.

60. Read, Ronald C. *Tangrams: 330 Tangram Puzzles*. New York: Dover Publications, 1965.

61. Rising, Gerald R. "The Egyptian Use of Unit Fractions for Equitable Distribution, and a Response from R.J. Gillings." *Historia Mathematica* 1 (1974), pp. 93–94.

62. Save-Soderberg, Torgny. *Pharaohs and Mortals*, trans. by Richard E. Oldenburg. London: Robert Hale Limited, 1963.

63. Singh, Paramanand. "The So-called Fibonacci Numbers in Ancient and Medieval India." *Historia Mathematica* 25 (1918), pp. 229–44.

64. Singmaster, David. "Some Early Sources in Recreational Mathematics," unpublished manuscript.

65. _____. "The Hundred Fowls, or How to Count Your Chickens," to appear in *Mathematics Review*.

66. _____. "Triangles with Integer Sides and Sharing Barrels." *The College Mathematics Journal* 21 (1990), pp. 278–85.

67. Smith, David E., and Jekuthial Ginsburg. "Rabbi Ben Ezra and the Hindu-Arabic Problem." *The American Mathematical Monthly* 25 (1918), pp. 99–108.

68. Stanton, R.G., and C.R. Zarnke. "Labelling of Balanced Trees," in *Proceedings of the Fourth S.E. Conference on Combinatorics and Graph Theory*, Winnipeg, Manitoba, Can.: pp. 479–95.

69. Stein, Sherman K. *Mathematics: The Man-made Universe*. San Francisco: W.H. Freeman & Co., 1963.

70. Steinhaus, Hugo. *Mathematical Snapshots*. New York: Oxford University Press, 1969.

71. Stern, Martin D. "A Mathematical Tosofot—A Case of Cross-Cultural Contact?" *Niv Hamidrashia* (1990), pp. 37–41.

72. Stewart, Ian. *Game, Set and Math: Enigmas and Conundrums*. Cambridge: Basil Blackwell, 1989.

73. _____. "The Riddle of the Vanishing Camel." *Scientific American* (1992), pp. 122–24.

74. Stewart, R.M. "Magic Graphs." *Canadian Journal of Mathematics* (1966), pp. 1031–59.

75. _____. "Supermagic Complete Graphs." *Canadian Journal of Mathematics* (1967), pp. 427–38.

76. Struble, Mitch. *Stretching a Point*. Philadelphia: Westminster Press, 1971.

77. Swetz, Frank J. "Using Problems from the History of Mathematics in Classroom Instructions." *Mathematics Teacher* (1989): pp. 370–77.

78. Swetz, Frank J., and T.I. Kao. *Was Pythagoras Chinese? An Examination of Right-Triangle Theory in Ancient China*. University Park: The Pennsylvania State University Press, 1977.

79. Temple, Robert. *The Genius of China: 3,000 Years of Science, Discovery, and Invention*. New York: Simon & Schuster, 1987.

80. Trudeau, Richard J. *Dots and Lines*. Kent, Ohio: Kent State University Press, 1976.

81. Tweedie, M.C.K. "A Graphical Method of Solving Tartaglian Measuring Puzzles." *The Mathematical Gazette* 23 (1939), pp. 278–82.

82. Varnadore, James. "Pascal's Triangle and Fibonacci Numbers." *Mathematics Teacher* (1991), pp. 314–16.

83. Waddell, Helen. *Medieval Latin Lyrics*. New York: W.W. Norton, 1977.

84. Wang, Fu Traing, and Chuan-Chih Hsiung. "A Theorem on the Tangram." *American Mathematical Monthly* (1942), pp. 596–99.

85. Westbrook, D.R. "The Desert Fox, a Variation of the Jeep Problem." *The Mathematical Gazette* 74 (1990), pp. 49–50.

86. Yong, Lam Lay. "Yang Hui's Commentary on the *Ying Nu* Chapter of the *Chiu Chang Shu* (*Nine Chapters*)." *Historia Mathematica* 1 (1974), pp. 47–64.

87. Zaslavsky, Claudia. *Africa Counts: Number and Pattern in African Culture*. Boston: Prindle, Weber, and Schmidt, 1973.

Grateful acknowledgment is made for permission to reprint from the following: Petr Beckmann, *The History of Pi,* 1971, by permission of The Golem Press; E. A. Wallis Budge, *Dwellers on the Nile,* 1985, by permission of Dover Publications, Inc.; A. B. Chace et al., eds. and trans., *The Rhind Mathematical Papyrus,* 1927, by permission of The Mathematical Association of America; Richard J. Gillings, *Mathematics in the Time of the Pharaohs,* 1972, by permission of the MIT Press; *The Original Rubaiyat of Omar Khayyam* translated by Robert Graves and Omar Ali-Shah, by permission of A. P. Watt Ltd on behalf of The Trustees of the Robert Graves Copyright Trust and Omar Ali-Shah; "Ishango," by Jean de Heinzelin. Copyright © 1962 by Scientific American, Inc. All rights reserved; Ross Honsberger, *Mathematical Gems III,* 1985, by permission of The Mathematical Association of America; Alexander Marshack, *The Roots of Civilization,* 1971, by permission of McGraw-Hill, Inc.; Geoffrey Mott-Smith, *Mathematical Puzzles,* 1978, by permission of Dover Publications, Inc.; James Newman, ed., *The World of Mathematics, Volume I,* 1956, by permission of Simon & Schuster, Inc.; T. H. O'Beirne, *Puzzles and Paradoxes,* 1965, by permission of Margaret A. L. O'Beirne; C. Stanley Ogilvy and John T. Anderson, *Excursions in Number Theory,* 1966, by permission of Oxford University Press; David Singmaster, "Some Early Sources in Recreational Mathematics," unpublished manuscript, by permission of the author; D. E. Smith and Jekuthial Ginsburg, in *The American Mathematical Monthly,* vol. xxv, no. 3, 1918, by permission of The Mathematical Association of America; Frank J. Swetz and T. I. Kao, *Was Pythagoras Chinese?* 1977, by permission of The Pennsylvania State University Press; Robert Temple, *The Genius of China: 3,000 Years of Science, Discovery, and Invention,* 1987, by permission of Simon & Schuster, Inc.; Helen Waddell, *Medieval Latin Lyrics,* 1977, by permission of W. W. Norton & Co., Inc.; (Figure 112 on page 241) Copyright 1979 by Claudia Zaslavsky. Reprinted from *Africa Counts: Number and Pattern in African Culture,* by permission of the publisher, Lawrence Hill Books (Brooklyn, New York).